COMPETITIVE DOMINANCE

BEYOND STRATEGIC ADVANTAGE and TOTAL QUALITY MANAGEMENT

COMPETITIVE DOMINANCE

BEYOND STRATEGIC ADVANTAGE and TOTAL QUALITY MANAGEMENT

Victor Tang   Roy Bauer

How to stun your competition,
surprise your customers, excite your allies,
and amaze the industry

VAN NOSTRAND REINHOLD
I(T)P   A Division of International Thomson Publishing Inc.

New York • Albany • Bonn • Boston • Detroit • London • Madrid • Melbourne
Mexico City • Paris • San Francisco • Singapore • Tokyo • Toronto

I(T)P™ Van Nostrand Reinhold is an International Thomson Pulishing
company. ITP logo is a trademark under license.

Printed in the United States of America

Van Nostrand Reinhold
115 Fifth Avenue
New York, NY 10003

International Thomson Publishing
Berkshire House I68–I73
High Holborn, London WC1V 7AA
England

Thomson Nelson Australia
102 Dodds Street
South Melbourne, 3205
Victoria, Australia

Nelson Canada
1120 Birchmount Road
Scarborough, Ontario
M1K 5G4, Canada

International Thomson Publishing
GmbH
Königswinterer Strasse 418
53227 Bonn
Germany

International Thomson Publishing
Asia
221 Henderson Road
#05–10 Henderson Building
Singapore 0315

International Thomson Publishing
Japan
Hirakawacho Kyowa Building, 3F
2-2-1 Hirakawacho
Chiyoda-ku, Tokyo 102
Japan

1 2 3 4 5 6 7 8 9 10 QEBFF 01 00 99 98 97 96 95

Library of Congress Cataloging in Publication Data

Tang, Victor.
    Competitive dominance : beyond strategic advantage and total
quality management / Victor Tang and Roy Bauer.
        p.   cm.
    Includes bibliographical references and index.
    ISBN 0–442–01966–1
    1. Competition.   2. Strategic planning.   3. Total quality
management.   I. Bauer, Roy A.   II. Title
HD41.T35   1995
658.4'012—dc20   95–2740
                                                      CIP

To our fathers,
Ray W. Bauer and Tang Wu

They provided us with the basic business
fundamentals

Contents

Preface

The core concept and theme of this book are simple. The core concept is that Strategy and Quality are fundamentally two sides of the same coin. The theme is that to become a winner you must drive both, you cannot neglect one for the other. Peter Drucker said that managers must not only do things right, they must also do the right things. Strategy deals with doing the right things, and quality deals with doing things right. It is fruitless to do the right things and do them poorly. It is fruitless and harmful if the things that are being done right are the wrong things. An executive is effective only when the right things are being done right and vice versa. In other words Strategy and Quality must come together. We call Competitive Dominance the unified practice of strategy and quality at the highest level of refinement and sophistication.

Competitive Dominance is about winning and staying a winner. It is about a style of management that seeks to achieve sustained leadership by out-thinking the competition with more effective strategies and by outperforming the competition with superior quality and customer satisfaction. Competitive Dominance is an attitude. It begins with a conviction that leadership is temporary, that the incumbent can be dislodged, and that to stay a leader, the firm must constantly create more customer value and must continuously surprise the competition. Nothing in this book about Competitive Dominance is unethical or illegal. No management principle, practice or methodology in this book will cause you to sacrifice any of your business ethics. Nothing herein will make your lawyers cringe. However, we do seek nothing less than to redefine and reconceptualize the notion of Competitive Dominance. Our objective is to cleanse this term of any negative connotations and nuances that it has acquired in the past. We want American companies to become the undisputed winners in the world.

In a real sense, what we are doing is nothing less than breaking the sound barrier in management disciplines of strategy and quality. We are doing this by introducing and describing the management practice of Competitive Dominance. The title of the book reflects the theme of our book, Competitive Dominance. The subtitle reflects the book's fundamental thrust, the presentation of managerial principles, methodologies, and tools that go beyond the conventional orthodoxy of Strategic Advantage or Total Quality Management.

Our thesis is that business leaders have addressed the major issues facing their business through the deployment of either strategy or quality initiatives, independently of each other. Our experience in strategy and quality leads us to the conclusion that sustained success requires the ability to integrate strategy and quality in a balanced approach. Through observation and practice, we are convinced that the appropriate balance of strategy and quality produces a powerful synergy that transforms the manner in which either discipline is applied independently. Each acts as a catalyst for the other to produce a substantially more effective management discipline. We describe in this book why and how this lack of balance between strategy and quality is creating dysfunctional results.

We have structured the book along the following lines. We begin with an Introduction, which contains a quiz and the answers. We developed this quiz for readers to calibrate their knowledge of Competitive Dominance. Our objective is to demonstrate that the subject is deeper than meets the eye. Along the way, we also demonstrate that conventional wisdom is simply incorrect and that myths are harmful and dangerous. Below is the overall logic and architecture of this book. Collectively, the chapters address the following key questions that business leaders typically ask themselves:

1. What is my current situation?

2. Given my current situation, what approach should I use?

3. How can I act on the approach?

4. What are the pitfalls that I should avoid in the implementation?

5. How do I know that I am getting the right results?

In Chapter 1, Competitive Dominance Theory: Integration of Strategy and Quality, we develop and describe a unifying framework for the integration of strategy and quality. Using this framework, we position and discuss

Baldrige and ISO 9000. We sketch four stages of strategy maturity and four stages of quality maturity. We argue that Competitive Dominance is the intersection of the highest stages of strategy and quality maturity.

Chapter 2, Paradigms in Crisis, describes the problems in the current practices of strategy and quality. We discuss the need for a richer and more robust unifying strategy and quality framework. This chapter owes its conceptual foundations to Kuhn (1962) where he discusses the phenomenon of crisis in valid paradigms. Kuhn very persuasively and convincingly argues that prior to the emergence of a new paradigm, existing ones undergo crises as new thinking stress old paradigms. Old paradigms are unable to accommodate new observable phenomenon or information. Paradigmatic tension and crises occurs. We think that the criticisms against strategy and quality are evidence of an emerging "crisis" in the current practice of strategy and quality. The critics are like blindfolded people feeling an elephant—they miss the shape and contour of the whole elephant. The critics may score on isolated points, but collectively they have missed the overriding point. The point is not that strategy and quality are outdated fads, but rather that a new unifying framework is needed. We formulate that unifying framework in the chapters that follow.

Chapters 3 and 4 establish the link among Competitive Dominance, strategy, and quality. The relationship between Competitive Dominance and Strategy are framed and discussed first in Chapter 3, Strategy and Competitive Dominance. In this chapter we argue that to achieve Competitive Dominance, strategic thinking, and practice must rise to a new level that goes beyond conventional orthodoxy. We show this by describing four stages of strategy maturity and argue that Competitive Dominance requires the practice at the highest level. Finally we discuss why Baldrige provides a good organizing framework for this new level of strategic thinking. The relationship between Competitive Dominance and Quality are framed and discussed in Chapter 4, Quality and Competitive Dominance. We parallel the development of Chapter 3 and describe four stages of quality maturity. We argue that to achieve Competitive Dominance, quality practice must rise to a new level that goes beyond the practice of Total Quality Management (TQM). We describe the key concepts that are required for this.

With the foundations of Chapter 3 and 4 in place, we proceed to Chapter 5 to describe the ten principles of Competitive Dominance. We do not claim that any one principle strikes new ground individually, but our observations and experiences as line executives tells us that their unified practice produces a powerful mixture. We do not claim that these principles displace or supersede existing and proven principles for strategy and quality. In the same manner that Calculus does not displace arithmetic, differential equations does not displace calculus, nor do the principles of Competitive Dominance displace known and effective practices of strategy and quality. The principles of Competitive Dominance merely elevate the level of strategy and quality thinking and implementation. However, through years of observation and practice in the disciplines of strategy and quality, we are confident, in claiming that consistent and disciplined practice of Competitive Dominance will provide a firm with a new level of effectiveness.

Chapter 6, Integrating Competitive Dominance into the Baldrige Quality Template, is a natural outgrowth of Chapters 3 and 4. In this chapter we take the Baldrige criteria and integrate into them the concepts and principles discussed in the previous chapters. When we were writing this chapter, we found that the integration was smooth and natural. We hope that readers will share our view that the integration of Competitive Dominance into the Baldrige template is not only natural and seamless but enriching as well.

Our firm conviction is that managerial principles are not meaningful unless they are also actionable. To that end we offer, in Chapters 7 and 8, tools and methodologies that we have found to be particularly helpful. Chapter 7 describes three tools. The first is a leadership diagnostic to calibrate and asses an individual's leadership capabilities to effectively operate in an environment of change. The second is Scenario Planning and Analysis. This tool is useful to describe the context of strategies to asses a broad range of different possible situations, which we call scenarios. The third tool is the Analytic Hierarchical Process (AHP). Most serious decisions in business are multidimensional with many variables that enter into the final decision. AHP offers a rigorous and disciplined process to parse complex decisions into an organized hierarchical set of variables and a means to analytically weigh importance of those variables in the final decision.

Chapter 8 discusses three methodologies that we have found especially useful. Customer Satisfaction is one of the hallmarks of Competitive Dominance. Our first methodology is a new way to address customer satisfaction. We discuss a life-cycle approach to customer satisfaction. The second methodology is Natural and Investment Markets. This methodology allows a company to systematically expand market occupancy. Our third methodology is an approach to create and sustain organization energy and enthusiasm. We call it Organizational Energetics.

This book was written for managers who are action oriented. Chapter 9 is written for those of us who have such a bias for action that we often forge ahead without carefully thinking about what we are doing. We discuss a dozen of the most frequently made mistakes we have observed and which we have made ourselves as line executives. These are the pitfalls to avoid as leaders of organizations. We call the practice of these misguided approaches "managerial malpractice." The book ends with a summary and conclusions.

Acknowledgments

This book is the culmination of many years of study and practical experience gained from the achievement of a number of unparalleled business successes and the learning gained from as many failures. Along the journey, many people and companies around the globe influenced our thinking about Competitive Dominance. Some were influential because their actions created the existence theorem of sustained leadership; the inaction of others led to major business downturns that resulted in dramatic shift of industry power and influence. The two constants that emerge from all this a forum for learning and an environment of change. We are grateful to those people and companies who gave us the opportunity to learn from experience and to participate in change.

We would like to acknowledge the contributions of those people and organizations identified in the bibliography who provided supporting evidence and facts to strengthen or convictions.

Our sincere thanks to those at Van Nostrand Reinhold, especially Jeanne Glasser, Editor, and Cyndi Dolcemascolco, Editorial Assistant, for supporting our initial book proposal and for guiding this book through the production process. Thanks to those unknown manuscript reviewers who provided extremely constructive input and encouragement. They were instrumental in the refinement of details in this book. A special thanks to Curt W. Reimann, Director for Quality Programs at the National Institute of Standards and Technology. He reviewed an early version of the manuscript and provided very insightful comments that were instrumental in extending the concepts far beyond the original approach.

Both of us had the opportunity to learn from very successful role models, our fathers. They provided us with the capability to perceive changes happening, the ability to learn from the changing environmental conditions, and the attitude to respond and capitalize on the opportunity. They taught us the value of integrity and honesty in responding to opportunity, and they showed us by their example the importance of sustained effort and decisive action. These characteristics were perhaps the common elements that created a bond between the authors. Our families also played a major role in the development of this book. They provided the encouragement to sustain the study required to refine the concepts and bring the manuscript to fruition. They sometimes forced us to get away from the word processor long enough to acknowledge their presence and to keep a balance between work and those most important to ultimate success, the family. For both authors, this is our third book. Without the support from those that love us for who we are, none of these books would have been possible. Thanks Wendy and Liz.

Introduction: Calibrate Your Competitive Dominance Knowledge

Accelerating environmental change, blurring of industry boundaries, shifts in markets, and new emerging global customer values dictate that management has to think and act differently than in the past. Maintaining a competitive position is becoming increasingly more difficult for business leaders and line mangers. It is even more difficult to close a competitive gap or extend a strategic advantage. Perhaps you have experienced some of the following problems:

• You have identified the right strategy, but cannot implement.

- You spend your time defending your old business and not growing new ones.
- The skill set of your management team is inconsistent with changing business needs.
- Your heavy investment to improve customer satisfaction does not yield expected results.
- You are surprised by unexpected or previously unknown competitors.
- Your own resources are limited, and you are unable to leverage others to gain advantage.

The major issues facing business leaders have traditionally been addressed through the deployment of either strategy or quality initiatives, independently of each other. Each discipline has been refined to high levels of sophistication in academic theory and practice but an integrated approach to both has not emerged until this book introduces Competitive Dominance theory. Our experience convinces us that a characteristic of companies that will enjoy long term sustained success will be the ability to integrated these disciplines in a balanced approach. *This balanced approach of strategy and quality can produce a powerful synergy that transforms the manner in which each discipline can be applied independently.* This ability permits a company to develop a sustainable leadership position throughout constant or intense environmental shifts. This the fundamental premise of Competitive Dominance.

Quiz

Test your knowledge of the synergy between quality and strategy. Read each statement below and answer "True" or "False." A "Not Sure" answer will be considered wrong. Answers are in this chapter, but this is not an open book test, so no cheating before answering the questions.

1.	Strategy and quality are separate management issues.	True ___	False ___	Not Sure ___
2.	Methodologies that can effectively forecast the future accurately will ensure strategy effectiveness.	True ___	False ___	Not Sure ___
3.	A Total Quality Management (TQM) objective to reduce cost and expense and improve customer satisfaction will yield long term company success.	True ___	False ___	Not Sure ___
4.	A company should not undertake major strategy initiatives unless there is a good fit with its capabilities and the environment.	True ___	False ___	Not Sure ___
5.	One of the most organizationally effective mechanisms for strategy is to have line managers perform strategy analysis, formulation, and implementation.	True ___	False ___	Not Sure ___
6.	Strategic planning must be done, at a minimum, yearly to continue to keep abreast of changes in the environment, industry, and competition.	True ___	False ___	Not Sure ___
7.	Companies must have disciplined methods, processes, and tools to analyze their culture, determine what needs to change, and implement the changes effectively.	True ___	False ___	Not Sure ___
8.	Ishikawa's seven basic tools of TQM form the analytical basis for all business improvement action.	True ___	False ___	Not Sure ___

9. There is a direct correlation between market share, customer satisfaction, employee satisfaction, and the cost of quality.	True ___	False ___	Not Sure ___
10. To ensure business success, the most important role for leaders is to participate, to be involved, and to be visible in day-to-day quality improvement actions.	True ___	False ___	Not Sure ___
11. Organizational renewal and transformation within the context of a meaningful vision represents one of the highest and most refined form of leadership.	True ___	False ___	Not Sure ___
12. All leaders do not have to be visionaries in order for a company to be successful.	True ___	False ___	Not Sure ___
13. If your company places all its focus on satisfying customers, business success will be assured.	True ___	False ___	Not Sure ___
14. Involving customers in the planning cycle is the best way to determine long term requirements.	True ___	False ___	Not Sure ___
15. When a company grows faster than the industry in each of its segments, it will grow market share.	True ___	False ___	Not Sure ___
16. The key to sustaining business leadership over a long period of time is keeping customers satisfied with superior product and service quality.	True ___	False ___	Not Sure ___
17. Historical trends with widening gaps between your company and the competition are accurate predictors of sustained success.	True ___	False ___	Not Sure ___

18. Considering all aspects of the competitor's company as a threat is one of the keys of successful strategy.	True ___	False ___	Not Sure ___
19. The Malcolm Baldrige National Quality Award is intended to raise the awareness of quality as an increasingly important element of competitiveness, to define requirements for excellence, and to establish benchmarks of excellence.	True ___	False ___	Not Sure ___
20. To sustain industry leadership, the quality system must be a closed loop system among suppliers and all functions of the company in support of the end customer.	True ___	False ___	Not Sure ___
21. True process reengineering must be a cross-functional activity involving all functional elements of the company.	True ___	False ___	Not Sure ___
22. Company-wide access to information bases that include customer, supplier, human resource, operational, and product related data is required to successfully implement TQM.	True ___	False ___	Not Sure ___
23. To reengineer processes, information flow and its use is fundamental to simplification.	True ___	False ___	Not Sure ___
24. Maximizing and optimizing the allocation of resources of the firm will also optimize strategy and quality effectiveness.	True ___	False ___	Not Sure ___
25. Companies can transform their business by developing effective Strategic Quality Plans.	True ___	False ___	Not Sure ___

ANSWERS TO THE QUIZ

Correct Answer	Your Answer	Explanation
1. False	____	Strategy deals with doing the right things and doing them in the right way. Quality deals with doing things right; consequently, strategy and quality are two sides of the same coin. The false belief that they are separate is what has given the Japanese a strategic advantage in so many markets. As this book shows, a balanced approach of the two, without sacrificing one over the other, creates an optimum degree of effectiveness.
2. False	____	This is the alchemy theory of strategy. It is like saying "by turning lead into gold, one can get rich." The concept is based on a false premise that we can forecast the future. Strategy effectiveness is based on understanding the dynamics, the configuration, and the intensity of the forces that impinge on a company. These conditions affect a company's ability to compete and to serve customers effectively on a sustained basis.
3. False	____	The characteristics of a highly effective, sustainable Total Quality Management (TQM) improvement system are ones that balance its priority on cost, expense, and customer satisfaction with revenue, market share growth, or competitiveness.
4. False	____	Lack of environmental fit does not mean a company cannot succeed. It can, provided the company is able to continuously learn, improve, and adapt relentlessly to the environment. Good environmental fit does

Correct Answer	Your Answer	Explanation
4. (Cont.)		not guarantee sustained performance. Failure to pick up weak environmental signals that are a precursor to major shifts and doing the same thing long after the environment has changed will certainly erode a strong initial position.
5. True	____	Historically these tasks were separated. Analysis and formulation were done by the planning staff, and the implementation was given to line managers. This caused many undesirable results. When both are done by line managers, the implementation is smoother, the organizational buy-in is higher, and the capability of detecting shifts, adjusting and learning is higher.
6. False	____	The dynamics of today's fast-paced industries with market shifts and rapid technology introduction require a continuous strategic process that is closed-loop in the way it monitors indicators and triggers of potential shift in order to anticipate and rapidly respond to change. This process must also be highly integrated into the company's management system.
7. True	____	While this is true, most companies have little or no systematic tools and methods to understand culture or to transform the organization from one culture to whatever it wants the new culture to be. Many companies also lack the capability to assess progress during the transformation.
8. False	____	While the Seven Basic Tools are important for analyzing and managing product and operational quality processes, where

Correct Answer	Your Answer	Explanation
8. (Cont.)		factual data exists for strategic analysis other tools and methods are required. These other tools are required to deal with strategic data that is sometimes voluminous, ambiguous, and conceptual in its nature. These tools are also required for synthesis to anticipate future dynamics and to make intelligent decisions for future competitive leadership.
9. True	____	Actual long term results from successful businesses presented in this book demonstrate the importance of an integrated business approach to successful quality implementation and demonstrate the need for a balanced approach to cost, expense, revenue, and market share growth.
10. False	____	While this day-to-day role is an important one for the leader(s) to emphasize, encourage, and support change, the more important role is one of developing a future strategic direction of the business, defining goals, and designing a transformation road map, and using quality to integrate and render the initiatives actionable within the extended enterprise (see Chapter 6, Item 5.1).
11. True	____	With the speed of change that is taking place today, with industry boundaries blurring and realigning, with markets shifting constantly, leaders must continuously find new ways to improve their products, to deliver better service and surprise their competitors. Pontificating and anecdotes do not ensure long term success.

Correct Answer	Your Answer	Explanation
11. (Cont.)		Leaders must develop a vision—a sense of direction and an inner guidance system. The leaders' responsibility to the employees, stockholders, customers, and the public is to integrate strategic management and quality for sustained long term company leadership. A major responsibility of a leader is the creation of Competitive Dominance strategies for the firm.
12. True	____	A company must understand the skills of its leaders and potential leaders and systematically place them in jobs that utilize their skills most effectively. Then it is important to create management systems that cross-functionally leverage the aggregate value of all key sets of skills—good administrators, managers, leaders, and visionaries.
13. False	____	Overemphasis on managing customer satisfaction within current customer base without a focus on new and emerging market opportunity can spell disaster for companies. New technology, new innovative designs, new service techniques, economic conditions, cost pressures, geographic shifts, and a myriad of other forces can change customer expectations overnight. Successful companies balance priorities between customers, natural and investment market expectations. Environmental scanning to understand market and industry forces and to anticipate changes is the way to achieve a sustainable competitive advantage.

Correct Answer	Your Answer	Explanation
14. False	____	Customers can provide requirements only on limited segments of the potential opportunity. Long term requirements can most effectively be determined by continuous environmental scanning, industry structure analysis, and market analysis. This is especially true for new businesses and market opportunities.
15. False	____	It is possible that a firm's market share is growing faster than the industry in every segment in which it competes, but in the aggregate, the firm is losing market share relative to the industry. To sustain market share in the aggregate a company must consider not only share growth in each segment, but the relative composition of its segments vis-à-vis the industry. For example, a company will not grow faster than the industry when it is gaining market share in a rapidly shrinking segment and simultaneously growing in a fast segment where the company has negligible share. This is described in detail in the chapter on Natural and Investment Markets.
16. False	____	The key to sustaining business over a long period is understanding natural and investment markets and the forces that affect those markets and then developing, introducing, and supporting differentiated products and services to continue to drive demand.
17. False	____	Past success is no guarantee of future success. Plans based on historical extrapolation to the future do not systematically consider or anticipate dramatic market shifts that can upset the status quo of the industry or the company.

Correct Answer	Your Answer	Explanation
18. False	____	Rigidly institutionalizing competitors is a bad approach to strategy. Identifying situations and conditions that create a competitive threat or opportunity is the correct approach. Competitors can be enemies in one segment and partners in another. For example, if IBM were to view Apple as the enemy, it could not have come out with the Power PC chip as quickly as it did. Yet this does not prevent IBM and Apple from competing intensely at the retail level in the PC market. Viewing competitors situationally is a strategically more flexible and less constraining perspective. Who is a competitor and when is it a threat must be determined on a case-by-case basis.
19. True	____	The Malcolm Baldrige guidelines provide a framework of how to develop and sustain a world class business. The key to successful implementation is understanding the guidelines, interpreting them in the broadest sense, and placing them in a future business context as described in Chapter 6.
20. False	____	The theory of Competitive Dominance states that all key stakeholders providing value to customers in the targeted markets need to be considered and involved in the processes that deliver value to customers and provide feedback to the company. This is a broader view than just company, suppliers, and customers. It extends the scope of quality improvement contributions to all constituents such as distributors, value added remarketers, and other channel participants.

Correct Answer	Your Answer	Explanation
21. False	____	Reengineering efforts that can produce meaningful results and sustainable impact must include all elements and functions of the company, but they must go much further. Reengineering must also include all value-providing stakeholders of the extended enterprise (inside and outside the company) and their combined and integrated business processes.
22. True	____	Broad sources of fact-based, company wide information are required to successfully implement TQM, but to sustain long term success, other data sources, such as market research and industry analysis, must be effectively and systematically used.
23. True	____	In fact, information flow and the use of information may be the most effective way to determine the redesign of processes to maximize the value-added steps throughout the extended enterprise.
24. False	____	There are never enough resources in any firm for quantum improvements of business performance above historical levels. Effective strategies and quality initiatives view the domain of maximization and optimization to include not only the company itself, but also business partners, customers, and other industry participants. The collective resources of this ensemble provide a reservoir of resources that can be optimized to the mutual benefit of all parties.
25. False	____	This is a common malpractice of TQM. The premise, as stated, is backward. Total quality initiatives must be designed and

Correct Answer	Your Answer	Explanation
25. (Cont.)		implemented within a transformational framework. If companies understand the future, can visualize its potential success, and develop a business strategy to implement, then quality concepts can be a power tool in the successful implementation.
	____	**Enter the number of correct responses.**

Range	Competitive Dominance Maturity
<10	Novice
10–15	Apprentice
16–21	Practitioner
22–25	Expert

If you scored less than ten, this book will provide you with the concepts and the means to improve your knowledge in integration of strategy and quality. If you scored ten to fifteen, you have a foundation to improve the depth of your knowledge and the skills of your management techniques in this area. If you score is between sixteen and twenty-one, you have a high degree of fluency and experience. Read this book carefully to hone discriminating skills so that you can deploy the power and synergy of Competitive Dominance. With a score above 21, our congratulations, you have acquired insight into the meaning and importance of the synergy between strategy and quality.

1

Theory of Competitive Dominance: Integration of Strategy and Quality

Competitive Dominance is the ability for a company to sustain leadership over a long period of time such that their products and services become the de facto standards. The "brand" becomes a power in the market. The brand generates extraordinary levels of confidence, trust, and, not incidentally, economic equity. It adds to the drawing power of a specific product or service. The company becomes simultaneously the most widely imitated and the most envied in the industry.

DuPont, General Motors, AT&T, Philips, Siemens, and Sony are just a few corporations that come to mind as historically dominant corporations. Take note of the words "historically dominant." Some of the corporate icons mentioned above have slipped from their dominant position to diminished status of "another strong competitor," and indeed, some to the ignominious position of "survivor." Consider IBM. Other competitors in the computer and information industry thought that no one would be able to unseat IBM in the seventies and eighties. IBM was the "most admired company" in Fortune magazine for four years in a row. Its brand, its extraordinary technical prowess, and its ability to compete were so lofty that the U.S. Department of Justice engaged in a protracted and invalid suit to show that it had "monopoly powers." Yet by 1992, IBM was showing poor business results and talking about layoffs for the first time in its history. By 1993, IBM had a new chairman, and it began a series of dramatic restructuring efforts in response to disastrous earnings and uninspired market performance. They slid from dominator to competitor. Digital Equipment Corporation is an even more dramatic example in the same industry. In 1987, Digital commanded the pre-eminent position in what the industry termed, "the mid-range" computer market. Its confidence was clear and unmistakable in its advertising slogan: "Digital has it now." Digital was the only company that was having success against IBM, which probably in Digital's view, did not "have it." Reasonable people argued then that IBM would forfeit that part of the market to them. But by 1990, Digital was down-sizing and reacting to market changes that took it from an apparently dominant position in the "mid-range" market to survivor status. Digital has demonstrated that it is unable to sustain its position in the industry and market. Sustaining leadership over an extended period of time is possibly the single most difficult challenge of a company. The only other more difficult challenge is reestablishing itself and contending for the leadership position again once a company has lost that position.

In the 1980s, Chrysler Corporation was barely in a survivor position. Yet today, Chrysler is a leader in the manufacture of Mini-Vans and four-wheel drive vehicles, and Chrysler has a complete new product line with innovative products such as the "cab-forward" designed automobile and the highly successful "Neon." In 1991, Chrysler had three consecutive quarters of net earnings loss. Yet it had three quarters of net earnings gains in each year during 1992 and 1993. The U.S. automobile manufacturers have regained a strong competitive position and re-established leadership in some product areas. This is impressive; especially when one considers the perceived invincibility of the Japanese in the 1980s.

Competitive Dominance is about sustained leadership (Figure 1-1). It is about levels of achievement beyond leadership. It is about undisputed excellence. Competitive Dominance is not about domination in the negative

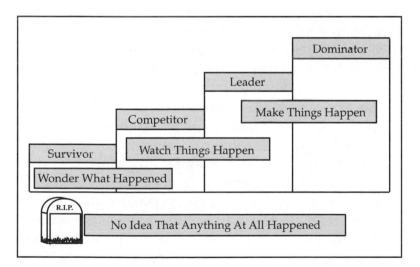

Figure 1-1 Strategic Choices.

sense of the word or in the context that makes corporate lawyers cringe. Competitive Dominance is not about competing unfairly to gain an advantage, and it is certainly not about unethical competitive practices to win over customers. Competitive Dominance is an attitude, an attitude that begins with a realization that a leadership position is no guarantee of long term success, especially in the global marketplace. It begins with a strong conviction that leadership is temporary and a belief that smart and competent competitors are always fully prepared to dislodge the leader or to displace the incumbent. In every endeavor, there is a leader. Competitive Dominance is the recognition that becoming a leader is only half the battle, at best. The other half is remaining a leader by consistently raising and creating new standards and levels of excellence. Leadership companies must continue to stretch goals and objectives. Leadership companies must consistently exceed objectives in a way that it surprises competitors and makes it difficult for followers to duplicate. They must continue to innovate, to deliver more value than any competitor, and strive continuously to dominate the competitive arena in this manner. They rewrite the competitive rules. They stun the competition. They delight their customers. Simply stated, they make things happen. They do this without sacrificing corporate and social responsibility and without deviating from ethical conduct in their business relationships.

Historically, dominant corporations lose their leadership position and succumb to competitive pressure and market dynamics because they fail to change the traditional processes and methods that made them successful. They do not recognize the environmental and technological changes that affect market demand and consumer expectations; nor do they recognize the rate of change. Frequently, it is not a case of these companies doing things poorly; rather it is a case of doing the wrong things so well. They rest on their laurels and begin to manage their business by rote. They forget the conditions under which the original strategies worked and why those strategies were effective. They spend their energies gloating about where they are and what they have accomplished, instead of what they should be and where they ought to be heading. Their very success drives them to an internalized view of their business instead of concentrating on the customer, the market, the competition, or those who will outflank them. They become predictable in their actions and their strategic approach, and therefore they become targets of companies with niche strategies, new ideas, or innovative repositioning.

Sears is an example of a company that was in a dominant position and saw its position erode. This example illustrates the irony of dominant firms. Sears became the profitable engine that served America so well that even today it is hard to find an American home that does not have Sears products in it. Sears was able to do this largely because it had an inspired leader, General Wood, who anticipated the population shift to the suburbs. He made sure that there was a Sears store in new suburban centers. Sears grew and prospered. General Wood recognized an environmental shift and took advantage of it to make Sears a leader. The same company, which had the insight to recognize an environmental shift, failed to recognize in the 1980s, that another shift was underway, and Sears ceded its position to Wal-Mart. Typically ignored because of their size or specialization, new competitors gain footholds in niche areas, and then all of a sudden, they emerge with irreversible momentum as strong industry forces propel them forward, ahead of traditional competitors. Many new, smart emerging upstarts gain dominant positions because they have strategies that create synergy and added-value with products and services from other companies. An example of two companies with different technologies that have emerged as leaders because of synergy are Intel and Microsoft. Intel produces the microchips that are used in personal computers, and Microsoft produces the software that makes the chips usable by application programs. Each company enhances the other. The more chips that are sold, the more software Microsoft sells. The more function that Microsoft develops in its software, the more the demand for more powerful microchips from Intel.

The typical response of the established leaders when confronted with vibrant and strong emerging competition is to go into reaction mode. They wonder, "What happened?" Predictably, they begin with quality programs or start reengineering initiatives targeted at the expense engine that complacency has created in the first place. Then they move to restructure, down-size, and lay off employees. Their prior success has caused them to internalize all actions. Without a strong external focus on market opportunities and new environmental dynamics, their revenue growth does not keep up with the market even though they are able to show improved financial performance because of cost-cutting. These are the symptoms of surviving, not of dominance. Without new strategic initiatives that will drive new sources of revenues and company growth, they continue to slide down the slippery slope of decline, they descend from the position of success to the lesser positions of "competitor," sometimes to "survivor," and perhaps, to obscurity. Very few companies today, if any, are able to sustain leadership over extended periods.

To become competitively dominant, corporations must have strategies, business processes, management systems, organizational culture, and values that extend beyond the excellence of individual executives, organizations, or generations of corporate structures. These characteristics form the genetic encoding of an organization. An organization must be genetically encoded to have the ability to respond excellently to external stimulus of global environmental conditions, market forces, opportunity, and industry dynamics. Those organizations that cannot respond are genetically deficient. In effect, they are retarded!

Historically, governments and large corporations controlled the pace of change to a large degree. There was geographic isolation due to lack of global travel and communications. People understood the "rules" and developed consistent expectations in different geographic regions. Large corporations tended to be dominant in specific market segments where competition was not as intense. Corporations were able to determine the pace of new product introduction, frequently by internal priorities and their own timing for competitive moves. In this regard, they were also largely self-sufficient; they had the resources to invest in research that led to new technology.

Today, in contrast, with global communications, affordable travel, and the emerging global economy, geographic and cultural boundaries are blurring. The old rules do not apply. Technologies that yield new products and services are being introduced at an increasingly rapid pace. Electronic communications has led to new organizational structures that enable networks of individuals and smaller companies to band together and become major participants in many technology and service opportunities that were once the sacred ground of "full-service" suppliers. In addition to the rapid pace of technology introduction, many technologies are converging to create new industries and new market opportunities. For example, the convergence of voice, image, computing, and video has created multimedia. Multimedia has application in information management, entertainment, education, government, and just about every other major industry. This creates new capabilities and markets like the high-tech companies that develop computer imaging for movies such as "Jurassic Park." And these changes are happening at an ever increasing rate.

Neither government, nor corporations can influence the changes as they did in the past. In fact, many are reacting to the changes affecting them. In this environment, it will be increasingly difficult for corporations to sustain a leadership position. It will impossible for corporations to achieve dominance without processes that recognize and anticipate future factors to respond in a way that gives them sustainable competitive advantage.

The objective of the theory of Competitive Dominance is to simultaneously synchronize, align, and integrate strategy and quality. Competitive Dominance seeks to position the company for future opportunities and growth through strategy and seeks to enable rapid and effective response to the opportunity through quality initiatives and offerings that delight customers. You must have both for Competitive Dominance. To sustain industry and market leadership, you must deploy policies that align and integrate strategy and quality initiatives. The principles and management practices of strategic thinking, strategic management, organizational transformation, organizational learning, and total quality management all address change, improvement, excellence, and industry and market leadership.

Competitive Dominance builds on these principles and goes beyond. In the same way that Calculus does not reject high school Algebra—it presumes you have mastered it and are ready to move on; Competitive Dominance does not reject effective principles of total quality management or strategic management. It does not discard the best practices from the experts of quality management, rather it extends them. *Competitive Dominance seeks to align, integrate, and synchronize strategy and quality to achieve future leadership and to be able to sustain it.* This definition of Competitive Dominance is illustrated in

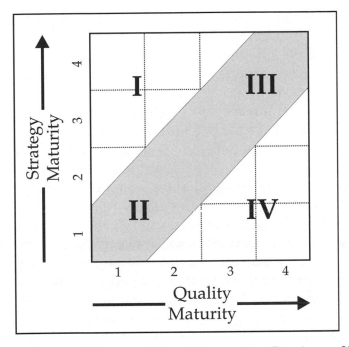

Figure 1-2 Alignment Map of Competitive Dominance Variables.

Figure 1-2, which demonstrates the relationship between strategy and quality.

Figure 1-2 shows the relationship of the two variables and illustrates the conditions under which effective alignment exists. There are four regions in this alignment map.

Region I, in the upper left hand corner, represents the companies that have strong strategic capabilities but weaker quality capabilities. For example, in the extreme case, companies in this region will formulate strategies that are skewed to gaining market share or the creation of a new market, but offer products that consistently fail to meet customer expectations because of poor reliability or lack of features and function. These are the companies that have a quality "blind-spot." They believe that their strategies can be effective without concentrating on quality.

These companies are most vulnerable to smart, relentless, and dogged competitors who will focus on quality to position themselves as the preferred alternative in the same markets. In recent history, these are the companies that have experienced the grim and consistent competitive quality pressure from Japanese products. Many of the automobile companies in the U.S. suffered this fate. One automobile company that falls in region I is Chrysler. They developed superior strategy to regain their position in the industry, but a lingering reputation for non-competitive quality has kept them from leadership.

Region II lies on the diagonal band along the 45° line. In this region are the companies that have strategies and quality programs that are consistently aligned. **Alignment here means that the strategic capabilities and the quality capabilities of the company exist to the same degree. The company is equally competent in strategy and in quality.** For obvious reasons, we call this band "the band of alignment." These companies may not be the stars of the market or the envy of the industry, but because their initiatives on the strategic and quality fronts are aligned, they are able to make progress along the 45° line and move in the direction of the upper right hand corner. Solectron from San Jose, California is an example of such a company that did become a star. Solectron submitted Malcolm Baldrige applications for a number of years, not because it wanted to win, but because it wanted world-class critiques of its business, and because it wanted to improve. Over time, Solectron moved up the diagonal in the direction of the right hand corner. In 1991, it won the Baldrige Quality Award for a manufacturing company. Time will tell whether it will move into Region III.

Region III is the region of Competitive Dominance, where strategic excellence and quality excellence come together in a mutually reinforcing way. These are the companies that can sustain their leadership position. These are the companies that have world class strategies and world class quality initiatives that produce unquestionable market performance, business results, and new levels of competitive performance. IBM Rochester was able to do this with the AS/400. It won the Baldrige Award in 1990, displaced Digital for the top position in the midrange computer market, and then set the standard.

Region IV, in the lower right hand corner, represents companies that have strong quality initiatives, but weak strategic capabilities. In the extreme case, these are companies that have a pathological fixation with quality management and lose sight of the market, competition, and other external environmental forces. Their quality initiatives are designed and deployed with little or no regard to market or industry conditions. In other words, these companies have quality initiatives that are inconsistent with the strategic necessities of the firm. Their quality initiatives are not tightly linked to corporate strategy. The absence of these links make companies unable to adjust their business to new or changing market or industry conditions. The Wallace company from Houston Texas, which won the 1990 Malcolm Baldrige Award for small business, but which was forced to undertake major financial restructuring soon after, is a stark example.

With this understanding of the Competitive Dominance Alignment Map, we now direct our attention to the two variables, strategic maturity and quality maturity. We segment the levels of maturity into four stages of progression, each punctuated by clear advance in sophistication of management practice, by increased scope of impact and effectiveness. The four stages of strategic maturity are summarized in Figure 1-3 for strategic maturity and in Figure 1-4 for quality maturity. The progression of strategy maturity is discussed in the next chapter. The progression of quality maturity is fully discussed in Chapter 4.

	Strategic Maturity	Focus	Response
1	Planning	• Operational control • Internal and functional • Short time horizon	• Fiscal discipline • Annual budget planning and reviews
2	Strategic Planning	• Planning effectiveness • Long time horizon	• Multi-year forecasts • Trends analysis • Investments based on capabilities and affordability
3	Strategic Management	• Respond to markets and competition • Cross-functional	• Environmental Analysis—markets, industry, competition, technology, etc. • Evaluation of strategic alternatives • Investments based on competitive outcomes and portfolio analysis
4	Strategic Leadership	• Competitive advantage • Flexibility and speed • Vision and transformation	• Opportunity driven strategy • Continuous scanning to create anticipatory capability • Tightly unified & integrated closed-loop business processes with operations • Culture and business transformation

Figure 1-3 Four Stages of Strategic Maturity (Adapted from Gluck 1983).

Strategic Maturity	Focus	Response
4 Strategic Leadership		• Strategic use of information technology • Investments based on core comp

Figure 1-3 Four Stages of Strategic Maturity (Adapted from Gluck 1983). *(continued)*

Quality Maturity	Focus	Response
1 Detection and Control	• Internal production focus	• Cost and expense reduction • Cost of quality focus • Conformance to specifications and procedures
2 Prevention and Efficiency	• Internal company focus	• Use of statistical tools • Cycle time reduction • Quality improvement teams • Root cause analysis • Fact based decisions • Process management
3 Management and Continuous Improvement	• External customer driven	• Customer satisfaction • Cross-function integration • Continuous improvement • Process reengineering • Supplier partnerships • Product and service focus

Figure 1-4 Four Stages of Quality Maturity.

Quality Maturity	Focus	Response
4 Anticipation and Creation	• External future market opportunity driven	• Future orientation • Customer and markets • Business and cultural transformation • Unified-systemic links • Stakeholder integration • Information and work process flow • Predictive and anticipatory tools and models

Figure 1-4 Four Stages of Quality Maturity. *(continued)*

Now that we have the Alignment Map and an understanding of the maturity levels for strategy and quality, we are able to discuss why the different regions produce different levels of competitive capabilities, organizational effectiveness, market impact, and customer satisfaction. The reasons can be stated very simply. Different alignments, which create the four different regions in the alignment map, are the result of companies taking approaches of different degrees of effectiveness, different levels of comprehensive deployment, the effect of which is different levels of results.

Before we continue, we describe what we mean by "approach," "deployment," and "results." "Approach" is the method or methods that a company uses to achieve its goals and objectives. "Deployment" refers to the extent to which the approaches are applied and institutionalized to key relevant areas and activities of the company. "Results" refers to the outcomes and effects of the approach and deployment.

In Region I, the strategic capabilities are strong, but the quality capabilities are lower by comparison. This results in two situations. One case is where the approach is strong, deployment is weak and therefore, results are weak. This is a situation where well-formulated strategy initiatives are poorly implemented, causing weak results. The other case is where the approach is also strong, deployment is adequate, and therefore results are effective. This is the case where well-formulated strategies with solid implementation can be effective.

In Region IV, there are also two situations. One is where the approach is weak relative to deployment. This is a result of the relatively lower strategy capabilities, but stronger quality initiatives. The effect is a situation where deployment carries the day and the results produced are adequate. The other situation is one where the approach is adequate and the deployment is strong. In this case strong implementation and quality processes that can learn and self-adjust will produce effective results.

We now turn our attention to the 45° band. Region II and Region III, where strategic capability and quality capability are consistently aligned. At the bottom of the band, strategic capability is lowest, and quality capability is lowest to the same degree. In this case, the approach is weak, deployment is weak, and, naturally, results are weak. Moving up the band slightly, strategic capability improves, and quality capability improves in the same proportion. In absolute terms, however, both are only reaching a level of adequacy, and mastery in neither has been attained. The result is then adequate approach, adequate deployment, and adequate results. Companies in this position are competing or surviving, and typically they are reacting to other participants in their industry. Moving up the band some more, these are the companies that have acquired strategic capabilities and quality maturity to the same degree. There is symmetry between the high degree of strategic capabilities and quality maturity. Typically, these are the companies that practice strategic planning, have strategic management capabilities, and simultaneously deploy fairly sophisticated total quality management (TQM) initiatives. They have good customer relationship processes, strong and well deployed approaches, results that strengthen and support the goals and objectives of the strategies, and an effective closed-loop learning system.

Moving up the band of alignment further, we are now in Region III, the region of Competitive Dominance. These are the companies and organizations that have integrated quality and strategic management fully. These are the companies that have business initiatives, business processes, management systems, organizational culture, and values that synchronize and integrate strategy and quality. These companies are very rare. Over an extended period of time they have been able to develop strategies that have transformed their business in a way that is consistent with new and emerging environmental changes. They are able to deploy new and reengineered business processes in addition to existing ones, to capitalize on new business and market opportunities. They create new competitive rules to their advantage and produce more value to customers. They can continuously improve to satisfy new customers to a degree that surpasses industry and customer expectations. The morale within the company is high; esprit de corps is the envy of the industry. These are the competitive dominant firms. In this region, the approach is superior, the deployment is superior, and the results they achieve are therefore also superior. These concepts are summarized and illustrated in Figure 1-5.

MCI is an example of such a firm. Under its visionary founder, Bill McGowan, MCI was able to create a long-distance telephone company by understanding the regulatory statutes better than anyone else and through a uniquely innovative strategy that used the facilities of its major competitor. And when the industry structure changed, driven by dramatic changes in regulatory con-

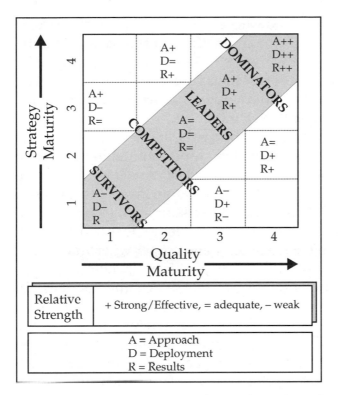

Figure 1-5 Approach, Deployment, and Results in the Alignment Map.

ditions, MCI was able to expand its business in the U.S. and overseas to create major new offerings. MCI appears able to constantly formulate new and effective strategies and innovative customer services that provides more value and economic benefit to its customers. It surprises the competition and its customers. It constantly rewrites the competitive rules. Its "Friends and Family" is an example of innovation that continues to fuel the growth and competitive capabilities of MCI. By the way, MCI is not the dominant firm in terms of market share—that distinction belongs to AT&T. But consistent with our definition of Competitive Dominance, MCI has an attitude that consistently surprises and catches its competition off guard. It continuously ups the competitive ante and is constantly striving to find new ways to satisfy its customers, redefine the meaning of customer value, and reshape the playing field. MCI is an example of a firm that lives by the rules of Competitive Dominance.

We have identified the areas in the alignment map where the various levels of approach, deployment, and results occur. *In business, sustainable results are what count.* Note that in Figure 1-5, we have delineated the areas in the alignment map where the results are the same regardless of the level of approach or deployment. The "survivors" are on the lower left hand corner where the results are the weakest. The next diagonal band where the results are adequate is the region where "competitors" aggregate. With inconsistent degrees of approach and deployment, one can only achieve adequacy. The next band, where the results are good, is the region where "leaders" aggregate. As in the previous band, one can achieve leadership through varying degrees of approach and deployment. However, because the level of approach and because deployment is higher, the results are better than "competitors." To be a "dominator," it is necessary to have superior approach and effective deployment to achieve superior results. This is the upper right hand corner of the alignment map.

With this broad understanding of the alignment map, we can now discuss the **operational domain** of the state-of-the-art strategy and quality methodologies. This is illustrated in Figure 1-6. It is our conviction, supported by many factual studies done in 1991, 1992, and 1993, that Total Quality Management is very effective in the domain shown where it can produce good results. ISO 9000 is effective along the band of alignment, but at a lower level than TQM and with less relationship to business results.

Figure 1-6 Domain of Strategy and Quality Methodologies.

We discuss the nature of this relative positioning in substantially more detail in subsequent chapters. At this time, we explore the relationship of quality and Competitive Dominance and contrast the key conceptual differences of the most effective and sophisticated of quality management principles in TQM.

Everything we have discussed so far is descriptive in nature. It is designed to provide a framework to think about quality and strategy integration. But what executives want most are not just descriptions that elucidate the behavior and dynamics of organizations. They are action-oriented. They want to know what to do. This book will have failed if it could not be prescriptive as well. We present a set of tools, methodologies, and practices, which, when used intelligently, can be very effective in moving an organization into the region of Competitive Dominance. We provide that discussion in Chapter 6 with what we consider the most important tool for Competitive

Dominance. In that chapter, we describe in substantial detail and discuss in depth how the Competitive Dominance principles can be integrated into the framework of the Malcolm Baldrige criteria as a guide to accelerate the achievement of Competitive Dominance.

For those who are anxious for a shortcut, who are impatient with the demanding and challenging task of quality and strategy, or who want results immediately, we offer a word of caution. Competitive Dominance is not achievable without effort, commitment, and continuous learning. Maturity and competence in strategic management and quality management are acquired over time. It is like playing the violin. To acquire virtuosity requires practice, patience, lots of mistakes, a passion for learning, and a set of uncompromising standards of excellence. In Chapter 9, we identify a dozen of the most common mistakes in strategic and quality management that we have observed from organizations that were impatient, in a hurry, looking for the quick fix, or unwilling to invest the time and energy. They represent a dozen mistakes of managerial malpractice. Not only are they ineffective; they are damaging to the business and the organization.

2

Paradigms in Crisis: Criticisms and Contributions of Strategy and Quality

Everyone believes that quality and strategy are essential elements to achieve business success. Criticizing the concepts of strategy or quality is akin to attacking institutions such as motherhood and apple pie. But debate and skepticism on approach, practice, implementation, and effectiveness rage in every business, in the trade press, and around the globe because these complex concepts have a multitude of variables and implementations. Almost everyone has a different perspective of strategy and quality depending on their background, experience, and point of view. The criticisms lodged have varying degrees of validity caused by varying degrees of interpretation, understanding, and implementation. A successful technology-based strategy may be right for one company, but it will fail in another, depending upon many different variables, such as innovation, market opportunity, excellent implementation, and product positioning. A team-based approach to quality improvement may be at the core of one company's successful quality implementation, while another company gains no business improvement with a strong team focus.

Common understanding must first be established before any intelligent conversation or debate on strategy and quality topics occur. Chapter 1 framed both strategy and quality within the context of Competitive Dominance. It is within this context that we address the criticisms and contributions of strategy and quality.

CRITICISMS OF STRATEGY

Everything, including the term strategy itself, has different meanings to different people. Some describe strategy as a set of actions to achieve plan objectives for the year. Others believe it is a long term view that has little pertinence to the current problems and challenges. Still others believe that it is a "blue-sky" approach that requires people with telepathic powers to prognosticate the future. Whatever the perception, the following five criticisms of strategy address much of the current debate.

Disconnected with the Real World

The strategy cycle in a company typically occurs in one-, two-, three-, or even five-year cycles. Most U.S. companies have a business cycle that includes a strategy review performed yearly with a five-year outlook. The strategy cycle is delegated to the "strategists" located in some remote part of the site or corporation in, what many people term, "the ivory tower." The image of the strategist is one of an academic—a desk covered with papers, books, computer printouts, and a statue of Don Quixote jousting a windmill. This image frequently includes former top performing executives who have plateaued in their careers. These people are good communicators, they are comfortable dealing with executive levels and board members, and they deserve a position of graceful transition to retirement.

Strategist's surface once a year to gather reams of data from finance, technologists, manufacturing, market research, competition, and the industry. The functional suppliers of data are too busy fighting the fires of the day and attempting to make their plan commitments, and therefore they perceive this cycle as added and unnecessary work. The strategists sift, consolidate, compare, and analyze information to develop a formal presentation carried up the chain to the executive offices. The executives see strategy as another input for corporate decisions, but many view it as a secondary set of data to supplement their own experience and knowledge. They view the strategy organization as a staff role, a necessary expense item, and a requirement to satisfy the Board of Directors. Planners and strategist skills are always on the "non-critical skill" lists.

Long, hard hours go into the development of the strategy. The climax is the CEO and operating committee review and approval. Everyone is congratulated on a fine piece of work, then the strategy goes into the file. There is minimal communication back down the organization on critical assumptions and strategic initiatives. The executives can now continue the business of achieving the plan targets as they have tucked away bits and pieces that may be useful someday.

Because very few line organizations see the strategy, and because the strategy itself is not a working document or process, critics question the value of the output, effort, and expense. The "buy in" from line organizations struggling to meet or achieve their plan goals is close to zero. Executive "buy in" is better, but only if it supports the current power structure and is non-threatening. Rather than analyze and study trends that may create a market shift or change the current status-quo, these executives attack the premise and analysis performed because it may threaten tradition and balance of power. The periodic planning cycle itself keeps strategy "out of site, out of mind" in the operational management and measurement systems creating a void between strategy development and strategy implementation. Even the best strategies succumb to the priorities of the day if not continuously integrated into the operational management system. The above circumstances cause strategy to become disconnected with the real world but this disconnect can be overcome by the following:

Make strategy a process, not a cyclical event. In competitive dominance, strategy is not an event, but a process. And just as in a manufacturing process, must be continuous. Environmental conditions, markets, and the industry do not stand still, nor do they change in periodic cycles. A dynamic environment requires a dynamic strategy tightly coupled to the operational management and measurement system.

Monitor feedback and adjust capability continuously. A disciplined strategy process has well-established listening posts, continuously monitored to identify and anticipate shifts in competition, market demand, or industry dynamics that create new business challenges or opportunities. Continuous closed-loop environmental scanning capability provides the powerful advantage of anticipating and responding before the competition. Companies that "make things happen," or always seem to be one step ahead of the industry, have developed this capability.

Implement a transformation road map. A company must translate its strategy into a set of initiatives that have identified owners responsible for the implementation, concrete goals that constitute success, and checkpoints or milestones that gauge progress on the changing journey. This is the action that renders vision and strategy actionable. The strategy cycle is not complete when the executive team reviews and concurs—it is just the beginning. Owners, checkpoints, and milestones enable the strategy to be integrated into the operational management system. This continuous system keeps the priority and focus on key strategic initiatives and provides the forum to rapidly adjust and respond to changes.

Make line managers the strategists. One of the major reasons for the disconnect of strategy is that the analysis and formulation is so frequently in the hands of staff or professional analysts. Their analysis and plans are done without line management participation. The way to solve this disconnect with line managers is to not have it in the first place. That is accomplished by making the line managers responsible for the strategy, but these line managers must be given tools and training in order to be effective.

Too Focused on the Short-Term

Another criticism of strategy is that it often only represents a short term focus of only one to two years. In this case, the terminology between strategy and plan becomes confused. The traditional five-year outlook has no specifics beyond the second year, and frequently even the second year lacks any concrete initiatives or goals. Then, every year when the new strategy surfaces, there is little relationship, or "bridging," back to the previous year. Out of frustration, critics complain that the time frame is insufficient to determine significant resource deployment changes, so all the company does is shuffle the same old deck of cards. A common characteristic of this approach in companies is continuous reorganization to solve the problem of the month or year. Companies that carry out this form of strategy development have "round heels" management. It is not uncommon to see a major reorganization every six months as executives roll back on their heels, reacting to marketplace dynamics that keep them off balance. These are the companies that "have no idea what is happening" or "wonder what happened."

Developing strategies that have the potential to establish long term leadership requires a perspective that is long enough to ensure that the significant resources deployed to achieve leadership can have constancy and continuity of purpose. Change takes time. New and significant initiatives require that processes and relationships be developed, deployed, and firmly established. Strategies founded with a short term view are typically developed from historical trends and current issues and opportunities. Many times, today's problems and opportunities are not the strategic issues, so resources are misdirected. Fact based analysis, modeling, and anticipatory tools provide more insight into the long range implications of the forces of today. Complementing this with a continuous scanning process helps manage the fine line a company walks in establishing the balance between long term commitment and the flexibility to adapt and respond to short term shifts.

No Need for Longer Term Focus with Rapid Changes Happening

No one disputes the rapid pace of change in the global marketplace. Speed is on the lips of most senior executives. Cycle time, time to market, and just-in-time have surfaced as key company initiatives in the last twenty years. Information technology continues to improve global intra-company communications, thereby increasing company capabilities to respond rapidly. So, with the rapid rate of change, what good is long term strategy? These are valid criticisms articulated by even some world-renowned business experts. The answer comes from the interpretation and understanding of how Competitive Dominance applies to strategy.

Strategy must be developed to address emerging and new market opportunities with a focus on market share and revenue growth. Strategy must consider the current company business heritage. More importantly, it must define the business of the future. The portfolio of tomorrow may be a different portfolio than today's. It must consider the value chain of the future business, and the other participants, both potential partners and competitors. That is to say, it must consider all the players that can provide value to the customer. In this context, strategy reconceptualizes the company's role, the business it is in, the critical success factors, and frames the "brand" image that provides the constancy of purpose for the company. Within this constancy of purpose, shorter term initiatives can address the transition from the legacy portfolio, respond to short term problems and opportunities, and adjust to anticipated shifts. An excellent quality system provides the basis for rapid and efficient short term response within the framework of an excellently developed longer term strategy.

To reinforce the long term direction and short term flexibility, consider this example from our experience. For years corporate task groups worked to reduce the product development cycle time. The technologists' position was one of "We can shorten the development cycle only if we have stable product requirements." Stable requirements would stabilize the process and make it easier to reduce cycle time. Of course, the developers knew that there was no such thing as stable requirements because market, competition, and customer needs determine requirements, and all these factors are uncontrollable to the product developer. Therefore, product requirement changes were a monthly occurrence. IBM Rochester decided to solve this problem differently. Its approach was to develop a long-term strategy that identified a new business context, a long-term product image or "brand," and a broader set of critical success factors. IBM Rochester identified those participants in the value chain who were critical to its success and brought those participants into the day-to-day activities of the product development process. IBM Rochester discovered that when it engaged external participants in the development process, those participants provided the product developers with day-to-day feedback (similar to monitoring and listening posts). With this feedback, developers could make changes "on the fly," improving the production in real time.

The result provided significantly improved flexibility and adaptability to a once rigid process. The results achieved speak for themselves. The development cycle was shortened by approximately 50 percent. More importantly, IBM Rochester was able to implement its long-term strategy by delivering to the marketplace a new and highly successful solution that established the reputation and basis for its future business success. A long-term time horizon for its planning and actions was critical. Without it, IBM Rochester would not have identified the future critical success factors that led to new and extended value chain partnerships. It would not have been able to identify the required shift in business context from a declining market to market segments with growth potential.

Strategy Is Too Qualitative and Judgmental

Strategy analysis and conclusions that are based on opinions and judgments become easy to challenge. Many times the conclusions are supported only by anecdotal evidence. Some factual evidence provided is based on the extrapolation of historical trends. This assumes that the conditions and assumptions of the past will hold true in the future. This becomes shaky ground to predict the future of the business, to say the least. In this all too common situation, two or three challenges that cannot be met with specific and concrete facts rapidly destroy the credibility of the strategy. Executives who see the strategy as a threat to their position can easily subvert the credibility of new strategic initiatives when proposals or analysis are supported with weak factual data and analysis. When the credibility of the analysis is suspect because the conclusions are not grounded in information, this attack is perhaps deserved.

Fact-based analysis is just as important to strategy development as it is to, say, manufacturing process control. An excellent strategist does not develop conceptual insight through the use of a crystal ball. Factual information analyzed by tools and predictive models is a hallmark of a mature Competitive Dominance system. Tools and models are even more important to strategy because the strategist must aggregate, correlate, and creatively synthesize massive amounts of data to identify concrete opportunities or problems from ambiguous sources of information. These tools typically supplement and compliment executive insight, experience, and knowledge, and they strengthen the overall decision making process, especially when dealing with the uncertainties of the future.

Factual information sources are the basis for a sound and systematic continuous environmental scanning process. They provide the foundation for listening post information and monitoring. The typical problem with strategy information is not a problem of enough data; it is the problem of how to aggregate and synthesize the data into usable information that can be translated to knowledge. It requires a disciplined and refined approach to information analysis and a high comfort level with analytic tools.

In Chapters 7 and 8, tools and methodologies to put more rigor and discipline into strategic decisions and processes are described.

No Accountability

Line operational managers, who are measured in performance by every way imaginable, are the most vocal critics that say there is no accountability for strategy. They are burdened by schedules, budgets, costs, sales, profit, morale, and other key criteria that measure an operational manager's performance. They view the strategist as having no schedule pressure, no operational commitments, and minimal responsibility for strategy actions that are unsuccessful. Their buy-in to strategy is biased according to their opinion of the strategist's role. This criticism is valid when strategy is disconnected from the day-to-day business or when very little factual information supports the strategy.

When strategy is highly integrated within the operational management and measurement system, everyone, including the strategist, is responsible for successful implementation. The entire team is working synchronously and in lock-step on both the tactical initiatives and the strategic initiatives. When organizations are able to do this, they are at the highest level of strategy maturity on the strategy-quality maturity grid. And when a company can couple this ability with quality maturity at a similar level, that company has gained the ability to sustain leadership.

The five criticisms described above are valid when the strategy practice of a company lacks maturity and seamless integration with the quality practice. When Competitive Dominance theory is applied to overcome the five criticisms, strategy and quality become highly integrated and refined, and the lines between quality and strategy become blurred and cease to exist as separate management practices. The solutions to the criticisms of strategy have a strong relationship to key quality concepts. Strategy is a continuous process with closed-loop evaluation and feedback cycles. Strategy must be grounded in fact-based analysis and supported with analytical tools that enhance the decision making process. Companies must integrate goals and milestones that constitute progress and success into the operational management system to ensure that strategic initiatives are deployed and producing results.

CRITICISMS OF QUALITY

Quality too, has its own set of critics and criticism. The introduction of many different quality methodologies has generated confusion and frustration for companies that have established or are beginning Total Quality Management (TQM) initiatives. What approach should they take? Should they use ISO 9000 standards? Should they use a quality award model, or is it better to focus on one of the "guru's" approaches? There is much discussion and debate around the globe on what is the best approach to quality improvement. Each method has its critics and supporters alike. What can be said is that all the approaches support a consistent set of quality theories and concepts that have existed for a number of years. They are: continuous improvement, teamwork, involvement, recognition, the importance of management involvement, customer focus, statistical analysis, defect prevention, and supplier partnerships. All these concepts and theories are embodied in the Malcolm Baldrige and other award criteria so it is from this base that we will discuss criticisms and contributions.

The Critics of Baldrige as a Quality Framework

Baldrige has enjoyed its share of acceptance and criticism. Much of the criticism leveled against Baldrige cites the cases of Baldrige winners with poor or failing business results. Most of the criticism, if not all, comes from lack in depth of understanding of the Baldrige criteria. Critics see Baldrige as a quest for an award more than a tool for overall business improvement. Just as strategy and TQM mean something different to everyone, the Baldrige guidelines are interpreted differently by everyone, critics, Baldrige Award winners, and those that use the criteria for self improvement. The Baldrige guidelines are broad and require intense study and experience to understand even one examination item. Moreover, many people, even those who have participated in Baldrige assessments, do not understand the critical links between the categories. And, the fact that Baldrige is not prescriptive, lends itself to a wide range of interpretation.

Curt W. Reimann, the Director for Quality Programs who administers the Baldrige Award through the National Institute of Standard and Technology (NIST) in the Department of Commerce, states best the value of Baldrige.

Reimann addresses critics and supporters alike by stating that, "All models are flawed, but some models are useful." The Baldrige model is useful because it puts quality into the context of a total and complete business framework. Those who use Baldrige without success have failed either in the interpretation of the guidelines, the application of practice, or the commitment required. Is it perfect? No, but it is continually improving and has become a rallying point for American industry. It is our belief that those not intimately involved in a Baldrige assessment are unqualified as critics. How thoroughly a company performs a Baldrige assessment, and what it does with the findings, determines the difference between valid criticism and interesting conversation. One can summarize all the criticisms of Baldrige in six areas:

It Is Bureaucratic and Stifling

The Malcolm Baldrige guidelines are very comprehensive and cover all areas of a business as well as interactions outside the company's boundaries with suppliers, customers, and the general public. So when a company decides to perform an assessment against the Baldrige criteria, it must include a broad base of people from all functions across the organization. This requires a project management effort with significant amount of planning and coordination. If a company uses "staffers" to perform assessment, they immediately create bureaucracy. Another common bureaucracy that develops when companies do Baldrige assessment is the creation of a person or group of people "administrators" to coordinate calendars, schedules, and checkpoints. These "non-value-added" participants tend to clog the airways and mail rooms with useless status and communications. With them, the administration of the assessment process takes priority over the content and outcome. Managers and employees that lack understanding of the company objectives do not see the value in performing an assessment. They see assessment as just another task on top of all their other priorities. Most people do not see the big picture that develops when an organization completes an assessment because they are only a "piece-player" in a Baldrige Item or a Category. It takes months and hundreds of hours to perform a through assessment. What is being done is a critical analysis of all areas of the business. If a company does not put rigor and discipline into an assessment, it is wasting its time—it is creating a bureaucracy.

In May 1993, Quality Progress magazine published an article from a study of the U.S. business community's opinion of the Baldrige Award (Knotts 1993). This survey of 285 U.S. businesses was performed in conjunction with the Faculty Research committee of Georgia Southern University. We use the results of this study throughout this chapter and refer to it as the QP study. Figure 2-1 shows the results of the survey. A high percentage of the businesses participating state that the process is useful for all types of firms. Almost half say the process is too complex. For large companies, the process demands a total business evaluation. People accustomed to working in functional areas find this task especially difficult because it requires that they understand cross-functional links and interdependencies. For small businesses, the criteria require data and interrelationships that may not be needed for effective small business operation. While the Baldrige process tries to take this into account as part of the examination process, many companies may take a prescriptive approach when none is required, or many that evaluate the application may interpret the guidelines too strictly. In other words, the criteria does not spell it out, so it must not be important. Even so, a large percentage of the companies surveyed feel that the criteria are useful as an evaluation tool, and the benefits are well worth the effort.

U.S. Business Community Perceptions about the Baldrige Process and Criteria	
Response Category	**Overall**
Is Useful	88%
Is as useful for small firms as for large firms	73%
Application process is too complex	44%
Criteria are useful as an internal assessment tool	80%
Benefits are not worth the effort	22%

Figure 2-1 U.S. Business Community Perceptions of Baldrige.

ISO 9000 and other total quality initiatives suffer similar criticisms because of the requirement for documentation, auditing, and compliance to specifications. Tracking and reporting requirements add workload to the system.

One other source that fuels the perception of bureaucracy comes from the origin of the Baldrige Award. People perceive that government involvement results in bureaucracy. The facts are that the Department of Commerce manages the process with only a small group of people. The Judges, Examiners, and much of the Administration are comprised of volunteers and non-profit organizations from industry, professional organizations, and academia.

The best method to avoid bureaucracy is to use senior line management as category "owners" in the assessment team. It requires their involvement and gains their commitment. As senior managers, they have the perspective to assure the scope is broad enough to complete a thorough assessment, as well as the resources and influence to make improvements identified. The senior management team, which puts the complete assessment picture together, has the opportunity to learn as a team and to see the major strengths, weaknesses, and opportunities throughout the total business operation. Dealing with these strengths, weaknesses, and opportunities as a management team is an inherent responsibility of senior management. It is also important to communicate the results of the assessment clearly to all, along with action plans for improvement. People must clearly see some value in the outcome, or they will see it as just "busy work." The organization must integrate the assessment process into the business operation so that it does not become the "quality action of the year." Half-hearted attempts to do "a category a year" is also a waste of time. All the categories have critical links throughout the operations of a business. When a company or business unit completes one category in a vacuum, the value for the effort is questionable and open to criticism because of lack of integration.

The strategy of the business must be the driving goal of a Baldrige assessment. Improvement actions do not happen overnight. If actions to solve historic and current problems are the only basis for quality initiatives, these issues may not necessarily be the emerging problems or opportunities in the future. By solving yesterday's problems, a company may find it has made no progress in the long run. Problems define where a company is currently; opportunity defines where a company wants to be. More simply stated, "If you do not know where you are going, you may find that you are someplace where you do not want to be!"

Criteria are Static and Unchanging
Only those with the most cursory knowledge of the Baldrige process lodge this criticism. They may have read the guidelines, have been involved in only one cycle of the process, or really do not understand the depth of the criteria. Less than half the business community in the QP study (44%) agreed that the criteria were easy to understand. The Baldrige Award criteria have changed every

year since its introduction in 1987. It has improved in both the examination contents and in structure. Each year, NIST requests feedback on the Award process and the criteria, from industry, Malcolm Baldrige Examiners, and companies involved in the process. They integrate best practices into the criteria. In the QP study, only 13% of the companies responded that the Baldrige needed additional categories of criteria. Figure 2-2 highlights the improvements to the Baldrige criteria and process since its introduction in 1987.

We have experienced the criteria's improvements personally during eight consecutive years of active Baldrige assessment. Some of those improvements came directly from our participation at IBM Rochester. For example, in the 1989 guidelines, little assessment criteria pertaining to analytical market segmentation techniques as a key method to gather requirements was included. In our 1989 application, the Examiners indicated this as a leading edge practice. NIST requested us to provide input to guideline changes for 1990. When the 1990 criteria emerged, there were examination areas related to market segmentation. With our input, and that of Xerox, the segmentation questions were more difficult for us to answer in 1990. The guidelines had improved more rapidly than our ability to improve our process.

Some believe that the Baldrige criteria are improving more rapidly than companies' ability to progress through the maturity stages of quality. Perhaps that is some of the reason for the lower score trends in Figure 4-8, Chapter 4. Introducing significant year-to-year change is a problem for companies attempting to make year-to-year improvements. It is like trying to hit a moving target. To address this problem, NIST is managing the amount of year-to-year enhancement. This does not preclude companies that have new breakthrough concepts from competing for Baldrige. The objective of the Baldrige criteria is not to

Year	1988	1989	1990	1991	1992	1993	1994	1995
Framework	Introduced						Refined	Refined
Examination guidelines						Introduced	Expanded	Refined
Performance Issues					Introduced	Developed	Refined	Linked to key business issues
Key concepts				6 concepts	10 core values	10 core values	10 core values	11 core values
Examination Characteristics				Incipient	12 areas	Simplified	Simplified	Tied to key business drivers
Business factors		Defined in overview	Defined in overview	Detailed explanation	Tied to application	Key to evaluation	Basis of quality system	Cont. imp., strategy, financials, innovation
Scoring method		Criteria	Dimensions	Dimensions and guidelines	Dimensions and guidelines	Guidelines tied to key business factors	Guidelines tied to key business factors	Linkage of criteria to business drivers

Figure 2-2 Changes in the Baldrige Award Process Since 1987 (Adapted from Neves 1994).

Year	1988	1989	1990	1991	1992	1993	1994	1995
Areas to address	278	192	133	99	89	92	91	54
Items	62	44	33	32	28	28	28	24
Sub-Categories	42	27	—	—	—	—	—	—
Categories	7	7	7	7	7	7	7	7

Figure 2-2 Changes in the Baldrige Award Process Since 1987 (Adapted from Neves 1994). *(continued)*

prescribe a method. It encourages leading edge concepts and practices that Baldrige Examiners are trained to recognize and consider in scoring. The Baldrige process itself has grown beyond a quest for an award. It has become an organizational learning tool that is continually improving, based on the most successful practices of industry and advanced theories of academia.

It Is Not Prescriptive

The fact that Baldrige is not prescriptive is a criticism from those that are looking for the cookbook approach. They have a problem and are looking for the answer. Baldrige cannot be effective as a prescriptive tool. It recognizes that there are demographic, resource, regulatory, and industry differences and that most companies do business differently. The "one fits all" philosophy would be ineffective and open to serious criticism.

Let's explore what the business community thinks about the criteria in the QP study (Knotts 1993). In Figure 2-3, only a small percent of those in the business community felt the criteria were not relevant to the organization or that the criteria were too broad. While Baldrige is not prescriptive, most felt that the criteria were applicable for their use with the right amount of qualitative and quantitative emphasis.

The value of Baldrige is that the criteria require companies to describe how their business operates to achieve its long term strategy within a framework of best practices benchmarks and theories. The effectiveness of the business operations is really in how well each of its processes integrates in the overall operation to achieve its objectives. Baldrige recognizes that different companies have different priorities and approaches. An important factor for success in one company might not have high priority in another. For example, one company may have account retention as its most critical success factor. In this case, the

U.S. Business Community Perceptions about the Baldrige Criteria	
Response Category	**Overall**
Criteria are not relevant to our organization	9%
Guidelines/criteria are too broad	12%
Criteria place too much emphasis on quantitative data	12%
Criteria place too much emphasis on qualitative data	6%

Figure 2-3 U.S. Business Community Perceptions of the Baldrige Criteria.

entire focus of the company's processes and resources is on this factor for customer satisfaction. Another company may be technology-driven to improve customer satisfaction. The objective of Baldrige is to assess the company approach, to determine how well this approach is deployed, and to evaluate if the actions deliver expected results. Overall approach, deployment, and results are assessed, not just in one or two areas of the business, but coordinated across the total business operation to achieve strategic leadership goals. This comprehensive approach is the least understood and most challenging aspect of Baldrige.

Weak Services Quality Emphasis

Few service companies have successfully competed for the Malcolm Baldrige National Quality Award. A common criticism of service companies is that the Baldrige criteria do not fit their business. "It's too production process-oriented" is a common complaint. Category five, the process category, tends to carry the brunt of the criticism. Data from the QP survey supports this criticism, as seen in Figure 2-4. Almost half the service companies felt a need for special criteria. Small service companies expressed stronger views than large ones.

U.S. Business Community Perceptions about the Baldrige Criteria—Manufacturing vs. Service			
Response Category	**Manufacturing**	**Service**	**Overall**
Needs special criteria for service firms	16%	48%	30%

Figure 2-4 U.S. Business Community Perceptions of Baldrige Service Orientation.

Those Baldrige winning service companies, such as Federal Express and AT&T, feel that the criteria fits service companies, but that some of the terminology needs interpretation for service-oriented firms. This criticism emanates from too narrow an interpretation of the guidelines. Interpretation of each of the examination questions is a difficult and humbling experience. One does not pick up the guidelines, read them over, and understand them immediately. The questions require intense and repeated analysis. What an assessor thought was the context of the question one day, may change entirely a week later, as a result of having been more deeply involved in a company's assessment.

As assessors, we have organized Baldrige assessments with service-oriented companies. Process, as a concept, has been the most difficult for them to understand, but once it becomes clear what process means in their business context, then they have a religious experience. For instance, one service company described some generic process theory to answer a Baldrige examination item on quality processes. It claimed that it did not have a formal process management system, so therefore it could not really address these items well. It kept referring to processes as things manufacturing companies did and that the guidelines did not "fit" service companies in this area. In reviewing the assessment, we discovered that each service representative customized his or her service to each customer. This was described in another key part of their Baldrige application as a major selling point and customer satisfier. This service "protocol" process was a guarantee that the company would perform every service call consistent with customer expectations. It was the critical success factor of their business, yet it was not apparent to the organization that this was the core process around which the business operated.

The realization of the importance of these "protocols" changed the structure of the entire assessment. The organization reset its perspective and went through the assessment again. This time, the pivotal role of service protocols became clear to the organization. The senior executive of the service business enthusiastically embraced the Baldrige process. For the first time he could see all the critical links and actions required for the company to move from an already-existing leadership position to domination.

IBM Rochester was active in the State of Minnesota Quality Award to introduce educational institutions to the Baldrige guidelines. Several state businesses partnered with educational institutions ranging from K-12 to the University level. Each institution performed an assessment over a 6 to 8 month period of time. The objective of this activity was to develop a set of Baldrige-like guidelines for Education. Most educators going into the assessment process felt there was a need for a special set of guidelines. At the end of the assessment, there was unanimous agreement that the criteria could apply, without change, to educational institutions. Interpretation and education-specific notes were all that were needed. In 1994, two of the three companies receiving the Malcolm Baldrige National Quality Award were service companies. No large manufacturing company won the Award in 1994.

Fails to Predict Financial Results

One area of Baldrige that has improved over time is the link between quality improvement and business results. Criticism that Baldrige lacks focus on financial results was valid at one time. When one Baldrige winner filed Chapter 11 the year after winning, anyone who was a critic of any aspect of Baldrige rode that bandwagon with exuberant cries of, "See, I told your so!" This situation damaged the credibility of the Award.

Yet the Award survived through this crisis of confidence because most companies understood the value of the Baldrige model. Companies know they must apply the model uniquely to themselves because each has different goals, priorities, approaches and processes. In its quest for continuous improvement, NIST implemented additional criteria that reinforced the link between quality and financial results. In 1995, additional points were added to the results category reinforcing its importance to the overall assessment. The National Institute of Standards and Technology trains Baldrige examiners to analyze company results more closely and to consider future projections of business performance. The European Quality Award criteria have a separate "Business Results" category as described in Chapter 4. The data presented from the QP study in Figure 2-5 demonstrates the confidence of the business community in the Baldrige link to business success.

So, at this stage of Malcolm Baldrige National Quality Award maturity, it is difficult to find anything lacking in the criteria to demonstrate the link between quality results and financial results. That is, of course, if people clearly understand and interpret the guidelines. If there is one financial risk area for Baldrige, it would be in the company's expected future success. A company could show outstanding quality and financial results, based on historical trends, but be at the edge of a cliff because of significant environmental forces that change the status

U.S. Business Community Perceptions about the Baldrige Criteria and Business Success	
Response Category	**Overall**
Criteria application results in quantifiable success factors	69%
Criteria measure excellent performance which improves competitive position	64%

Figure 2-5 U.S. Business Community Perceptions About Baldrige and Business Success.

quo. This is the real problem with Baldrige winning companies that experience difficulty in successive years.

Winning the Baldrige heightens visibility, raises expectations, and creates significant industry and competitive attention. These companies have demonstrated leadership results but have planned using historical projections. Unless they analyze and prepare themselves for industry and market shifts, the recipes of the past will not prepare them for the future. This is where Competitive Dominance theory strengthens a Baldrige assessment and provides some tools and methods to prepare for future leadership. Chapter 6 renders Competitive Dominance theory explicit in the Baldrige criteria.

More Emphasis on the Award Than on Improvement
This criticism is usually internal to the organization by those who feel that the only objective the company has is to win the Award. Therefore, the company should not waste money and resources to develop a Baldrige application. These critics are usually people not involved in the assessment or who feel that the company compromises other important priorities in its zeal to win the award. These critics believe in quality, but not in the value of the Baldrige assessment process. They view it as form over substance.

While this criticism is valid in some companies, the value of the Baldrige Award is that it requires a quantitative measure to identify winners, and thus enables a company to establish improvement goals. Many companies have used the Baldrige model to set a quantitative base-line with yearly improvement goals. In the QP study, 44% of the companies use the criteria as an internal assessment instrument and 10% have internal quality awards based on the criteria. Everyone can understand number-based goals. Executives can use these goals to establish unit targets, to recognize achievement, and as incentive compensation. Critics of the Baldrige process inside an organization usually disdain all forms of measurable objectives.

Goal orientation is a basic requirement for change and progress. Goals can bring common focus and commitment. Those companies which have set a goal to win the Baldrige award agree that there is an increase in commitment and accelerated improvement. But, when companies set their goal to only win the Baldrige Award and accomplish it, they run the risk of not sustaining the improvement momentum. The objective of a Baldrige assessment is to identify company strengths and areas for improvement. If the company loses this objective in its "quest for the gold," then it, and the Baldrige Award process, have lost.

The value of the Baldrige Award process is the feedback report and site visit (assuming there is one). Some participants have stated that this process is worth at least a $150,000.00 consultant analysis. Figure 2-6 illustrates how companies feel about the Baldrige feedback.

More importantly, though, if the Baldrige application is done with rigor and commitment, it smokes out the critical business issues. The Baldrige process is a valuable tool to guide organizational transformation. There is significant organizational learning by the participants in an assessment. They are the people who most intimately

U.S. Business Community Perceptions about the Baldrige Feedback	
Response Category	**Overall**
Feedback report is of great value (37 applicants responding)	73%
Information from site visit is of great value (17 finalists responding)	71%
Feedback from previous winners is very valuable	67%

Figure 2-6 U.S. Business Community Perceptions of Baldrige Feedback.

discover how well or poorly the business operates. They understand the critical business links and ask the salient questions in meetings. Companies should use the Baldrige assessment as an executive development tool.

Just as in any new endeavor, the maturation of the Baldrige Award has not been a smooth transition. Anything new requires "shake-out." The introduction of a new concept requires systematic closed-loop monitoring and improvement process that works. Baldrige has that process, and NIST is responsible for the management of the continuous improvement. Each cycle of learning enhances the strength, depth, and value of the Baldrige criteria as a business model and framework for organization excellence. Much of the criticism has varying degrees of validity based on interpretation and implementation. When quality maturity and strategy maturity levels are high, and the two are highly integrated, then all criticism can be easily overcome as the company gains and sustains leadership and competitive dominance. So now we turn the focus from the criticism and dwell on the positives.

Baldrige has made many important contributions to the practice of quality management in the United States.

It has contributed significantly to raising the industry's literacy and professionalism of the practice of quality management. For businesses, whether in products or services, Baldrige principles have been able to improve operational effectiveness, customer satisfaction and employee morale and well-being.

Industry Literacy

To effect change in any management practice, a base level of domain knowledge based on a commonly accepted conceptual framework is fundamental. This intellectual construct combined with a common vocabulary provides the foundations for an effective management practice. A managerial practice that lacks these attributes is one where there is a distinct absence of industry literacy. Baldrige has given American managers the foundations for accelerating industry literacy in quality management.

In the QP study, the U.S. business community responded positively that the Baldrige Award is accomplishing its industry literacy goals as shown in Figure 2-7.

NIST estimates that it has distributed over one million copies of the Baldrige award criteria to companies and individuals through 1994 (Baldrige, 1994). If we conservatively assume that three people read the Baldrige criteria, then at least three million people in the U.S. have tried to understand Baldrige quality management. Baldrige winners have made approximately 10,000 presentations, and between 5,000 to 8,000 presentations are given yearly by program participants. After winning Baldrige, IBM Rochester gave over 5,000 presentations to an average group size of 20; addressing over 100,000 people. This figure is consistent with Xerox which estimated that they have talked to over 125,000 people a year, many of whom are customers and suppliers. It is, therefore, appropriate to say that in the U.S. millions are familiar with Baldrige quality.

U.S. Business Community Perceptions about the Baldrige and Industry Literacy	
Response Category	**Overall**
Accomplishing quality awareness	92%
Clarifying the understanding of quality requirements	82%
Sharing of quality strategies	78%
Recognition of excellent firms	78%

Figure 2-7 U.S. Business Community Perceptions of Baldrige and Industry Literacy.

Benchmarking is one of the most important Baldrige practices. It is the practice by which companies try to learn from each other the most effective managerial techniques or processes to produce better quality results. This mechanism serves to spread effective practices and to elevate the literacy level in quality management. IBM Rochester benchmarked over 150 activities that spanned close to 60 business processes. We can confidently say that the rising tide of Baldrige quality is raising all boats.

Operational Effectiveness

One of the key results of quality is improved operational effectiveness. A recent study by the Government Accounting Office (GAO) of the twenty highest scoring Baldrige applicants over a period of two years indicates that there is a direct correlation between Baldrige quality management and operational effectiveness (Management 1991). The study shows that the average annual improvements in reliability, on time delivery, and errors or defects (cost of quality) to be 4.7%, 10.3%, and 9.0% respectively. Motorola has an accrued annual savings of $250 million, on sales of $12 billion, which are a direct result of its Baldrige quality initiatives. Similarly, Globe Metallurgical has reached $10.3 million in annual savings, on sales of $100 million by embracing the Baldrige principles of quality (Baldrige 1992). IBM Rochester records show that the reliability of IBM's products improved from 200% to 300% over a six year period. Over the same period, engineering costs and write-offs declined by 50%. Simultaneously, supplier lead times have improved by 80% and defect rates for incoming parts have improved over 58% (IBM Rochester 1992). Over a period of four years another IBM site, the Santa Teresa software development laboratory, has been deploying Baldrige for quality improvement. During that time, their internal calibration of Baldrige has improved from about 350 to over 750. During this period, there has been a dramatic reduction in the number of defects. Defects have decreased by 100%, and at the same time development productivity has increased by 50% (Kaplan, Clark, Tang 1995).

Customer Satisfaction

Operational effectiveness is very important, but it is hollow and pyrrhic unless customers experience an increased satisfaction in the use of the product or service. The GAO study shows that the average annual increase in customer satisfaction and reduction in customer complaints was 2.5% and 11.6% respectively (Management 1991). IBM Santa Teresa, over the same period cited in the previous paragraph, experienced an improvement of about 20% in customer satisfaction by direct application of Baldrige principles. The experience in IBM Rochester with Baldrige quality showed the importance of customer satisfaction and the critical nature of reducing customer complaints. Through an intensive study, IBM Rochester estimated that a 1% increase in customer satisfaction would produce incremental revenues of $250 million. A longitudinal analysis of statistics collected from thousands of customers convincingly told that customers who had a complaint but whose problems were fixed promptly had a higher propensity to purchase again. Furthermore, these customers would also provide an unsolicited positive recommendation at a higher frequency than a customer who never experienced a problem (Bauer, Collar, Tang 1992).

Employee Morale and Well-Being

Since the seminal studies by Taylor and the Hawthorne experiments, managers have known that there is a very strong causality between employee morale and well-being and the performance of an organization. Because quality is one of the most important performance indicators, it is natural that Baldrige has a special focus on morale and well-being of people. Not surprisingly, the GAO study indicates that the annual improvement in employee satisfactions and turnover has improved 1.4% and 6% respectively (Management 1991).

Our experience as line executives in the IBM Santa Teresa software development laboratory strengthens our conviction on this subject. For example, we used four indicators from our annual employee opinion survey—Buy-In Index, Empowerment Index, Participation Index, and Cooperation Index. Buy-In measures the degree to which employees accept the concept of market-driven quality. That is to say that customers' perception of quality is as important as internal conventional measures. Over a period of three years, this index has improved by about 50%. The Empowerment Index determines whether employees feel that they have the responsibility, accountability, and the means to get the job done. Over the same period, this indicator has also increased over 50%. The Participation Index determines the degree by which employees feel that they are directly participating in the deployment of quality improvement initiatives. Over the same period, this indicator has risen by 25%. Cooperation Index calibrates the extent to which employees feel that the quality management environment increases cooperation among employees in problem solving and in their day to day work. This has improved by about 13% to reach a high water mark of about 85% (Kaplan 1995).

At IBM Rochester, employee morale led all company manufacturing and development units, and continuously improved to a high water mark of 83%, with over 95% of the employees participating in the survey (IBM Rochester 1992).

Business Effectiveness

With all these internal improvements, the external business results were equally impressive. A four year snapshot of IBM Rochester demonstrates continued revenue growth, thirty percent faster than the industry. IBM Rochester's net earnings were twice that of U.S. and Japanese competitors. With the integration of strategy and quality IBM Rochester achieved continuous growth in market share. Even though IBM Rochester had revenue and net earnings growth in years previous to Baldrige, only when it began to implement an integrated approach to quality and strategy, did it discover that it had been losing market share at a dramatic rate. This key element of Competitive Dominance is described in subsequent chapters.

In 1992, IBM performed a company-wide study of unit business results compared to its level of attainment in Baldrige assessment score. The best Baldrige units' customer satisfaction was 18 points higher than the best competition and 28 points higher than average IBM units. The best units also increased customer satisfaction year to year. The best Baldrige units experienced double digit revenue increases year to year, while the average IBM units lost revenue. The best Baldrige units' market share over a three year period grew at 2% faster than the industry, while the average IBM units lost market share.

The most extensive analysis of the business benefits of quality within the United States was performed by the General Accounting Office (GAO) in May, 1990 (Management 1991). This study evaluated twenty companies who scored high in 1988 and 1989 Malcolm Baldrige competition. The GAO concluded that there was a cause and effect relationship between Total Quality Management practices and corporate performance as illustrated by Figure 2-8.

The evidence from the U.S. Business Community in the QP study in Figure 2-5 further supports quality contribution to business effectiveness.

The Importance of a Balanced and Integrated Approach to Achieve Business Leadership

We attempt to present a balanced view of the criticisms and contributions of quality and strategy. If one can ac-

Financial Performance from GAO Study

		Direction of Indicator			
Financial Indicator	Number of Responses	Positive	Negative	No change	Average Annual improvement (%)
Market share	11	9	2	0	13.7
Sales per employee	12	12	0	0	8.6
Return on assets	9	7	2	0	1.3
Return on sales	8	6	2	0	.4

Figure 2-8 Financial Performance from GAO Study.

cept that the criticisms are valid in specific cases and depending upon the interpretation and implementation, then one must accept that the contributions are also valid. The critics will continue to question the value and the supporters will continue to pontificate the virtues. So where does that leave us? It leaves us at a point where we must understand, more fully, the root cause of the issues. Why are the strategy and quality criticisms valid? Why are continual studies being performed to validate contributions? Why are the Baldrige scores trending lower? Why has learning plateaued?

Our assertion is that most companies are progressing at various stages of quality and strategy maturity without a balanced, integrated approach between the two. Some companies have demonstrated successful quality approaches, but cannot sustain them. Their approach has targeted historic or current problems and opportunities, ignoring future opportunity and factors that may change the status quo. So when change occurs, the traditional systems and processes cannot respond. Others develop grand visions and mission statements based on a future view of where they want to be and fail in implementation. Executive desire and will alone are not enough to take a company to a future leadership position, and sustain the position over time. Still others apply quality concepts with the objective of reducing cost and expense as a strategy to become more competitive when the issue that is causing lack of competitiveness may be market shifts that change consumer preferences or buying habits.

Gaining and sustaining industry leadership to achieve Competitive Dominance requires a balanced and integrated approach between strategy development and deployment and quality improvement. A balanced and integrated approach between cost and expense (efficiency, speed, effectiveness) and revenue and market share (growth, opportunity, and positioning). The theory and practices that form the foundation of Competitive Dominance are grounded in quality and business success. Competitive Dominance emerged from Baldrige Award winners with the highest scoring applications that have demonstrated clear and sustained business leadership in their markets. Competitive Dominance is the success formula for these companies. These concepts have been applied in other businesses with the same degree of success. The importance of the integrated and balanced approach can be demonstrated with the following factual analysis.

Figure 2-9 presents ten years of data that demonstrates a strong correlation between quality, business, and people factors. This information is from IBM Rochester AS/400 business unit. The business unit results would put IBM Rochester in the Fortune 50 as a stand-alone company. Their business results have continuously shown profit and growth over this ten-year period, despite the business problems of IBM in general. In this case, quality is defined as warranty cost and customer satisfaction. Business results are defined as market share and revenue per employee. Employee satisfaction is overall employee morale as measured by yearly opinion surveys. The negative correlation in the Warranty Cost columns and rows is because of the inverse relationship between warranty cost and other indicators. For instance, when warranty costs increase, customer satisfaction and market share decrease. Figure 2-9 illustrates the strong relationship between these three factors (greater than .7 correlation) and reinforces the importance of an integrated approach to achieve business success. This balanced and strong integration is also the reason for high Baldrige scores and demonstrates that the robustness of the Baldrige model as a framework for business success.

To improve employee satisfaction, focus on improving job satisfaction, satisfaction with manager, and having

Correlation Analysis—IBM Rochester AS/400—1984–1993

	Business		Quality		People			
	Market Share	Produc-tivity	Warranty Cost	Customer Sat.	Employee Sat.	Job Sat.	Sat./w Manager	Right Skills
Market Share	1.00	0.97	-0.86	0.71	0.84	0.84	—	0.97
Productivity	0.97	1.00	—	—	0.93	0.92	0.86	0.98
Warranty Cost	-0.86	—	1.00	-0.79	—	—	—	—
Customer Sat.	0.71	—	-0.79	1.00	0.70	—	—	0.72
Employee Sat.	0.84	0.93	—	0.70	1.00	0.92	0.92	0.86
Job Sat.	0.84	0.92	—	—	0.92	1.00	0.70	0.84
Sat./w Manager	—	0.86	—	—	0.92	0.70	1.00	0.92
Right Skills	0.97	0.98	—	0.72	0.86	0.84	0.92	1.00

Figure 2-9 Relationship Between Business, Quality, and People Indicators—IBM Rochester (Hoisington, Huang, Cousins, Suther 1993).

the right skills for the job. To improve job satisfaction, focus on improving satisfaction with the manager and having the right skills for the job. Improving skills will improve employee satisfaction, job satisfaction, and it will directly impact productivity, market share, and customer satisfaction. Improving employee satisfaction will directly impact productivity and market share. Improving productivity will directly impact customer satisfaction, and improving customer satisfaction will directly impact market share.

To reinforce the theory of Competitive Dominance further, consider a similar factual analysis from another equally successful unit with an entirely different focus (Kaplan, 1995, Clark 1993). IBM Santa Teresa is a software and service unit. IBM Santa Teresa scored in the "GOLD" level (750–875 Baldrige points) in IBM's internal award improvement process. The correlation is extremely high due to only three years of data. With ten year of data similar to Figure 2-9, one can expect the data to go down, but still show high correlation among the three factors. In this case, business results are defined as profit per employee. Quality is defined as software code defects, and customer satisfaction. The people factor is an employee well-being index that is created from yearly employee opinion survey data. The data used to create the index is consistent with the people elements in Figure 2-9. This correlation supports the same conclusions stated above.

Savings and improvements can be achieved at any maturity level of strategy and quality implementation. A strategic perspective and integrated approach offer the potential to realize dramatic overall business results for the benefit of all stakeholders and stockholders. Competitive Dominance defines the relationship between strategy and quality. The facts shown demonstrate that this approach is fundamental to sustaining leadership. In the following chapters, we describe the details of competitive

Correlation Analysis—IBM Santa Teresa—3 years of data				
	Business	Quality		People
	Productivity (Profit/ Emp)	Cost of Quality (Code Defects)	Customer Satisfaction	Employee Well- Being Index*
Productivity (Profit/ Employee)	1.00	.99054	.99054	.99594
Cost of quality	.99054	1.00	−.99999	−.98718
Customer Satisfaction	.99054	−.99999	1.00	.98718
Employee Well- Being Index	0.95594	.98718	.98718	1.00

Figure 2-10 Relationship Between Business, Quality, and People Indicators—IBM Santa Teresa.

dominance and the methods and tools to implement successful approaches.

3

Strategy and Competitive Dominance

We will argue in this chapter that to achieve Competitive Dominance, strategic thinking and practice must be extended to a new level. To rise to this new level, we will show why we believe that the conventional orthodoxy of strategy must be extended. We provide a new organizing framework for strategic thinking and practice, and we demonstrate why we think that the Baldrige framework meets that need. This is not to say that the Baldrige criteria apply as they are currently defined; it does say that the Baldrige framework is a robust one. In Chapter 6, we show very specifically and directly how the principles of Competitive Dominance integrate readily, naturally, and synergistically with the Baldrige principles.

We must begin with "Strategy," its meaning, and the way it is practiced. At this point, we loosely define "strategy" as efforts to out-wit and out-perform your adversaries while they are trying to do the same to you. Later, we provide a more rigorous definition within the context of Competitive Dominance. Next to Quality, Strategy is possibly the most abused word in the English language. It is arguably the most abused word in business. It is used indiscriminately, it is used without precision or accuracy, and it is used as a synonym for other simpler words that are far more communicative and accurate. It is also used to endow the speaker with mystique and authority that he or she probably does not deserve. Strategy is most frequently used as a substitute for "plan." For example, we often hear, "this is our product strategy," or "our marketing strategy is...." The term "strategy" gives the speaker legitimacy and authority for which the speaker is searching, and it endows the "plan" with analytic rigor and thoughtfulness which the word "plan" is not able to convey. Strategy has plans, but not all plans are strategies. "All men are mortal, but not all mortals are men" is a rule of logic. Strategy is used interchangeably with "important," as in "we must pay attention to this project because it is strategic." Again strategies are important, but because it is important, is it also strategic? Strategy is also used as a qualifier to mean "long range." For example, we hear frequently, "this initiative is strategic, deployment and investments begin three years from now," or "this is not tactical, it is strategic. We don't have to decide now."

Strategy deals with the urgent decisions of today to create a meaningful future. Strategy is not entirely about future decisions, and this distinction is lost on many. It is also used to mean "future." We hear frequently, "we can barely make it in the market, why worry about strategy?" Or we hear, "the competition is bashing our brains in, we have to do something; what we don't have time for is a strategy." Arrogant executives, brash young MBAs, and superannuated staff use "strategy" to mean "policy," as in "this is our strategy," which really means "don't argue with me," or "I can't explain it, just do it," or "someone else has made a decision, and we are here to implement it," or "you are not smart enough to understand it, you are here to take orders."

Strategy is also used interchangeably with the word "rule." For example, "under these circumstances and conditions, our strategy is to do the following..." This we hear most frequently in functional areas where operational rules have being codified to a high degree to ensure consistent operational actions under specified conditions. For example, when the cost and quality from a supplier fail to meet specified range of acceptability, the "strategy" is to negotiate different terms and search for another supplier. As these examples show, "strategy" is rich in meaning, complex in nuance, subtle in conception, vague and apparently precise at the same time.

The fundamental reason the word "strategy" is so widely misused is because the level of maturity and sophistication of those who use the term are so widely divergent. In Chapter 1, we postulate four levels of strategy maturity and capability, from the most elementary to the most sophisticated and mature. They were Planning, Long Range Planning, Strategic Planning, and Strategic Leadership. Those at the lower level of maturity use the word "strategy" rather loosely and imprecisely. Those with more maturity endow the word with more meaning and substance. This is like mathematics. To a high school student, mathematics is Algebra and perhaps Calculus. To the graduate student, mathematics includes Partial Differential Equations and Reimannian Geometry. Graduate students do not reject the principles of Algebra; rather they have moved to a more elevated level of knowledge and practice. In the same way, each stage of strategic maturity and capability does not reject the principles or practices of the previous stages; rather each subsequent stage moves forward a higher level and brings to bear more powerful ideas and management techniques that make the practice of strategy more effective. A highly developed and refined practice of strategic leadership makes a business enterprise competitive, admired, feared, envied, and dominant in the markets and industries where its presence is felt. Simply stated, it becomes dominant. The practice of strategy at the highest level provides a company with the machinery to become competitively dominant. This practice does not guarantee dominance, but it does provide the methodologies and processes which, if practiced well, enable a company to rise above its competitors and remain there for a sustained period of time.

Let us discuss briefly the distinction among the four stages of strategy maturity. The first stage we simply call "planning." At this stage, the emphasis is on operational control of the internal business functions. Its principal objectives are to make sure that the budget is met, bills are paid, and costs are not overrun. Fiscal discipline and variances from yearly budgets are the key and most important managerial responsibilities. In some companies, this function is called appropriately "Plans and Controls." Their staffs hover over line executives counting dollars and looking over expense accounts. Invariably what happens is that the best "plans and controls" fail to close variances, not because the accountants have not done a great job, but because unpredictable situations arise that planning and controlling will not cure. For example, fluctuations in the market may cause revenue shortfalls, or runaway demand cause spiraling expenses

If there were a way to look at a time horizon that is longer than the yearly budget cycle, then these fluctuations could be better managed. These processes and increased maturity cause companies to migrate to "long range planning." They move to multi-year forecasting and begin to use trend analysis to look beyond the present. Their hopes are to avoid financial surprises. They also begin to invest more wisely by determining what is affordable not only from a longer time frame, but also considering their capabilities in the markets they are competing. This approach improves their planning effectiveness and begins to smooth out the vagaries of fluctuations.

Long Range Planning works, but not well enough for many companies. Many experience the rude and stochastic shocks from the external environment. A new product emerges out of nowhere, and it embodies technological innovations that makes the product cheaper, more functional, and less expensive. Overturning conventional wisdom, a competitor finds a new way to distribute its product, end-running the company, and dramatically reducing sales expenses or the Federal Reserve increases interest rates to defend the dollar and control inflation. Any and all these situations can render the best "long range planning" and trend analysis academic. In response to this, many companies move to the next level of strategy maturity, they begin to analyze the fundamental forces in the external environment rather than reacting to them, and rather than simply "trending" the past. For example, they analyze the direction and speed of technological change, they study the configuration of suppliers and the economic underpinnings of that configuration to understand the structure of an industry, they examine what keeps companies in or out of specific markets to understand the barriers of markets. Through analytic intensive studies, they formulate plans that more sophisticated, insightful, and robust. They have moved to the level of Strategic Management. The way they marshal resources is also more sophisticated than in previous stages; it has a strong bias to markets and competition. These analyses provide the means for allocation of the resources of the

firm in more sophisticated ways, such as portfolio structures. Cross-functional execution is more pervasive than
the past to gain efficiencies, reduce redundancies and improve operations.

We call the fourth stage of strategic maturity "Strategic
Leadership." We draw a big distinction between leadership and management. Management deals fundamentally with the issues of planning, organizing, budgeting, and
controlling. The core of good management is implementation and execution, optimization, and predictability.
Leadership deals with the issues of renewal and transformation. The core of good leadership is vision, seeing
what others don't, acting decisively, being agile and flexible, but at all times moving in a consistent direction.
Good leadership doesn't reject the past entirely, it knows
what to shed and what to keep, and is able to give the past
newer and richer meaning. Exceptional leadership is able
to tap the reservoir of energy, creativity and commitment
of people. Driven by this kind of leadership, strategy
practice begins to depart from conventional and its historical practice. Strategy is fully integrated into the fiber
of the organization. It is no longer a periodic exercise, or
a major review of plans, or a style of management, but it
permeates every aspect of the enterprise. What separates
strategy practice that enables Competitive Dominance
from the conventional practice of strategy? For reasons
we elucidate in the remainder of this chapter, we divide
the practice of strategy into two schools: the deterministic
and the contingent schools. This contrast is summarized
in Figure 3-1, Contrast of Deterministic and Contingent
Schools of Strategy.

This is similar to Kay (1993) who divides the pattern of
strategic thinking and practice into two major schools: the
rationalist and the contingent schools. We think that calling it deterministic is more descriptive than rationalist,
because in both schools of thought rational thinking is

Schools of Strategy Practice	
Deterministic	Contingent
Stages I, II, III	Stage IV Strategic Leadership
Competitive Advantage.	Competitive Dominance.
Forecasting Based.	Scenario Based.
Predicated on environmental "fit."	Predicated on intent and aspirations.
Separation of Formulation from Implementation.	Integrated, iterative and continuous Formulation and Implementation.
Assumes strategic thinking can be delegated. Staff formulation, line implementation.	Strategic thinking cannot be delegated. Line managers = the strategists and implementers.
Quality and Strategy as discrete and separate.	Quality and Strategy as an integrated concept.
Biased to analysis, planning, and strategy processes.	Biased to businesses processes, implementation, and reengineering. Analysis, planning are tools.
Rigid, institutionalized view of competitors.	Situational perspective of competitors.
Business is rooted on products, services, or markets.	Business is rooted first in the core capabilities of the company.

Figure 3-1 Contrast of Deterministic and Contingent Schools of Strategy.

mandatory; furthermore, we think that "deterministic" and "contingent" contrast more precisely the differences between two approaches to strategy. Our first three stages of strategy maturity fall into the deterministic camp, and our last stage, Strategic Leadership, falls into the contingent school of strategy. The deterministic school represents the practice of strategy that is rooted in classical strategic orthodoxy and the doctrine of separation of strategy formulation and implementation. The contingent school of strategy has evolved the practice of strategy into a higher, more refined and sophisticated form. Major environmental stochastic shocks, which have humbled so many apparently invincible companies, have sown the seeds of dissonance and are signaling paradigm shifts in the conventional and orthodox model of strategic thinking and practice.

To enable us to understand why this is so, and to appreciate the subtle but profound difference in these two schools of strategic thinking, let us briefly review the evolution of the discipline of strategy.

The deterministic school of strategy has its roots in the orthodox definitions promulgated by the leading thinkers and pioneers in strategy. In a classic textbook authored by experts from the faculty of the Harvard Business School (Christensen, et al. 1982), strategy is defined as: "the pattern of decision in a company that (i) determines, shapes, and reveals its objectives, purposes, or goals; (ii) produces the principal policies and plans for achieving these goals; and (iii) defines the business the company intends to be in, the kind of economic and human organization it intends to be, and the nature of the economic and non-economic contribution it intends to make to its shareholders, employees, customers and communities." In another classic collection of publications on strategy (Andrews 1983), strategy is defined as three propositions: (i) as "pattern of objectives..." and is almost an exact duplicate of the above definition, (ii) as "entailing two interrelated tasks: strategy formulation and strategy implementation," and (iii) as requiring general management "to create fit among: the opportunities in the external industry environment, the strengths and weakness of the firm, the personal values of the key implementers, and the broader societal expectations of the firm." Ohmae (1982), the noted Japanese consultant simplifies the definition for "strategy" as "actions aimed directly at altering the strength of the enterprise relative that of its competitors." He takes a strong competitive perspective. In a more recent and very thoughtful book (Kay 1993), Kay devotes the whole book to the conceptual foundations, to discussions and to lucid and instructive examples of what is and is not strategy. The author eschews providing a direct definition; rather he chooses the pedagogical approach, he explains: "strategy is a sequence of united events which amounts to a coherent pattern of business behavior...business strategy focuses on the relationship between the firm and its environment...a meaningful strategy is not a statement of corporate aspirations, but it is rooted in the distinctive capabilities of the individual firm." For decades, these definitions and other similar ones have provided the intellectual underpinnings for the study and the practice of strategy. Research and practice have resulted in an approach and a framework that can be illustrated and summarized with the following diagram.

Figure 3-2 shows the interaction between a company and its environment. The environment is set by the participants external to the firm that create forces and exert pressure on the firm. Among the external participants are the company's incumbent rivals—its competitors. Although direct competitors are important, they are not the only external participants that shape the environment. External participants also include other important players, for example, government bodies, regulatory agencies, other firms, suppliers, distributors, service companies, etc. In the aggregate and collectively, external

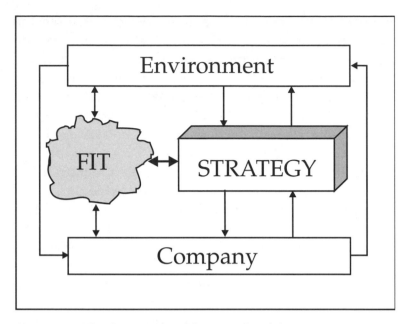

Figure 3-2 The Conventional Strategy Model.

participants create forces that shape the environment in which a company has to compete and distinguish itself. These forces create a set of dynamics that alter the equilibrium of forces and dislocate the status quo for a company. In this situation, the firm creates initiatives and actions to alter the direction and magnitude of these forces. The goal of these initiatives is to create a more favorable situation for itself by creating new forces and deflecting and neutralizing existing ones. The sum total of these initiatives is the operational expression of a company's strategy. Through strategies, every company is constantly seeking to change the playing field so that it is unlevel and optimized to its own capabilities. Sanctimonious protestations notwithstanding, all firms seek to create an unlevel playing field. When the other fellow has a head start it is so inconvenient for us, and that is what makes us so righteous and mad. Initiatives, in this conventional orthodox model, are designed so that they are consistent with its capabilities relative to the environment. This is the concept of "fit."

To maximize fit or to develop an improved fit, strategy is divided into two activities: strategy formulation and strategy implementation (Christensen, et al. 1982). This is illustrated in Figure 3-3. The fundamental focus of the strategy formulation process is to analyze the environment and to decide what to do. The focus of strategy implementation is to organize and to allocate resources for the execution and achievement of results. (Yavitz, Newman 1982; Hamermesh 1986).

Historically, the major effort of strategy has been expended to analyze the environment so as to determine the extent and depth of a company's fit relative to the environment. By developing insight into the areas where fit is present and absent, intelligent strategies can be formulated for subsequent implementation. Practitioners of strategy developed elegant analytic methodologies for

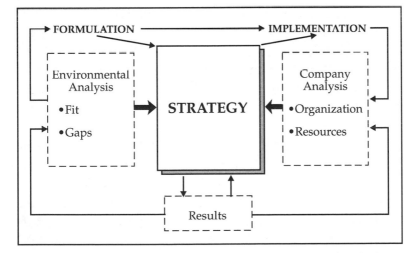

Figure 3-3 The Strategy Formulation and Implementation Model.

environmental analysis to find areas of fit and areas where gaps exist. One of the pioneers and original thinkers in this area was Henderson from the Boston Consulting Group (BCG). He developed the celebrated BCG model. In this model businesses are variously described as dogs, cash cows, stars, or wildcats, according to their position in a two-by-two matrix, the growth-share matrix. The dimensions of the matrix are market share and market growth. Depending on which cell a business is categorized, prescribed strategies are identified. A.D. Little, a management consulting firm, took a different approach. It used the stages of the Product Life Cycle and five distinct competitive business positions to create a twenty-cell matrix array of business situations. Then it specified twenty distinct strategies a company can take depending where it is positioned competitively in the life cycle of its offering. At one time GE used what it called a "screen," a nine cell matrix where the dimensions of the matrix are market attractiveness and company strength. The matrix is divided into three zones, and distinct strategic approaches are prescribed for different zones of this matrix. These approaches proved effective because they injected a degree of analytic rigor into "environmental analysis," which was heretofore absent. Porter elevated the rigor to another level when he created the five forces analytic methodology for environmental analysis (Porter 1985). In this model he considers the power of incumbent rivals, potential rivals, substitutes, buyers, and suppliers. This model established a high-water mark in environmental analysis because it provided a new level of analytic rigor and provided a robust framework for further analytic elaboration and deduction. From this and other analysis, Porter formulates strategies based on cost, differentiation, and scope of strategic coverage. Ohmae created the 3-C model for environmental analysis (Ohmae 1982). The three Cs are: the company, the competition,

and the customer. The interaction of these three participants determine the optimal strategies of a company. He
discusses company-based strategies, competitor-based
strategies and customer-based strategies. There are many
other strategic models, but these represent the best
known and most widely adopted tools for strategic analysis. They are representative of classical approaches to
strategy. They are summarized below in Figure 3-4.

Source	Methodology	Strategies
Boston Consulting Group	Growth-Share Matrix	Specific strategies for Dogs, Stars, Cash Cows, and Wildcats.
A.D. Little	Product Life Cycle (PLC) and Competitive Position Matrix	Specific strategies for each cell of this matrix, ranging from Aggressive Push for Market Share, ... Maintain, ... to Divest.
GE Screen	Market Attractiveness and Company Capability Matrix	Matrix is divided into 3 zones, each zone has specific strategies.
K. Ohmae	Company, Competitor and Customer Analysis—3 Cs	Strategies based on Company, Cost, or Competition.
M.C. Porter	5 Forces Analysis	Strategies based on cost, differentiation, or scope.

Figure 3-4 Best Known Methodologies for Strategy Analysis and
Formulation.

The models for strategy shown in Figures 3-2 and 3-3 have served us well, and the methodologies exemplified in Figure 3-4 have proven to be useful. But, in the sense of Kuhn (1962), signals of paradigmatic discontinuities are evident. An increasing number of dissonant counterexamples in the world of strategy and business have given reason for executives, strategists, and consultants to pause and, with some degree of skepticism, reflect on the robustness of conventional orthodoxy. Honda is an example of an upstart company that did not follow the rules but made it to the ranks of a world-class competitor. It was inconsistent with the conventional orthodoxy of fit that Honda should consider taking on the Big Three from Detroit. It is an understatement to say that there was not a good "fit" between Honda's capabilities and the American competitive environment it was facing. In fact, it was the overwhelming gap and lack of fit that was most startling. Nevertheless, today by the thinnest of margins, Honda is the second largest car seller in the U.S. Similarly, it was by no means clear that there was a good fit between the capabilities of Intel and the semiconductor industry. Although it may not be apparent today, it was a stretch to imagine that Intel would try to take on the likes of Texas Instruments, the Japanese semiconductor foundries, Motorola, or even try to surpass IBM.

There are also strong and capable U.S. companies that had a very strong fit with the environment that have not made it. RCA is an example. This is the firm that created the business model for the broadcasting industry. This is also the firm that invented the first television, held all the key patents in color television, and had a world-class research laboratory, the David Sarnoff Research Center. RCA didn't make it, and it was acquired by GE. Its high powered research laboratory was sold to Stanford Research Institute. GM is another example of a company that also had a strong fit with its industry and market environment. Although being advised by strategic power-houses of the world, GM had to suffer the ignominy of competitive assault and setbacks from lesser Asian car manufacturers. It is also hard to imagine that Toyota had a robust fit with the American competitive environment.

Something is amiss. Here we have counterexamples to one of the pillars in the orthodoxy of strategy—fit. One of its articles of faith does not seem to pass the test of universal truth. Hamel and Prahalad (1989, 1993) are creating powerful arguments that are overturning this concept of fit. They argue that we ought to be thinking about strategy in new and different ways. They think that strategy has less to do with fit and depth of resources of the firm and far more to do with the aspirations, tenacity, and constancy of purpose. They argue persuasively that ambition is a powerful motive to successful strategy. In our opinion Hamel and Prahalad have fired a powerful salvo against the conventional definition of strategy.

The second problem with conventional approach to strategy also arises from the conceptual separation of formulation and implementation. Although the conventional definition stresses "inter-relatedness," the starting assumption is that they are distinct and separate. Kay (1993) appropriately raises the question whether Napoleon's defeat in Russia was a failure of strategy or of implementation. He concludes that it is a meaningless question because for one who has mastery of the subject, "the two are inextricable." But this separation and distinction are very real in the conventional practice of strategy. Because of the importance of environmental analysis and determination of fit, formulation has been left in the hands of analysts, consultants, and staff. This has lead to the situation where a priesthood of strategists has emerged who are disconnected from the operational side of the business. The result is that formulated strategies are not implementable for a variety of reasons. There is little or no buy-in from the line organizations who have to implement. The so-called strategies are too vague and abstract for them to be useful; the formulation process becomes a ritual of form rather than substance, and the intellectual content of the strategy, arguably the most important function of a business, is delegated to staffs. This has led to the "fallacy of detachment," as Mintzberg (1994) has written.

The third problem with conventional practice is that our enchantment with models has resulted in "strategic recipes." The methodologies have created generic strategies. The weakness of generic strategies is that they are predictable by the competition. This allows them to formulate countermoves that neutralize the effectiveness of the strategies being formulated.

For every example of firms that are not successful or have failed, there are dozens of examples of companies that have been successful applying the conventional model for strategy. It is not that the model does not work, rather that the model now applies to a considerably narrower range of problems. The participants in any given industry are far more sophisticated today than they were at the time these models were first created. The forces at play in the environment are far more in number, far stronger, far more diverse, and, most importantly, they are moving at a far greater speed. For example, a small island like Taiwan is the twelfth largest trading economy in the world, the product life cycle in the Personal Computer industry is six months, the telecommunications industry around the world is being privatized and deregulated. The result is that by the time the cycle of formulation and commitment to implementation is complete, the environment has already changed. The definitional assumption that analysis, in particular fit assessment and gap assessment, can be separated from implementation is not operationally effective in a world that is moving at the speed it is today or with the level of complexity we see today. The literature that is trying to strengthen the link between analysis and implementation, and the dramatic changes in the practice of strategy, all point to the definitional weakness of separating formulation and implementation. (Yavitz, Newman 1992; Hamermesh 1986; Montgomery, Porter 1994; Mintzberg 1994)

To avoid the above problems, Wack (1985a, 1985b) in his seminal papers, documents the approach to environmental analysis and strategy formulation he used while at Royal Dutch Shell. Wack created the innovative approach of scenario planning. The reason Wack's approach was brilliant is because in one approach, he was able to attack the major weakness of conventional strategic planning in three ways. One, he was able to link the analysis and the strategy formulation in one seamless process. Two, he was able to cope with the speed of environmental change in such a way that Royal Dutch Shell was able to respond when change did come. Three, he was able to escape the straight jacket of single point forecasting which is the analytic prison of conventional strategic planning. While doing that, he was liberated from the deterministic approach of strategy based on fixed assumptions. He moved in the direction of the contingent approach to strategy. In the effective scenario planning processes we have led, line management constructs different scenarios, develops different contingency plans, and monitors the conditions that will signal a significant change in the environment. In that way, strategy is a continuous process, not an event that takes place periodically. Strategy is not something that can be delegated to staff; learning cannot be delegated. Strategic thinking cannot be outsourced. Our view is that strategy is like rebuilding an airplane in the air while you are flying it. Fly it you must, and change it you must. (Bauer, Collar and Tang 1992). We believe that history will judge Wack's work to be seminal in its innovative approach and significant in the evolution of the discipline of strategy.

Kay (1993), with a great deal of insight, identifies two schools of strategic thinking: the rationalist and the contingent schools. The rationalist, which we are calling the deterministic school, is exemplified by the models in Figure 3-1 and 3-2. Strategy is optimizing fit with the environment through environmental analysis and then formulating a strategy which is then implemented. The contingent school began with the disenchantment with the diminished effectiveness of strategies that followed traditional orthodoxy of fit assessment which separates formulation from implementation. Wack fired the first salvo in favor of the contingency approach to strategy. Hamel and Prahalad further provided insights by saying that strategies have less to do with fit, but more to do with strategic intent and the core competencies a company has. Mintzberg (1987) says strategy is less about formulation but more about crafting. DeGeus (1988) says strategy is about learning. Aspirations, stretch, contingency, learning, competency, and crafting clearly represent a different model and a departure from the rigid and generic approaches of the past.

While this transition is taking place, what has the world of business being doing? What are the current practices? Clearly businesses are bearing the brunt of change. To deal with these changes, companies have created and adopted a plethora of diverse new approaches in strategy. A summary of the best known and most widely practiced approaches is shown in Figure 3-5. The order in which we have chosen to present them is not significant.

The list can actually go on to a considerable length. Is anything wrong with this list? Actually there is nothing wrong with any individual item. Each item on the list is addressing a symptom of the problem. No one item on

Reaction	Approach
Do it faster.	Compete on the time dimension.
Do it better.	Produce a product/service that is defect free. Increase customer satisfaction, service, better warranty, etc.
Do it with less.	Leverage assets from outside the company and lower your cost. Be efficient, jettison all meaningless work, e.g., "workout."
Do it with different processes and organizational constructs.	Organize with cross-functional teams, or with reengineered business processes. Or transform your firm entirely, e.g., ABB, GE, etc.
Do it with better information.	Use computer systems and improve your competitiveness.
Do it so that it is customizable.	Mass produce so that it is customizable. Mass customize.
Do it with vision and leadership.	Develop an overarching, inspiring view of a more desirable state and mobilize people and energy in that direction.
Do it the Japanese way.	Emulate the Japanese; they got it right.
Do it by trial and error.	Keep trying until you get it right. The Japanese approach in consumer electronics, or the Honda approach, is learn, learn, learn.
Do it overseas.	Manufacture elsewhere to lower cost.
Don't do it.	Outsource as much as you can. The Nike, Sears appliance approach: no manufacturing, package and sell only. Divest from businesses that are not "strategic."

Figure 3-5 Reactions to New Realities in Strategy.

Reaction	Approach
Do it with somebody else.	Form alliances, consortia, partnerships, etc. Do so even with your apparent competitors.
Do it first.	Be first to market, price to value, and appropriate profits early.
Don't do it first.	Let the first one make the mistakes; learn from them and profit.
Do it with planning and learning.	"Craft" strategies, plan intelligently, create a learning organization.
Do it by empowering.	Train and give people responsibility and resources to succeed.
Do it by optimizing in the value chain	Focus on stages of value chain to gain competitive advantage.

Figure 3-5 Reactions to New Realities in Strategy. *(continued)*

that list is capable of definitively providing a foundation or a framework for a more sophisticated model of strategy. The list has to be seen not only for the elemental pieces, but in its aggregate to discern a structure it may suggest. For it is in the underlying fundamentals that a more robust and sophisticated strategy model can emerge. We are not against lists; they give us a glimpse and a hint of what is ultimately possible and they are useful specially when under stress to perform something quickly. But lists only help us to see through a glass darkly. Although they are useful, as a conceptual piece of machinery they are not as useful. They may be harmful. Ohmae (1994) writes:

"The reflex, of course, is to provide a headache pill for a headache—that is, to assume that the solution is simply the reverse of the diagnosis. That is bad medicine and worse logic.... Getting back to strategy means fighting that reflex, not giving in to it. It means resisting the easy answers in the search for better way..."

When one steps back to examine what each item on the list is trying to do, one finds that the focus is fundamentally on improving the operational side of the business and on bridging the disconnect between strategy formulation and implementation in a way that it produces no time lag between the two. Strategy formulation and implementation are merged and synchronized into a seamless management discipline. The goal is to produce excellence in the market and the industry in a way that is sustainable. Make the rules, don't accept them the way they are. We further note that the key improvements in Figure 3-4 fall into very distinct categories. They deal with leadership and vision, with how planning is done and the supporting data and analysis that is used for making decisions, and with how people and organizations are engaged in improving the strategic position of the company. They deal with restructured and reconceptualized business processes that are supposed to generate competitive advantage and with results which go beyond making a buck, but they also improve customer satisfaction and force the competition to follow. Force the competition to emulate you. On deeper scrutiny, one realizes that, at the core, the actions deal with the integration of the goals and objectives with the operational side of the business in a way that they are seamless and fully integrated to give the organization sustainable and enduring staying power.

The astute observer will note that when the list in Figure 3-4 is viewed in this structural manner, the principles they represent are congruent with the Baldrige principles and framework. In effect, the state-of-the-art practitioners in strategy are integrating the principles of quality and strategy into a single discipline and they have independently discovered the synergy that this integration brings. They are making the operational principles of quality and the imperatives of strategy seamless. They have developed a more sophisticated view of strategy and of quality. We postulated earlier that what was needed was an organizing framework in which to hang the items of the list in a organized and logical manner. We believe that Baldrige is a natural framework in which to do this. It passes the Kay test (Kay 1993):

> "A good organizing framework is minimalist—it is simple as is consistent with illuminating the issues under discussion—and it is memorable. …The organizing framework provides the link from judgment through experience to learning. A valid framework is one which focuses sharply on what the skilled manager, at least, distinctively, already knows."

We would like to paraphrase the definitions of strategy that we have seen as follows: Strategy is a continuous business process which takes resources out of bad businesses and puts new resources into good businesses to drive current and potential competitors out of business, so that the company can achieve and sustain industry and market leadership. If we parse this definition, strategy has the following components and deals with the issues and fundamental assumptions about:

- the nature of the strategy process
- the determinants of good and bad businesses
- the core determinants of a business
- the means by which resources are allocated and optimized
- the approach to analyze what is current and potential

- competitors, their assessment, positioning and conditions that create a competitor
- what constitutes industry and market leadership

Figure 3-5 illustrates strategy within the context of Competitive Dominance and draws a contrast between conventional strategy discipline and Competitive Dominance. In Competitive Dominance, strategy does not separate formulation from implementation; rather it is a continuous and iterative process of learning and adjusting to reach a goal. The goals are not necessarily rigidly predicated on environmental fit. Rather, on goals are focused aspirations and intent, on continuous environmental scanning, and on responding to shifts. Objectives are not founded on forecasts or deterministic dynamics, but on flexible goals that are consistent with strategic direction that extend the aspirations and reach of the company. The process in Competitive Dominance is like "rebuilding the airplane in flight," because action, change, and purpose are also fused into a single implementation. Because formulation, implementation, deployment are continuous and integrated, it is natural that quality is part of the strategic process, not just a functional activity. In conventional practice, resources are to be maximized and occasionally extended with alliances or partnerships. In Competitive Dominance, the company views itself as a member of a community of stakeholders who depend on and leverage each others' assets to establish supremacy in the market and the industry. It views the collective capabilities and the collective value chains as a single value delivery system to serve customers, rather than narrowly sub-optimizing its segment of the complete value chain. (Charan, Tichy 1991). Business performance is not only profit, market share, and portfolio performance; it also includes customer satisfaction, quality, learning, competitive stealth, and surprises. To them these are also important indicators of superior strategy and leadership. In Competitive Dominance, competitors' indignation, running and seeking governmental succor, fear and envy are all the successful companies preferred indicators of progress and business success. A business is no longer defined only as products, services, markets, or abstractions of benefits; rather it begins to be grounded on core competencies and capabilities.

Competitively dominant firms are not content to maneuver within established or known market or industry boundaries; they create new value by breaking stereotypical and artificial boundaries. They are not content in following rules, they make them, and thereby forcing the competition to follow. They surprise the competition. Over a sustained period, they are simultaneously admired, feared, and sometimes intensely disliked. Rather than relying on rigid and deterministic forecasting models, the approach of these firms is more flexible and richer.

Scenario planning is one of the preferred approaches of these firms. Rather than relying on predictions, they rely on insight and understanding of the interplay of forces. They look for clues and signals to know when environmental shifts are taking place. And because their processes are flexible, their ability to respond is superior than those companies that rely on formalistic rigid processes. In the conventional model, competitors are frequently viewed institutionally. That is to say, firms are rigidly viewed as competitors. In Competitive Dominance, competition is viewed situationally. Only specific conditions make a company a competitor. Thus a company can be simultaneously a customer, an ally, or a competitor. This not only limits the number of adversarial confrontations in the market, it also increases the opportunities to serve customers better (Kelly, 1993, Konselka 1993). Leadership is established by integration of the principles of quality and strategy and the relentless pursuit and deployment of the principles discussed here. These principles are summarized in Figure 3-6.

This is the contingency approach to strategy. We believe that this is the essence of a new and emerging strategy model, where strategy and operations are seamless and integrated into a single principle of Competitive Dominance and where the goal is sustainable leadership. This fusion of formulation and implementation is completely consistent with the Baldrige principles of Approach, Deployment, and Results (Baldrige 1992).

By the way, we are not throwing the baby out with the bath water. As we said earlier, we do not reject and discard the conventional strategy model, nor do we imply that the conventional model is ineffective in all cases. We do suggest that the conventional model is effective in a narrower range of situations than they have applied historically. Not all industries, not all markets, not all customers around the world, and not all companies of all sizes, necessarily view strategy in the advanced and sophisticated manner we are discussing here. For these companies, differences in the industry's competitive intensity, complexity of markets, or customer sophistication may very well mean that the conventional approach to strategy will work very well. This is not a statement to minimize and discredit those who do not need this machinery to solve their business problems. In fact, all things being equal, the best choice is always the simplest approach and the simplest tool to solve a business problem. That is what is known as an elegant solution. As the English say, "Horses for courses." Apply the right approach for the right situation.

	Conventional Orthodoxy	Competitive Dominance
Process	• formulation and implementation separated • focus on environmental fit • focus on efficiency and effectiveness • quality is a separate process • deterministic, rationalist approach	• integrated, continuous and iterative • focus on intent, stretch • focus on learning, transformation and reengineering processes • quality is seamless and integrated • contingent, self-adjusting approach • "rebuild the airplane in flight" approach
Resources	• concentrate on company resources • portfolio approach • extend with alliances, partnerships, etc.	• leverage resources from community of stakeholders • businesses and competencies • portfolio leverage stakeholders
Good & Bad Businesses— metrics and parameters	• profit, market share • portfolio performance	• Competitive Dominance • consistency with vision, intent • profit, market share • portfolio of businesses and competencies • quality and customer satisfaction • learning • redefines and creates new metrics

Figure 3-6 Strategy and Competitive Dominance.

	Conventional Orthodoxy	Competitive Dominance
Good & Bad Businesses—metrics and parameters *(continued)*	• performance within established market and industry boundaries • follows rules	• redefines rules and makes new rules
Business	• grounded on products, services, function, or markets • within known markets and industries or combinations	• grounded on products, services, function, markets, and ... • grounded on core competencies and intent • creation of new businesses and markets
Current and Potential	• deterministic approach • forecasting based approach • rigid, fixed assumptions	• contingency based • analysis of forces and scenarios • "expeditionary" in nature • continuous monitoring of environment for triggers that signal change

Figure 3-6 Strategy and Competitive Dominance. *(continued)*

	Conventional Orthodoxy	Competitive Dominance
Competitors	• rigid institutional view of competitors • rivals, potential entrants, substitution	• flexible institutional view of competitors • prefer situational view of competitors to limit number of enemies. • rivals, potential entrants, substitution
Industry and Market Leadership	• served markets • competitive advantage • quality is a separate leadership concept	• served markets • market creation and new opportunities • competitive advantage • quality is an integral leadership concept • continuous adaptation to change

Figure 3-6 Strategy and Competitive Dominance. *(continued)*

4

Quality and Competitive Dominance

Two fundamental quality approaches are in practice today:

1. Conformance to specifications and standards, and

2. Theories and practices of the quality experts (gurus)

In approach 1, all business methods, practices, and procedures should conform to a specific set of documented standards or specifications. This quality practice is governed by audits, inspections, and tests to ensure conformance. The focus is on products and services, and typically it is internal, within the company or extending to suppliers of goods and services. Quality in this context is applied to physical things—parts, equipment, and so on. Military specification, ANSI (American National Standards Institute) Standards, and ISO 9000 (International

Organization for Standardization) Standards are typical of this approach.

The second approach, the quality experts, or gurus, more broadly addresses the company and organizational aspects of quality implementation. This approach complements standards and specifications with additional focus on the role of management, planning, people contributions, customer focus, teamwork, and business process. These elements tend to be less physical and more of the "soft" technologies such as building teamwork, involvement, changing attitudes, building and maintaining relationships, and understanding the nature and flow of work. This approach is less audit and inspection oriented and more prevention based.

Procedures and specifications have been with industry since the beginnings of the industrial revolution. The practices of the quality gurus began in the post-World War II era. Edward Deming and Joseph Juran are considered the fathers of modern total quality management theory. Crosby, Feigenbaum, and Ishikawa are also considered the leading authorities on total quality. Each has brought his own philosophy and practice. Deming is famous for his "14 point approach" (Deming 1986, Walton 1986); Juran, his "quality trilogy" (Juran 1988); Ishikawa, his "7 statistical tools" (Ishikawa 1985). Feigenbaum has the "nine M's" (Feigenbaum 1983) and Crosby has "Zero Defects, "14 steps" and his "quality is free" philosophy (Crosby 1979). It is not our intent to cover all these approaches in detail as there are already many books that describe the theories and approaches of each guru in detail. Figure 4-1 summarizes the theory and key elements of each of the gurus.

This figure represents an overview of the majority of the current global practice in total quality management today. While each has its own approach, the elements are basically common.

Theory and Definition

	Crosby	Deming	Feigenbaum	Ishikawa	Juran
Quality definition	Conformance to requirements	Three corners of quality: product, user, instructions for use	What the customer says it is	Satisfactory to the customer	Fitness for use
Philosophy	Defect Free	Constancy of purpose; Statistical analysis	Full customer satisfaction at economical cost	Company-wide quality control	Project approach; in order of importance
Approach	Motivate the people	Statistical techniques	Systems approach to total quality control	Talk with data	Quality trilogy; planning, control and improvement
Mechanics	Fourteen steps	Fourteen obligations of management	The nine "M"s	Seven Statistical Tools	Diagnostic and remedial journeys

Figure 4-1 Relationship of Philosophies and Key Elements of the Quality Gurus.

Quality Improvement Elements

	Crosby	Deming	Feigenbaum	Ishikawa	Juran
Quality Planning	Good things happen when planned	Plan, do, check, act (PDCA) cycles	...Must deliver satisfactory product quality	Cause and effect diagram	... Will result in minimal need for subsequent improvement
Process Control	Zero Defects	Improvement of the production process	Significantly important	Detect any abnormality	Variables are not equally important
Measurement	Cost of quality: Price of non-conformance	Reduction of variation	Quality cost data	Physical, chemical, and human sense perception	Quantification of characteristics
Education	Formally structured	Education and self-improvement For everyone	Quality education never ends	Participation by ALL employees	Use basic skills as team member and problem solver

Figure 4-1 Relationship of Philosophies and Key Elements of the Quality Gurus. (*continued*)

Quality Improvement Elements

	Crosby	Deming	Feigenbaum	Ishikawa	Juran
Improvement	...A long while before it becomes permanent	...Constancy and forever	...From all the men and women	...Never in the short term	Do better than the standard
Management	Start at the top	Cannot be delegated	Organized company-wide	Not exclusive domain of Q. C. specialists	Start at the top
Employee Participation	Each person	Everyone's job	Genuine management involvement	All employees	Entire Hierarchy
Suppliers	Oriented to needs of the company	Long-term relationship with key suppliers	Important ingredient	Select two subcontractors	Multiple sources

Figure 4-1 Relationship of Philosophies and Key Elements of the Quality Gurus. *(continued)*

- Strong executive management leadership and involvement is required to ensure success;
- A well educated and involved employee base that operates in a teamwork environment within and between company units;
- Inclusion of suppliers in quality product and process improvement;
- Continuous and closed-loop process improvement,
- A fact-based measurement system for cost of quality, statistical control, priorities, and reduction in variation;
- A focus on planning for continuous quality improvement; and
- A customer orientation that drives everything.

The philosophy and key elements form the reference point for most discussion on TQM today. But when one talks quality today, ISO 9000 is always part of the conversation.

ISO 9000 is a European standards and specifications approach to quality that is emerging globally. Compliance with these European quality standards has increased in importance since the beginning of European unification. For non-European businesses, ISO 9000 registration is becoming a requirement to do business in Europe, and many companies are scrambling to comply.

ISO 9000 is comprised of five major documents (three standards and two sets of guidelines) and some subsidiary documents created by the International Organization for Standardization. The standards outline twenty elements defining how to establish, document, and maintain an effective quality system. The five documents are shown in Figure 4-2.

Each country which has adopted these standards (currently more than 90) has its own set of standards techni-

ISO 9000 Standard		
ISO 9000	Guideline	Determines which standard is applicable to an organization
ISO 9001	Standard	For organizations doing both development and manufacturing
ISO 9002	Standard	For organizations doing manufacturing only
ISO 9003	Standard	For organizations doing inspection and test, and software
ISO 9004	Guideline	Describes the elements of quality management and the quality management system

Figure 4-2 ISO 9000 Guidelines.

cally equivalent to the ISO series. For instance, in the United States, the American National Standards Institute (ANSI) and the American Society for Quality Control (ASQC) approved these standards incorporating customary American language usage and spelling. A company is required to perform its own audits based on company processes and procedures and demonstrate compliance and improvement to these independent auditors. Twice a year surveillance visits are conducted to maintain registration by independent organizations like Underwriters Laboratories and British Standards Institute.

IBM Rochester received ISO 9001 registration for its computer hardware and software, as well as its hard disk drive facilities one year after winning the Malcolm Baldrige National Quality Award. The process calls for continuous evaluation and improvement of processes and procedures. If well implemented, it can be the foundation for a very systematic continuous improvement process. On the other hand, some consider the process one that introduces a great deal of paperwork and bureaucracy into a system. In our judgment, a company must spend a great deal of mental energy determining how to meet the ISO standard efficiently or the project will become a paperwork nightmare. The current ISO standards are specifically internally focused and lack a customer perspective. It is focused on doing things right, not necessarily doing the right things from a customer perspective. This is a limitation that the ISO recognizes, and future improvements to ISO 9004 will address this. Figure 4-3 provides a comparative view of ISO 9000 with the quality gurus.

Successful implementation of quality in a company requires the combined approach of standards and total quality concepts articulated by the quality gurus. While everyone believes that quality is important, many question the economic value of either approach.

Many cost benefit studies have been performed to demonstrate the relationship between company results and quality improvement. All of these studies yield the same conclusion—quality improvement pays. The broadest study to date of business improvements from quality is perhaps the PIMS Associates study of 3000 businesses in Europe and North America (Buzzell 1987). The results of their data base show a positive relationship between quality and profit, consistent between North American companies and European companies. Figure 4-4 shows that the higher the relative quality, the higher the average return on investment (ROI) and return on sales (ROS). Relative quality is perceived customer quality compared to competitors.

Further analysis shows that the better the quality system, the higher the return on investment. Figure 4-5 shows 600 companies divided into five groups based on relative quality. Only twenty percent of the group with low relative quality achieved a return on investment greater than twenty-five percent, while almost sixty percent of the

Theory and Definition

	Crosby	Deming	Feigenbaum	Ishikawa	Juran	ISO 9000
Quality definition	Conformance to requirements	Three corners of quality: product, user, instructions for use	What the customer says it is	Satisfactory to the customer	Fitness for use	Conformance to procedures and specifications
Philosophy	Defect Free	Constancy of purpose; Statistical analysis	Full customer satisfaction at economical cost	Company-wide quality control	Project approach; in order of importance	Documentation defines and reflects practice
Approach	Motivate the people	Statistical techniques	Systems approach to total quality control	Talk with data	Quality trilogy; planning, control and improvement	Self audit with independent review
Mechanics	Fourteen steps	Fourteen obligations of management	The nine "M"s	Seven Statistical Tools	Diagnostic and remedial journeys	Three ISO 9000 standards and two guidelines

Figure 4-3 Comparison of ISO and Quality Gurus Philosophy and Key Elements.

Quality Improvement Elements

	Crosby	Deming	Feigenbaum	Ishikawa	Juran	ISO 9000
Quality Planning	Good things happen when planned	Plan, do, check, act (PDCA) cycles	...Must deliver satisfactory product quality	Cause and effect diagram	...Will result in minimal need for subsequent improvement	Defined in ISO 9000 and 9004 guidelines
Process Control	Zero Defects	Improvement of the production process	Significantly important	Detect any abnormality	Variables are not equally important	Procedures and specs define level of control
Measurement	Cost of quality: Price of non-conformance	Reduction of variation	Quality cost data	Physical, chemical, and human sense perception	Quantification of characteristics	Adherence to procedures and specifications
Education	Formally structured	Education and self-improvement For everyone	Quality education never ends	Participation by ALL employees	Use basic skills as team member and problem solver	All education tracked and reported

Figure 4-3 Comparison of ISO and Quality Gurus Philosophy and Key Elements. *(continued)*

Quality Improvement Elements

	Crosby	Deming	Feigenbaum	Ishikawa	Juran	ISO 9000
Improvement	...A long while before it becomes permanent	...Constancy and forever	...From all the men and women	...Never in the short term	Do better than the standard	Continuous review and update
Management	Start at the top	Cannot be delegated	Organized company-wide	Not exclusive domain of Q. C. specialists	Start at the top	ISO 9004 defines the quality management system requirements
Employee Participation	Each person	Everyone's job	Genuine management involvement	All employees	Entire Hierarchy	Addressed in ISO 9004
Suppliers	Oriented to needs of the company	Long-term relationship with key suppliers	Important ingredient	Select two subcontractors	Multiple sources	Addressed in the ISO standards

Figure 4-3 Comparison of ISO and Quality Gurus Philosophy and Key Elements. *(continued)*

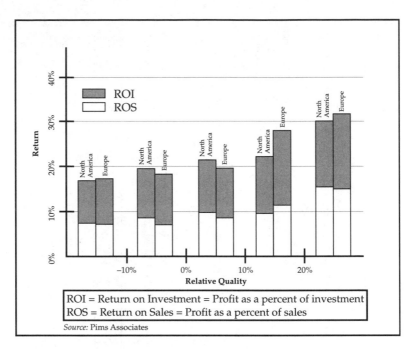

Figure 4-4 Relative Quality and Rate of Return for North American and European Companies.

group with high relative quality exceeded twenty-five percent return on investment.

The evidence that quality improvement yields business improvement is clear. But one subtle element that surfaced in the PIMS report was that market differentiation is the key to both quality and business leadership. Implementing quality programs focused internally can have some benefit to operational improvement but will not sustain long term growth for the company. It's like rotating bald tires and expecting to get a different result. Company strategies that identify new approaches, surprise the industry and competition, discover new business opportunities, find new methods to generate demand, and then have efficient and effective systems to supply the demand are those that become the leaders and dominators.

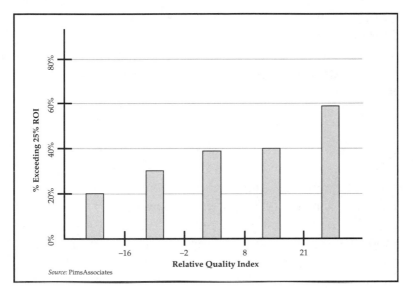

Figure 4-5 Return on Investment of Groups of Companies With Various Levels of Quality.

A heightened emphasis on the global importance of quality began with the emergence of Japan in the 1960s as an international economic power, primarily as a result of the Japanese reputation for superior quality. The reputation that Japanese manufacturers acquired for mass produced, superior quality products was almost mythical to U.S. and European captains of industry. We used to say that a tour of the Japanese manufacturing industry was a basic requirement for executive development programs. The threat of worldwide industry dominance by the Japanese as a result of their total approach to quality was motivation enough for the U.S. Government and American industry to do more than travel to Japan on tours.

The basis of Japan's quality movement was the Deming approach, and the "Deming Prize" was implemented to recognize superior quality performance. The idea for the Malcolm Baldrige National Quality Award emanated from the aura of the Deming Prize. Florida Power and Light (a Deming Prize winner), McDonald Douglas, and a number of other corporations combined with the National Institute of Standards and Technology to develop the Baldrige criteria in the mid-1980s.

Since its promulgation by the Department of Commerce in 1987, Baldrige has elevated the literacy level of quality management throughout the country. The objective of the Award is to raise the level of awareness, provide guidelines for excellent quality implementation, and promote sharing of best quality practices. The Baldrige criteria, for the first time, rendered explicit the requirements for excellent quality implementation. It provided a foundation to put the best practices of Ishikawa, Deming, Juran, Crosby, Feigenbaum, and others into a definitive model to guide American industry in the pursuit of leadership quality. By codifying the principles for quality management and by creating a framework to calibrate progress, Baldrige has given managers a comprehensive set of instruments to improve quality. It has injected new rigor on how managers should address the traditional areas of operations. And because it integrated all the best theories into a framework, the Baldrige model presented a much broader view of quality excellence than had previously been thought of. It took quality to a new plane by integrating information technology, customer satisfaction focus, new areas of leadership, employee well being and morale, and public responsibility.

The Baldrige also brought forward its usual set of critics. When theories are rendered explicit and documented, it provides an opportunity for additional study and challenge to the written word. Some of the criticism has been constructive, leading to continuous improvement of the Baldrige model itself. Other criticism has significantly challenged the Baldrige process. Chapter 2 analyzed this criticism and contribution in detail. Despite the criticism, one can safely say that the Malcolm Baldrige National Quality Award as met its objectives in grand fashion. It certainly has raised the level of awareness and sharing, and has improved overall quality practice and its importance as a business imperative.

The Baldrige Award process and criteria has also sparked renewed emphasis on quality across the globe. Europe, Australia, New Zealand, and Mexico are just a few continents and countries that have introduced their own quality structures and award initiatives. All of these are variations of the Baldrige to address unique cultural differences and to learn from the best and worst practices of other countries. Figure 4-6 contrasts the Baldrige model with the European Quality Award Model. During the development of the European Quality Award, there was a great deal of debate in the U.S. over the emphasis (or lack thereof) on business results in the Baldrige criteria. Hence, the increased emphasis in the European Quality Award on results.

Quality awards are the best attempt to establish a framework around all the different quality approaches. They do not prescribe a solution, rather they present a series of examination criteria that represent leading edge practices of companies and define "world class." All the approaches described above can apply to meet the examination criteria, and new approaches can be applied if substantiated by results. For example, Figure 4-7 demonstrates how the 20 elements of ISO 9000 apply to the Baldrige criteria.

Baldrige is a uniquely effective American approach to quality management. In the United States, it has become the single most important catalyst for the transformation of quality management practices (Garvin 1991). Companies scrambled to apply for the award, but after understanding and interpreting the criteria, they found that their quality approach did not meet the standards re-

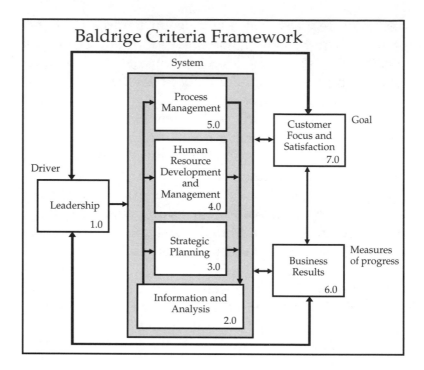

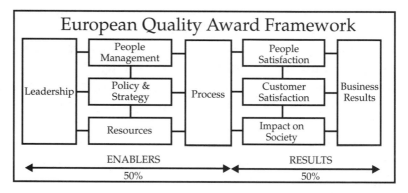

Figure 4-6 Baldrige and European Quality Award Models.

quired to win the award. Some companies did not continue to pursue the award, others put renewed emphasis on
improvement. After the initial few years of emphasis and
excitement generated by the introduction of the award,
there were two kinds of companies remaining. Those that

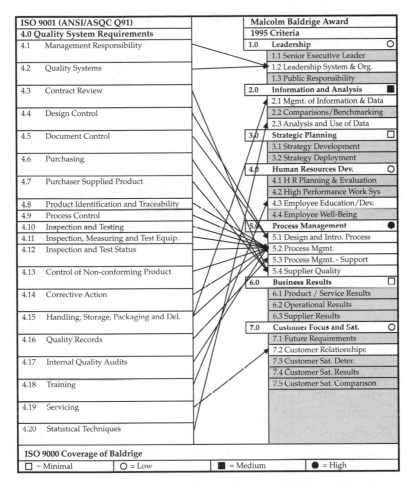

ISO 9001 (ANSI/ASQC Q91)	Malcolm Baldrige Award	
4.0 Quality System Requirements	**1995 Criteria**	
4.1 Management Responsibility	1.0 **Leadership**	○
	1.1 Senior Executive Leader	
4.2 Quality Systems	1.2 Leadership System & Org.	
	1.3 Public Responsibility	
4.3 Contract Review	2.0 **Information and Analysis**	■
	2.1 Mgmt. of Information & Data	
4.4 Design Control	2.2 Comparisons/Benchmarking	
	2.3 Analysis and Use of Data	
4.5 Document Control	3.0 **Strategic Planning**	□
	3.1 Strategy Development	
4.6 Purchasing	3.2 Strategy Deployment	
	4.0 **Human Resources Dev.**	○
4.7 Purchaser Supplied Product	4.1 H R Planning & Evaluation	
	4.2 High Performance Work Sys	
4.8 Product Identification and Traceability	4.3 Employee Education/Dev.	
4.9 Process Control	4.4 Employee Well-Being	
4.10 Inspection and Testing	5.0 **Process Management**	●
4.11 Inspection, Measuring and Test Equip.	5.1 Design and Intro. Process	
4.12 Inspection and Test Status	5.2 Process Mgmt.	
	5.3 Process Mgmt. - Support	
4.13 Control of Non-conforming Product	5.4 Supplier Quality	
	6.0 **Business Results**	□
4.14 Corrective Action	6.1 Product / Service Results	
	6.2 Operational Results	
4.15 Handling, Storage, Packaging and Del.	6.3 Supplier Results	
	7.0 **Customer Focus and Sat.**	○
4.16 Quality Records	7.1 Future Requirements	
	7.2 Customer Relationships	
4.17 Internal Quality Audits	7.3 Customer Sat. Deter.	
	7.4 Customer Sat. Results	
4.18 Training	7.5 Customer Sat. Comparison	
4.19 Servicing		
4.20 Statistical Techniques		
ISO 9000 Coverage of Baldrige		
□ – Minimal ○ = Low	■ = Medium ● = High	

Figure 4-7 The 20 Elements of ISO Placed in Baldrige Criteria Context.

lost interest because they discovered that quality improvement required a long term commitment, and those that continued to doggedly pursue the quest to become a world class quality company. The criteria also kept improving year to year, faster than companies' ability to keep up with improvements in their own operations. This has created a great deal of executive frustration and slow progress in translating quality improvement to the financial bottom line.

In an ASQC/Gallup Survey on quality leadership roles of corporate directors and executives, of those with a formal quality program in place, only thirty-nine percent reported that they are "pleased with the results" (ASQC/Gallup 1992). The result from McKinsey & Company is the same (Shorman 1992). Their experience is that:

> Two out of three quality management programs in place for more than a couple of years are stalled; they no longer meet the CEO's expectations for tangible improvement in product or service quality, customer satisfaction, and operating performance.

The story is similar in Europe. A study by the London Business School reported that many companies in Europe have some form of quality initiative but few have made a sustained effort to implement an integrated approach to Total Quality (Technologist 1993).

The trends in Baldrige scores since 1988 (Figure 4-8) show a gradual reduction in scores over time.

From Figure 4-8 it is apparent that the average scores are dropping and the percent of top scorers is plunging. It is our conviction that three situations are leading to the dropping scores:

1. The rate of new quality learning in industry is improving at a slower pace than refinements to the Baldrige criteria.

2. Quality learning as defined by the gurus has plateaued and therefore, companies have failed to keep pace with the rate of improvement in the Baldrige guidelines. Additionally, the trickle down effect of learning is not yielding industry improvement because significant

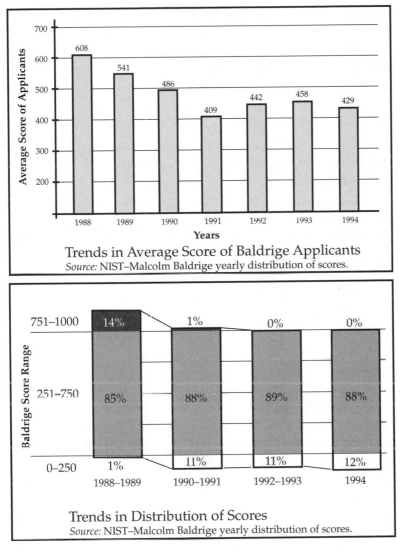

Trends in Average Score of Baldrige Applicants
Source: NIST–Malcolm Baldrige yearly distribution of scores.

Trends in Distribution of Scores
Source: NIST–Malcolm Baldrige yearly distribution of scores.

Figure 4-8 Trends in the Range of Baldrige Winning Scores.

new concepts and ideas beyond current practice and theory have not emerged.

3. Companies have not implemented a highly integrated strategy and quality approach.

IBM Rochester's Baldrige score was almost 800 points in 1990, the year they won the Baldrige Award. In 1991, IBM Rochester performed a worldwide assessment that scored over 850 Baldrige points as judged by independent, non-company examiners. The winning Baldrige feedback report indicated that IBM Rochester quality was "strategic" and recommended that the company expand this view in aiding American business competitiveness. At the time, IBM Rochester really did not fully appreciate the examiner's perspective. What they were doing was such a natural part of their day to day action that it was not apparent there was anything uniquely profound. As this business unit continued to perform Baldrige assessments, began to share with other companies, and watch the subsequent Baldrige winners results, the difference became apparent.

What the examiners meant by "strategic," was that IBM Rochester had *a highly integrated and balanced approach between quality improvement internally focused on cost, expense, and cycle time, and quality improvement externally focused on a strategy of future growth based on market opportunity.* Competitive Dominance theory was created from this successful practice. It is a new paradigm in quality management that will raise the top tier; increase the intensity of trickle down; improve Baldrige practice; accelerate industry learning, and most importantly, enable companies to gain and sustain leadership. Just as strategic thinking must expend to a new level, quality practice must also apply broader thinking and concepts to achieve competitive dominance in the market. Quality learning must progress and adapt its principles to cope with the turbulent market dynamics of today's competitive environment. That does not mean that all current practice is obsolete. Just the opposite. Progressing to a level of competitive dominance requires basic building blocks from current quality and strategy practice. The malpractice of "leap-frogging" will not work, and those who attempt it will find themselves in over their heads. On the other hand, a company at one stage of quality maturity can improve its strategy maturity and see expanded business benefits from the derived current level of quality maturity. The competitive dominance level of quality is: (1) the further refinement of practice; (2) the introduction of new tools and methodologies to manage in a future environment; and (3) the integration of quality with strategy.

Strategy and quality theory, tools, and methodologies are progressing through distinct stages of maturity and companies are progressing through the journey at different rates. This progression can be segmented into four sequential stages, each punctuated by clear advances in quality and strategy maturity, refinement and insight over its predecessors in terms of managerial emphasis, effectiveness, and results. Figure 4-9 illustrates the four stages of quality management maturity.

Detection and control characterize stage 1 of quality maturity. The company strives to make its systems conform to specifications and procedures to ensure consistency. In stage 2, the company uses quality to drive internal efficiency. It begins to use data to analyze trends and problems, and prevent defects from occurring. Stage 3 represents the current level of maturity of most Baldrige-winning quality organizations or those that enjoy superior quality reputations. Their systems are designed to provide excellent external customer response and drive customer satisfaction. The processes are well understood and continuously improved by benchmarking other leaders. There is a direct cause and effect relationship between company actions and the repeatability of the results they expect. In stage 4, quality deployment progresses from methods to improve the current processes, products, and services to a strategic weapon to drive for future oppor-

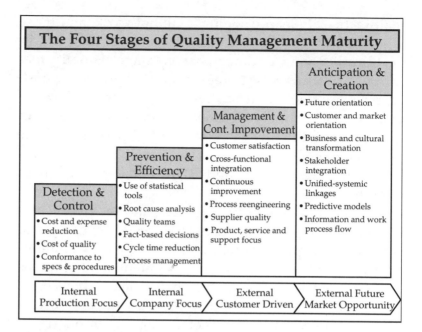

Figure 4-9 Four Stages of Quality Management.

tunity. Stage 4 shifts the excellent quality company into overdrive by introducing new tools, methodologies, and practices that expand company capabilities to anticipate and create the future. As in the movie "Star Wars," stage 4 companies have pushed the hyperspace button.

As the maturity level increases, the company moves from an internal focus to an external focus. At this level of quality maturation, the improvements in business results and competitiveness achieved from quality improvement initiatives become more and more amplified by the maturity level of the strategic approach. When the two dimensions of strategy and quality become highly integrated, competitive dominance is achieved.

Each of the twenty elements of ISO 9000 can also be positioned, based on the authors' experience, into stages of quality management maturity and summarized in Figure 4-10. None of the current ISO 9000 elements fit stage 4,

20 Elements of ISO 9000		
Stage 1: **Control**	**Stage 2:** **Prevention**	**Stage 3:** **T Q M**
2. Quality System	3. Contract	1. Mgmt.
5. Document	Review	Responsibility
Control	4. Design	6. Purchasing
8. Product I. D. and	Control	7. Purchaser-
Traceability	9. Process	Supplied Prod.
10. Inspection and	Control	15. Handling,
Testing	14. Corrective	Storage,
11. Inspect,	Action	Packaging, and
Measure, and	17. Internal	Delivery
Test Equip.	Quality	19. Servicing
12. Inspection and	Audits	
Test Status	18. Training	
13. Control of Non-	20. Statistical	
conforming	Techniques	
Product		
16. Quality Records		

Figure 4-10 Positioning ISO 9000 Within the Four Stages of Quality Maturity.

but, as in the other quality elements of stage 1 through stage 3, these can be primary building blocks essential for stage 4 success.

Stage 1: Detection and Control

Quality management had its roots in the discipline of production management where it intersected naturally with accounting. It was in production that managers first discovered that manufacturing defects increased product cost and after sales expenses. In order to reduce and eliminate these additional costs and expenses, managers concentrated their attention on detecting and repairing defective parts. They then developed specification and procedures manuals to ensure repeatability of the operations. These procedures became the guiding documents to control conformance to specifications. ISO 9000 registration is grounded in this discipline. This action produced the desired results. It reduced scrap, warranty costs, and field repair expenses. Figure 4-11 illustrates the stage 1 quality management model.

At this stage, the quality management system is based on identification and repair of defective parts. Inspection gates and defect detection form the basis of the management model focused on controlling line and field defects. The dominant perspective is a functional one, inwardly directed at the production areas, and fundamentally driven by the accounting imperatives of production and warranty costs. The key motivation is to control costs and to ensure conformance to requirements. Typically, the leaders of quality management at this stage of quality maturi-

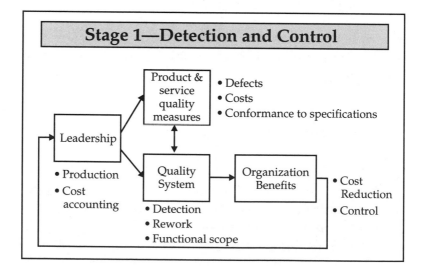

Figure 4-11 Stage 1 Quality Maturity.

ty and sophistication are in the operational areas— manufacturing, manufacturing engineering, production control, and accounting. In rare cases where a senior executive is in charge of quality management, the motivation will also include increasing profits and improving manufacturing efficiencies.

Having a defined quality system is one of the key ISO 9000 element important to stage 1 quality maturity. The ISO 9000 standard defines the maintenance of quality procedures to ensure that a product conforms to requirements. ISO 9000 requires the establishment and maintenance of procedures for controlling documentation through approval, issue, change, and modification to ensure that all procedures, process documentation, and specifications are up to date and regularly reviewed for currency. ISO 9000 evaluates procedures for identifying the product during all stages of production, delivery, and installation by individual product or batch. Another stage 1 ISO 9000 criteria is centered within three elements of defect detection—inspection, measuring, and testing. These elements require:

1. procedures for inspection and test at various stages of production;

2. procedures for selection, control, calibration, and maintenance of test and measurement equipment; and

3. appropriate markings, stamps, or labels affixed to product or equipment throughout production and installation to show conformance or non-conformance to tests and inspections.

ISO 9000 also requires procedures for identification, collection, indexing, filing, and storage of quality records from all its 20 elements.

Stage 2: Prevention and Efficiency

Seasoned managers in stage 1 learn that inspections and repairs deliver initial cost reduction, but not enough to sustain continuous improvement. Cost reductions bottom out at a level beyond upon which manufacturing can significantly improve. They discover that to reduce costs they have to staff inspection gates and repair stations, all of which detract from production efficiencies. Soon they come to the pivotal realization that elimination of defects can be more effective than repair. If no defects exist, then no repairs would be needed; consequently, no defective products would be leaving the factory, and service could be delivered more efficiently. Quality can be free if only there were no defects. The "zero defect, and quality is free" model of quality management emerged from this realization. Sophisticated managers at this stage spend their energies preventing defects from occurring. They focus in improving the production process, reducing its cycle time, and assuring the consistency of the output. They begin to apply statistical tools to increase consistency and fact-based analysis to understand root causes of repeatable defects. At this stage, there are seven frequently used basic instruments (Ishikawa, 1985) for quality improvement: five statistical analysis tools and two process tools. The five statistical tools are:

- the trend chart, which plots a measurement against time;
- the histogram, which plots frequency distribution by class or category;
- the Pareto chart, which plots the relative distribution of the constituent parts of the total;
- the control chart, which plots a measure against a control band that contains an upper and a lower limit; and

• the so-called "scatter chart" that correlates two variables to show their relationship.

Figure 4-12 illustrates these tools.
The two process tools are:

• the flow chart that depicts the sequence and branching of activities; and

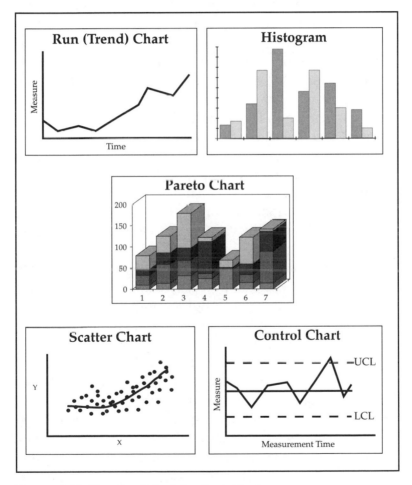

Figure 4-12 Five Statistical Analysis Tools.

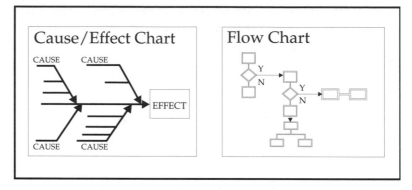

Figure 4-13 Two Process Tools.

•the "cause and effect" chart that shows the contributing factors that lead to a final result.

These are shown in Figure 4-13.

Taken together, these tools enable the quality manager to monitor processes, take action before a defect propagates to the finished product, and determine the contributing factors that can lead to a defect. These tools begin to drive the collection and analysis of meaningful data. They drive the organization to manage to trends rather than events.

The thrust for quality improvement is internal, but company-wide. Product defect isolation and removal is the joint responsibility of engineering and manufacturing. Effective service and support requires the synchronization of all elements of the sales and service organization. The company begins the formation of cross-functional improvement teams to address company wide issues and opportunities. Effective managers at this stage realize that anyone in the company, no matter how humble his or her position, can contribute to improvement. They also learn that groups of people working together can significantly improve the number and the effectiveness of the improvements. They learn that the specialized skill of each individual on the team works synergistically to produce better ideas that everyone understands and can implement because collectively they participated in the design. These quality teams become increasingly more widely deployed throughout functional areas and into cross functional organizations. Leaders discover that the effectiveness of the quality improvement teams increase when they communicate the goals and rationale for defect free products and services in a comprehensive manner that unifies the diverse interests of the group. This practice has the effect of increasing the team's understanding and capacity to make contributions.

When they do, these cross-functional teams realize that process issues cut across functional boundaries, and that process management discipline is required to obtain definable, repeatable, and predictable results. As they accept ownership and implement process management initiatives, cycle time improvement emerges as a major opportunity because it is a natural outcome of prevention-based quality systems and typically requires cross-functional cooperation to achieve.

Effective leaders at stage 2 begin to train and educate members of quality teams to work together as a group and contribute within a context that is larger than their immediate job descriptions. They must be good communicators—they must be able to act as coaches and teachers to groups larger than their own. They can no longer merely operate with excellence in reaction. They must anticipate and respond to prevent problems and seize opportunities. They must motivate groups larger than their own to act within a context which has a larger purpose than their immediate tasks. Quality improvement teams begin to integrate suppliers as a key participants in product improvement. Together they focus on product, process, and cycle time reduction to optimize operations between them.

Figure 4-14 illustrates the stage 2 quality management model. Note that the stage 2 process does not reject stage 1 principles; rather it builds on it by adding new processes and extending existing ones. In this way it enriches the overall approach of stage 1 to reach the level of stage 2.

Stage 2 quality management is more effective than stage 1. A shift from defect detection to defect prevention produces results which go beyond those experienced in stage 1. Analytic tools provide the means for disciplined planning and monitoring. Quality improvement teams expand the scope and level of participation. Both personal and organizational learning are taking place, although they are still centered on the production or service function. A new and more effective leadership style emerges. Organizational priorities are on the ability to be proactive and communicate the rationale for these actions.

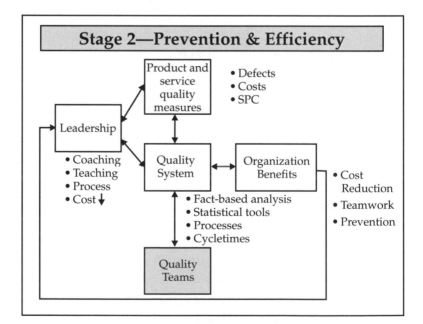

Figure 4-14 Stage 2 Quality Maturity.

In stage 2, ISO 9000 element 20 requires procedures for identifying the adequate use of statistical techniques in process, product, and service. These process and design control elements stress the monitoring and control of important process and product characteristics. Element 17, requires a system of internal audits to verify whether quality activities comply with requirements and to determine the effectiveness of the quality system. The ISO 9000 standard requires procedures for identifying and providing training and education needs for all personnel. Procedures for investigating causes of non-conformance, taking action to rectify them, and creating processes to prevent future occurrences is an important consideration in the ISO standard.

Stage 3: Management and Continuous Improvement

There is a fundamental shift, which delineates quality management in stage 2 from stage 3. There is an expansion from an inward orientation to a broader orientation that becomes driven by external factors. The focus for quality management expands from internally-driven functional factors to ones that are influenced by customers, suppliers, competitors and other industry participants. Simultaneously, the scope of internal functional participation expands to include a larger set of company-wide constituencies. Customer relationship management and satisfaction and process reengineering are stage 3 imperatives. Baldrige-winning companies' scores reflect current stage 3 quality practice.

In stage 3, process reengineering differentiates itself from process management in stage 2 by the scope and breadth of processes addressed. Process management tends to address refinements to current processes within the company, while process reengineering addresses new process structures to support changes required in the business (Hammer, Champy 1993). Companies realize that process reengineering must extend to business support areas and suppliers as well as those processes that provide goods and services to customers. Internal customer and supplier relationships develop between functional organizations. The company includes process reengineering and improvement as part the management and measurement system. Process owners and quality improvement achievements are recognized in communication and recognition events.

In stage 2, the emphasis is on energizing cross functional groups of people to quality improvement by participatory leadership rather than supervisory coercion and on the application of tools to prevent defects. In stage 3, cross-functional teams expand in their scope from related functions to company-wide units that may include supplier and customers (Charan, Tichy 1991). Managing such diversity makes it imperative that analysis of facts and trends becomes a common practice. People begin to understand their roles and responsibilities in support of the customer. They also begin to realize that there is valuable learning from the best industry practices. Management becomes acutely aware of the necessity to continuously improve, because knowledge and awareness of quantitative facts and practices from external sources bring into high contrast any ineffective practices and poor results.

A key factor that differentiates stage 3 cycle time improvement from stage 2 is the external orientation. Addressing cycle time for customer and competitive advantage versus cost advantage (Stalk 1988). Cycle time reduction actions in stage 3 expand to include suppliers and other stakeholders throughout the value chain. Support service areas consider cycle time reduction a key part of internal customer satisfaction. Some support service cycle time actions address days' sales outstanding, support service turn around time, and employee benefits processing.

A key contributing factor that drives the external orientation is the discovery by management that its best efforts at defect prevention and removal often fail to meet customer expectations. Many customers remain unsatisfied with the product or service in spite of the best of efforts. Customer complaints and related problems persist. What distinguishes stage 3 quality management is the degree of commitment to customer satisfaction and the depth and scope to which a company addresses customer dissatisfaction issues. The management practice includes solving the symptoms of customer dissatisfaction and providing a closed-loop solution that will identify and eradicate the source of complaints. Management practice also includes business process improvements in areas that resulted in customer dissatisfaction. Collectively these practices provide a systemic solution to customer dissatisfaction. The systemic solution prevents the same problem from cropping up again. Because every customer complaint or dissatisfier is addressed in this systematic way, quality is constantly improving. The company begins to aggregate this information and use it to determine trends and to understand the reasons for sales wins and losses. It uses this information for market advantage and refinements to products and services.

In an attempt to solve customer dissatisfaction comprehensively, quality management extends the parties that can contribute to the solution. This extension includes not only key functional areas internal to the firm, but also include parties external to the firm, such as customers and suppliers. The integration of these parties to the customer satisfaction process is a key distinguishing feature at stage 3 of quality management. All these parties who participate in the systemic solutions of customer satisfaction now become stakeholders in the process. The process now becomes closed-loop.

Because of the diversity of participants and the externally-driven actions, it is no longer sufficient to address problems or solutions by anecdote, by intuition or uninformed opinion. The solution has to be grounded on facts—quantitative analysis that provides the firm with reliable information about customers and competition within markets. At this stage, external, factual information supports and enhances the internal indicators common to stage 2 quality practice. The shift from an internal focus to an external one where the emphasis is on customer satisfaction demands a high level of marketing literacy and fluency. Usually in quality management initiatives, marketing is one of the last organizations to be involved. To focus quality initiatives externally requires timely and accurate analysis of customer information, market behavior, customer preferences, and expectations. Fact-based market intelligence is also an indicator of increasing strategy maturity. When the company's quality system begins to merge operational data with market planning information, it begins to emerge into competitive dominance.

At stage 3, management discovers that there are pivotal processes to support customer satisfaction where they feel their ability and knowledge is still insufficient. Benchmarking becomes the method to discover effective improvements to address problems or create opportunities. Stage 3 firms share their best practices with other firms, and they search for best practices to improve their ability to meet customer satisfaction. Cross-industry benchmarks provide companies with leading edge ideas from the best processes and practices. For example, Xerox wanted to improve its distribution system, so it sought out the company with the best distribution system. The company they benchmarked with was L.L. Bean. While L.L. Bean's products and services were uniquely different, the processes were similar enough to gain effective improvements.

Figure 4-15 illustrates the overall quality management model for stage 3. Just as stage 2 extends the stage 1 model, stage 3 quality management extends the stage 2 model. Thereby, it enhances the organization's overall capabilities for quality management, and improves its potential for effective results.

In the quest to meet customer expectations, companies learn that they cannot meet all expectations of every existing or potential customer. They realize they can satisfy expectations well for only specific customer groups or markets. This is the situation in which millionaires who want to purchase a Rolls-Royce will never be satisfied with a Honda, no matter how defect-free it is, or how outstanding the service from the dealership. Communicat-

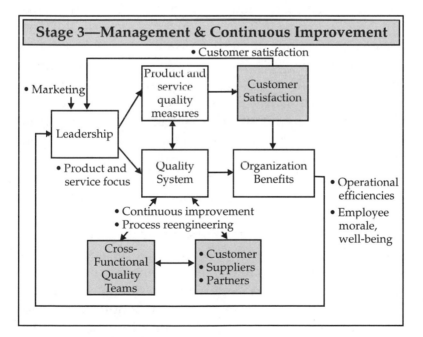

Figure 4-15 Stage 3 Quality Maturity.

ing expectations and implicit or explicit commitments to customers becomes part of the quality planning process and another area where marketing information is important. One note of caution is that companies must understand the difference between marketing and sales. Sales is the front line of customer support; marketing is the industry intelligence arm of the organization.

The focus on customer satisfaction imposes new requirements on the style and breadth of leadership. Stage 3 leadership requires multi-disciplinary skills, a high level of marketing literacy, and the ability to team with external groups, such as customers, suppliers, distributors, etc. In this environment, an important leadership attribute is the ability to work across functional boundaries to make business decisions, not work unit decisions. Leaders must create an environment where all the internal functional areas work together harmoniously to achieve quality that will meet customers' expectations. They realize that they must not only work as a team across functions within the firm, but also with organizations outside the firm. Leaders find that this teamwork spans the length of the value chain— all the links within or outside the company that provide some added value to customers (see Chapter 6, Item 5.1) (Norman, Ramirez 1993). This is necessary because, from a customer's perspective, the functional area(s) that contributed to his or her dissatisfaction is irrelevant. The customer just wants the problem solved. Customers have a right to expect a high level of satisfaction when they use a product or a service.

Employee morale and well-being are important indicators of effective leadership and characteristics of stage 3 quality maturity. At stage 2, leaders involve all people in improvement teams. A leadership imperative in stage 3 is to ensure a healthy environment for people to develop and grow their own skills, and to contribute positively to company results. The leadership responsibility extends beyond people involvement, safety, and morale on the job to include external influences such as family, community, and social responsibilities.

ISO 9000 elements have less importance in stage 3 quality maturity because they are more internally focused. Two ISO 9000 areas that do apply to stage 3 are

- the requirement for on-going subcontractor assessments, clear and accurate purchasing data, and verification of purchased product; and
- the requirement for evaluating the service performed on products.

Stage 4: Anticipation and Creation

There are two major distinctions between stage 3 and stage 4 quality. The first is the level of integration between quality management and business management; the second is the future orientation. In stage 4, management has the sophistication and the insight to prioritize its quality initiatives to meet its future business goals. The resources deployed and the quality improvement initiatives can be directly tied to future critical success factors. Too often, companies implement improvement initiatives to address current or historic problems only to find that after 2 or 3 years of working the problem, the industry and marketplace have shifted, and new problems with higher priorities need to be addressed, rendering all the prior effort wasted. The internal focus of stage 1 and stage 2 open companies to this risk. In fact, the heavy focus on customers in stage 3 maturity also has risk associated with it. Today's customers in today's market may not be tomorrow's customers if the company shifts its strategy or consumer buying habits change. The tobacco companies have had to shift product and market focus in order to remain a growth business. The customers they cater to today are a different set than a few years ago. In this case, external factors of environmental safety and health drove consumer buying habits. Quality improvement initiatives to create more efficient tobacco processing would have not yielded the business results expected. On the other hand, quality improvement initiatives to address new growth market opportunities were the right priority, provided the company anticipated the shift in consumer buying habits.

Another example is the company that changes its strategy from low volume, high profit, high service quality to high volume, low profit products because it sees more long term growth opportunity in this market. If this company has quality initiatives targeted at improving service quality and profitability, it cannot support the structure required to compete in a high volume, low profit business. The quality initiatives it must concentrate on for success in this business are cycle times, time to market, inventory turns, and return on assets.

In both above examples, one fundamental difference emerges between stage 4 and the other stages of quality. Most companies see quality as a way to avoid or respond to problems. In stage 4, quality becomes a weapon to anticipate, create, and respond to opportunity. In the case of the tobacco company, it clearly would have been reacting to a serious business problem if it did not recognize the future market shift. The fact that it was able to anticipate the future trends, enabled it to respond to a changing environment. Many times companies recognize the opportunity, but their structure does not enable them to respond. They blame culture or bureaucracy when in fact they have not applied quality theory to address the opportunity. Figure 4-16 illustrates stage 4 quality maturity.

Stage 4 quality requires a time horizon anchored in the future, a single-minded commitment to competitive dominance, organizational structure and management

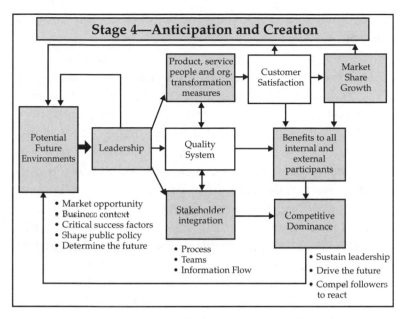

Figure 4-16 Stage 4 Quality Management Model.

system transformation, and revenue and market share growth focused on new business opportunities. Again, as in previous stages, stage 4 extends the stage 3 model in four key areas:

1. Understanding of market forces and industry dynamics;

2. Implementation of analytical tools and predictive models to enhance planning and goal setting;

3. Transforming the organization and the leadership to the future goals;

4. A focus on revenue and market share growth to achieve competitive dominance in new, emerging markets.

These four key areas provide the integration between quality and business, and the future orientation. When coupled with strategy, they form the basis for competitive dominance.

Understanding of the future market forces and industry dynamics: The basic premise in stage 4 is that any successful quality system must have, as its foundation, an understanding of the nature of future demand and the industry structure that can fuel and maintain it. For business, demand comes as segmented market opportunity; for public sector, non-profit, education, and/or health care organizations, the nature of demand derives from other industry forces such as government funding, needs of the public, or societal trends, just to name a few. The nature of demand and the industry structure, determines the context of the business or the business model. Ask yourself this simple question "What would motivate you, as a customer or potential customer, to write out a check for a company's goods or services." This question can uncover new and emerging patterns or "niches" in traditional buying habits that enable a company to form a new context for its business. Customers told IBM Rochester that they purchase its computer systems because of the large software application portfolio available. The nature of demand was for applications, not for computers. The business of IBM Rochester, until then, was defined as a provider of computers to small- and intermediate-sized businesses. All the focus was on the computer hardware and operating system software, not the applications. Applications were provided by other participants in the industry for our computer and other competitors' computers. IBM Rochester found that other factors outside its control determined its success or failure as a business. From this realization, IBM Rochester redefined its own business as that of a supplier of application platforms and redefined its business context within the framework of four critical success factors—products (application platform), the channels (participants who provide applications), the applications themselves, and the service and support structure for products and applications (Bauer, Collar, Tang 1992). These four critical success factors formed IBM Rochester's "extended enterprise," or new business context, and drove all its quality initiatives. Every participant within the new business context became a "stakeholder" in success. Process management encompassed the extended enterprise. IBM Rochester included applications providers in teams and involved them in all aspects of the product cycle processes. IBM Rochester was able to tie applications to high growth market segments to re-shape the "mid-range" industry and shape its future. Instead of reacting to the forces affecting its business, it became a master of its own destiny through alliances, quality initiatives, and management systems that organized around all the critical success factors of the business.

Implementation of analytical tools and predictive models to enhance planning and goal setting: Planning processes founded in extrapolation of historical trends are no longer sufficient, and must be augmented and enhanced with future modeling and predictive analysis tools. Stage 4 expands the traditional quality approach using the "7 basic tools" to an additional set of tools that help companies analytically deal with uncertainties of the future. This subject is discussed in detail in Chapters 7 and 8.

Using fact based processes to systematically analyze and understand the range of potential and alternative futures as a means to set appropriate and achievable leadership goals is a fundamental requirement of stage 4 quality maturity. The "crystal ball" approach in developing a strategic perspective is as unacceptable to stage 4 quality as lack of statistical process control is to production quality. The same rigor and anticipatory capabilities that the best quality disciplines have mandated in production processes must apply to strategic planning. Analytical and statistical analysis applies to planning just as it does to production with one key difference. Accurate historical trends must be complemented with future projections that are sometimes ambiguous and clearly have more margin for error. Therefore, planning tools must be able to deal with vast amounts of dissimilar information and creatively correlate and synthesize this information into actionable opportunities. These tools must also provide the capability to model alternatives and determine optimum approaches. And just as in production planning, analysis must be a continuous process, not an event that happens once a year. In a dynamic marketplace, the extended enterprise must be able to monitor the environment continuously and adjust to changes. Planning tools and methodologies as described in Chapters 7 and 8 will help the organization anticipate change, identify and create opportunity, respond before the competition, and sustain leadership.

Transforming the organization and the leadership to the future goals: In stage 4 maturity, transformation of the organization and the leadership becomes an integrated quality initiative. The organization definition must include all participants in the extended enterprise. The stage 4 quality system recognizes that product, service, and traditional operational quality measures are complemented with measures of progress in organizational transformation and cultural change. Leadership skills in both operational excellence and strategic perspective are required to grapple with the future and deal with organizational (extended enterprise) and external challenges throughout the change journey. Exceptional leaders will also be able to anticipate and shape evolving key forces such as health, safety, and diversity issues. Instead of reacting to governmental regulations, public opinion, and politically correct issues, the leader in stage 4 takes a proactive role in shaping public policy and establishing the benchmark of how business, government, and community improve through mutual cooperation.

A focus on revenue and market share growth to achieve competitive dominance in new, emerging markets: Stage 4 quality maturity emphasizes the closed-loop customer satisfaction and customer relationship management processes but expands practice to include closed loop feedback on market growth. This is a broader perspective where the business continuously adjusts to market dynamics and industry forces that shape and influence the changing nature of demand. Stage 4 does not assume a stable customer base, a stable marketplace, or a stable industry structure. The stage 4 quality system is designed to anticipate, even shape change, and adapt the organization to meet these changes before the competition. It is designed to recognize opportunity, seize it, and develop a commanding position. Opportunity may not necessarily be determined by the current customer base or industry structure. Therefore, a key element of this quality system is a market share information process and industry analysis that measures and analyzes detailed market segments continuously to ensure market acceptance, revenue growth, and competitive dominance.

Figure 4-17 positions Competitive Dominance within the context of other quality approaches.

Theory and Definition

	ISO 9000	Crosby	Deming	Feigenbaum	Ishikawa	Juran	Competitive Dominance
Quality definition	Conformance to procedures and specifications	Conformance to requirements	Three corners of quality: product, user, and instructions for use	What the customer says it is	Satisfactory to the customer	Fitness for use	Balanced approach between cost, expense, growth, opportunity, organ.
Philosophy	Documentation defines and reflects practice	Defect Free	Constancy of purpose; Statistical analysis	Full customer satisfaction at economical cost	Company-wide quality control	Project approach; in order of importance	Integration of strategy and quality
Approach	Self audit with independent review	Motivate the people	Statistical techniques	Systems approach to total quality control	Talk with data	Quality trilogy; planning, control and improvement	Extends practice beyond current approaches

Figure 4-17 Competitive Dominance Relationship to ISO and Other Quality Gurus.

Theory and Definition

	ISO 9000	Crosby	Deming	Feigenbaum	Ishikawa	Juran	Competitive Dominance
Mechanics	Three ISO 9000 standards and two guidelines	Fourteen steps	Fourteen obligations of management	The nine "M"s	Seven Statistical Tools	Diagnostic and remedial journeys	Baldrige as foundation; ten principles, new tools and methods

Quality Improvement Elements

	ISO 9000	Crosby	Deming	Feigenbaum	Ishikawa	Juran	Competitive Dominance
Quality Planning	Defined in ISO 9000 and 9004 guidelines	Good things happen when planned	Plan, do, check, act (PDCA) cycles	...Must deliver satisfactory product quality	Cause and effect diagram	...Will result in minimal need for subsequent improvement	Must consider customer, environment, and market opportunity

Figure 4-17 Competitive Dominance Relationship to ISO and Other Quality Gurus. *(continued)*

Quality Improvement Elements

	ISO 9000	Crosby	Deming	Feigenbaum	Ishikawa	Juran	Competitive Dominance
Process Control	Procedures and specs define level of control	Zero Defects	Improvement of the production process	Significantly important	Detect any abnormality	Variables are not equally important	Closed loop across the extended enterprise
Measurement	Adherence to procedures and specifications	Cost of quality; Price of nonconformance	Reduction of variation	Quality cost data	Physical, chemical, and human sense perception	Quantification of characteristics	Market share, efficiency, productivity, morale
Education	All education tracked and reported	Formally structured	Education and self-improvement For everyone	Quality education never ends	Participation by ALL employees	Use basic skills as team member and problem solver	Future skill needs-based, including leadership

Figure 4-17 Competitive Dominance Relationship to ISO and Other Quality Gurus. *(continued)*

Quality Improvement Elements

	ISO 9000	Crosby	Deming	Feigenbaum	Ishikawa	Juran	Competitive Dominance
Improvement	Continuous review and update	...A long while before becoming permanent	...Constancy and forever	...From all the men and women	...Never in the short term	Do better than the standard	Milestones that define progress and success
Management	ISO 9004 defines the quality Mgmt. system	Start at the top	Cannot be delegated	Organized company-wide	Not exclusive domain of Q. C. specialists	Started at the top	New leadership skills required
Employee Participation	Addressed in ISO 9004	Each person	Everyone's job	Genuine management involvement	All employees	Entire Hierarchy	Customer culture across extended enterprise
Suppliers	Addressed in the ISO standards	Oriented to needs of the company	Long-term Relationship with key suppliers	Important ingredient	Select two sub-contractors	Multiple sources	Broadly defined as partnership with all stakeholders

Figure 4-17 Competitive Dominance Relationship to ISO and Other Quality Gurus. *(continued)*

In the stage 4 quality system, a strategic perspective permeates the major quality initiatives to sustain leadership and compel followers to react. It is designed to anticipate and create future opportunity, and apply systematic processes that include all stakeholders to seize that opportunity. It is designed to integrate all the responsibilities of quality management with those of general management within a strategic framework to achieve competitive dominance in a market.

The mastery of the two domains of strategy and quality is demonstrated by the extent to which they are seamlessly integrated. The next chapter describes the ten principles that address this seamless integration to achieve Competitive Dominance.

5

The Ten Principles of Competitive Dominance

Competitive Dominance results in sustained leadership and acceptance of the firm's product and services as the standard by which all others are judged. In this environment competitors are forced to react and follow. These goals are achieved by being visionary and a creator of opportunity, but doing this ethically and fairly, while being a very tough competitor. However, competitively dominant firms are toughest on themselves; they relentlessly practice the following principles of Competitive Dominance. They consistently appear to be steps ahead of the competition. They anticipate, create, and act. They don't react; they don't wait, and they don't follow. They shape the future rather than adjust to it. They are viewed as role models in the industry and they are the envy of the competition. The goal for Competitive Dominance fuels the will to make things happen and to create a future that will compel competitors to react and follow. This desire nourishes the tenacity to sustain leadership, and sustained leadership establishes the firm's products and services as the de facto standard. Their supremacy is acknowledged by customers and competitors. Having the goal for Competitive Dominance creates the will for sustained competitive leadership, and it is in this way that firms not only continuously improve, but make innovative breakthroughs that separate them from the pack and also-rans. This is illustrated in Figure 5-1.

The following ten points are the guiding principles that integrate strategy and quality into a refined system that achieves Competitive Dominance.

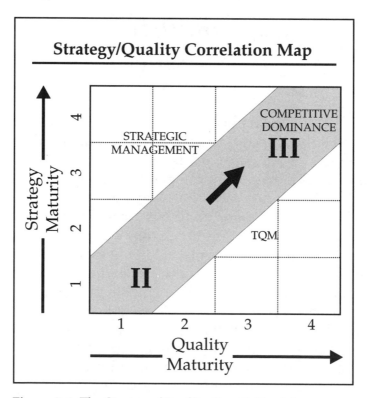

Figure 5-1 The Strategy/Quality Correlation Map.

1. Strategic and Visionary Leadership

Strategic leadership is the competence to manage in two time-frames simultaneously and it is also the capacity to simultaneously manage two structures. Visionary leadership is the unique ability to conceptualize and give meaning and significance to these actions and create a rallying point. The capacity to manage two time frames is an issue of balance. It deals with the capacity to act on issues and decisions of today, which will yield results in a short time; and it also deals with the capacity to act today on the tough decisions which will yield results in a longer time horizon. The ability to manage two structures is also about balance. It deals with the capacity to focus on cost and expense, without losing sight of the importance to grow revenue and market share. This is illustrated in Figure 5-2, Locus of Strategic Leadership. However, visionary leadership requires an additional, rare, and exceptional dimension. Visionaries are able to formulate and articulate a vision that captures the imperatives of the enterprise, as well as the aspirations of the people. In this manner the visionary leader gives meaning and significance to the two time frames, the two structures, and their actions.

2. Continuous Environmental Scanning

No firm can assume it is competing in a static environment where competitive forces are stable and predictable. Firms risk being surprised. New forces are constantly emerging which abolish cherished assumptions, create new industry structures, re-segment the market, re-level the playing field, and facilitate entry of hungry and smart new competitors. In recent years, the velocity of these changes has accelerated at an unprecedented pace. Any

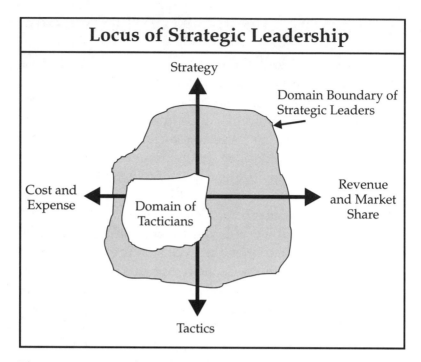

Figure 5-2 Locus of Strategic Leadership.

firm that does not wish to be overtaken must be constantly alert for shifts in existing forces and for new, emerging environmental shifts. Environmental scanning is the means by which a firm can continuously analyze the intensity and direction of existing market and industry forces, the configuration of new market forces, and the potential impacts on their ability to sustain Competitive Dominance. This process requires the continuous analysis and study of industry trends, customer attitudes and values, capabilities of current and new technologies, capabilities of the competition, policies of governments and international organizations, and positions of important thought leaders such as consultants and other opinion makers (Stanat 1990). Simply stated, market and industry intelligence are key processes to support environmental scanning.

3. MODELING TRENDS AND DYNAMICS

Fact-based analysis of trends must consider the past and historical data, but must also project into the future through analysis of the dynamics of forces and trends. Fact-based analysis of trends is fundamentally important and absolutely necessary, but insufficient when it considers only historical information. This is the flaw of "rearview mirror" analysis. Also beware of the corollary flaw of straight-line extensions of the past into the future. That is fallacy of "momentum forecasting." This is valid only if the future is a natural extension of the past; it assumes there are no environmental shifts, that no new forces emerge, and that competition is complacent. This one of the fundamental reasons why seemingly first-rate quality firms fail in the marketplace or lose their position in their industry. Environmental scanning enables a firm to acquire unique insight into the potential configuration of forces and thus develop unique and differentiated strategies. Industry and market intelligence results from environmental scanning can be used as a basis for modeling the dynamics of environmental forces and scenario analysis about alternative futures. Modeling and scenario analysis provide a basis for prediction in a way that is similar to that of the seven basic tools for historical data. The difference is that the Competitive Dominance set of tools helps companies deal with ambiguity and uncertainty of future decisions.

4. LISTENING POSTS

Companies must have well-deployed listening posts to gather fact-based information about the market and industry; they also have management systems that continuously monitor, analyze, and model this information.

Just as sales and production require fact-based information to understand their current position, listening posts assess the environment and the market to determine if the direction the company is headed is the right one. Some examples of external listening posts are industry-wide data bases, consultant reports, industry trade journals, government reports, market research studies, and competitor analysis. Listening posts provide the fact-based information for environmental scanning, the input to predict analytical modeling, and the trend data to assess shifts and anticipate change in consumer, industry, or market preferences. While many companies claim to have effective listening posts, they have difficulty translating all the data into information that provides knowledge to the organization because the data is spread out all over the company. Sales has some data; planning has some data, and finance has other data. Typically these data rarely come together, and even if they do, there is probably no aggregate analysis or conclusions formed. Strategic leadership is rarely gained by experience or intuition alone. Those leaders with perceived visionary capabilities will typically have effective listening posts that provide consolidated facts from many different sources. The information that is obtained from these different sources can then be synthesized into potential opportunities or problems. Companies must gather and analyze important sources of data from listening posts to create a competitive advantage through information.

Another key listening post required for a company to achieve Competitive Dominance is internal. Personnel attitudes, opinions, and concerns must be monitored continuously to keep a pulse on the support for company goals and the acceptance of change. Yearly opinion survey trends, while important, do not provide timely information to respond to problems or to seize the high ground.

5. CHANGE AND ORGANIZATIONAL TRANSFORMATION

This is a call to action for self-renewal through continuous transformation, systematic, and thoughtful change. Change and organizational transformation are business imperatives. The dominant firm must continuously "reinvent" itself to maintain its position. If it fails to do this, a smart competitor will predict the dominant firm's actions and create a way to improve on the product or service or find a way to deliver more value. Change and organizational transformation are also imperatives for the firm that is not dominant, but has aspirations to become so. For, it will not be able to dislodge the leader or break away from the pack without breakthrough innovations. These goals do not come without change and transformation. They come from doing the unpredictable. Firms must develop a plan, formulate the initiatives and create a road map to accomplish their transformation. This includes an ability to rethink what business they are in, how they can serve customers more effectively, how to reengineer key business processes to be more competitive, and whether the culture and values of the firm are sufficiently robust for the new journey. Successful companies must launch their initiatives with unambiguous milestones to signal progress and success to future goals.

6. CUSTOMER-CENTRIC CULTURE

The purpose of business is to keep existing customers and to create new customers by consistently delivering more value than the competition. All too often, successful firms begin to develop an internal view of value and miss the mark with customers. In order to maintain an externalized perspective, companies must develop processes that integrate customers into all aspects of the business. It must develop a customer-centric culture. Customer satisfaction is not a one-time event. It occurs at all "moments of truth" with the products or services that the firm provides. Essentially, the moments of truth are the pivotal events during the life-cycle of the product or service when customers observe and judge their experience. For an airline, it begins with reservation, and it is followed by check-in, in-flight service, luggage handling, safety, etc. For a car, it begins with the professionalism of the salesman, and it is followed by the car's performance, the dealership, etc. To make every customer life-cycle experience memorable, and to exceed the performance of the competition, every business process must be customer-centric. To develop this cultural characteristic, an effective approach is to have customers actively participate in key business processes of the firm such as product development, product introduction, and product planning cycles, to name a few. This accelerates employees' understanding of their role in value creation and learning about the direct impact of their contribution to customer satisfaction. This continuous contact with customers reinforces a market and service orientation and culture.

7. UNIFIED-SYSTEMIC LINKS

To achieve dominance requires the alignment and integration of an extended set of processes and resources within the enterprise and outside the boundaries of the enterprise. In effect, the processes must be "boundaryless," but they must also be meaningfully linked and integrated. Linking key processes—so that in unison they create more customer value, or provide sustainable competitive advantages—forms the foundation for dominance and leadership. Unified and systemically linked processes can produce results which are more difficult to imitate or duplicate by a competitor. Unlike product attributes, or technology, a competitor cannot take a process to a laboratory for reverse engineering or imitation. At best the competition can guess or imagine how it was done. Systemically-linked processes are one of the most powerful strategic actions in a firm can launch when key processes are re-conceptualized to deliver more customer value to improve product or service quality, or to reduce time to market, or to change the economic structure of the product or service. A simple example is the link of a computer-aided design system with plant-floor manufacturing and with the business planning system of a manufacturing firm. Another example is SABRE, the airlines reservation system, which is linked to the frequent flier system, with a bank's credit card system, and with rental car agencies, hotels, etc. These unified links enable a firm to provide superior, seamless, and differentiated customer satisfaction.

8. STAKEHOLDER INTEGRATION

Sustained leadership is impossible without tightly knit participation of stakeholders in the firm's key business processes and information systems (Kosynski 1993). Industry participants who have a stake in the success of a firm's product or services are stakeholders. The most significant stakeholders are those that play an active role in the value-chain of the firm's products and services (Norman, Ramirez 1993, Porter 1985). They are important because, collectively with the firm, they have the means to create the conditions that can enhance customer satisfaction and, individually, they are able to improve their competitiveness. As a unit they form a community of shared goals, a pool of extensive resources which can pro-actively launch integrated initiatives to produce results that can create substantially more impact at all moments of truth. This community of stakeholders also forms a broader and more robust base for continuous improvement and organizational learning than just suppliers or distributors.

9. ORGANIZATIONAL ENERGETICS

Firms that have achieved or are striving for Competitive Dominance have a discernible and palpable level of energy and enthusiasm. This level of excitement and emotional commitment goes well beyond high morale. They are on a mission, there is purpose in what they do. This special characteristic we call organizational energetics. All ranks in the organization feel they are special, and because they feel that way, they are able to produce extraordinary results. Many firms are able to achieve a high level of organizational energetics for brief periods of time, but they are unable to sustain it. Effective leaders sustain organizational energy by a tightly-focused sense of where the firm is going and why, by empowering the workforce, by constantly improving their skills, and by celebrating the achievements people make. A strong customer-centric culture reinforces and nourishes organizational energetics. It is also nourished by continuous and credible feedback that employees are doing the right thing from the people that count—customers. Participation with stakeholders in key initiatives is another effective way to reinforce this. Sustained leadership is impossible without a high level of organizational energetics.

10. OPPORTUNITY GROWTH

Competitive Dominance means establishing and gaining market-share in new opportunities. It means that the firm is able to increase its customer base at a rate that exceeds the growth rate of all other key traditional and established businesses. It also means that it is able to create new business before, or faster than, any competitor. The ability for a company to establish and create a new businesses is proof that it has been able to anticipate and create new customer value. The company has turned an opportunity into a reality by rapid growth in new revenue sources. The simple fact that more customers are voting with their money on the firm's product and services indicates that they are more satisfied with the benefits they experience and the value they receive. We are all familiar with firms that had humble beginnings but with outstanding innovative products and services have established themselves as the dominant firm. These are the firms that had a very small market share but, with innovative ideas, were able to grow faster than the established firms. They were able to steal a march and move into an occupied space, while the dominant firm was complacent and slow. We are also familiar with firms that had a high and dominant market-share but underestimated the abilities of small and rapidly growing firms to be ultimately threatened by these upstarts. The focus on opportunity growth permits large firms to be alert for upstarts and recognize major shifts in customer expectations or market/industry dynamics. It also enables small firms to become upstarts.

We do not believe that these ten principles of Competitive Dominance are a substitute for other quality or strategy management principles that have been articulated by other leading thinkers. Our ten principles are built on the foundation concepts which have already been established, accepted, and widely practiced. One question that may now come to mind is, "Which one do I address first?" or, "Are these ten principles listed in the order that they should be addressed?" The answer is that they are all interdependent. You will find that when effectively addressing one principle, you will be implementing parts of another. Therefore we have chosen to use the Malcolm Baldrige National Quality Award criteria as the foundation within which to integrate the ten principles. Baldrige is by far the best foundation because of its breadth and scope in addressing all areas of a business enterprise. Figure 5-3 demonstrates the link between the Malcolm Baldrige categories and the ten principles.

In the following pages, the ten Competitive Dominance principles are placed in the context of the Malcolm Baldrige guidelines highlighting the key salient features in bold strokes. Our intent is not to prescribe actions, nor is it to propose additions to the Baldrige criteria. Our intent is to expand the thinking of companies toward Competitive Dominance theory using the Baldrige framework as a foundation for differentiated strategic advantage and broad-based deployment.

10 Principles of Competitive Dominance	Malcolm Baldrige National Quality Award Criteria						
	Leadership	Information	Strategy	Human Resources	Process	Results	Customer Focus
Strategic Leadership	X		X	X		X	X
Cont. Environmental Scanning	X	X	X				X
Modeling Trends & Dynamics		X	X			X	X
Listening Posts	X	X	X	X	X	X	X
Change / Transformation	X		X	X	X	X	
Customer-Centric Culture	X			X	X		X
Unified-Systemic Links	X	X	X	X	X		X
Stakeholder Integration	X		X		X	X	X
Organizational Energetics	X			X			
Opportunity Growth		X	X			X	X

Figure 5-3 Ten Principles of Competitive Dominance Cross-Referenced to Baldrige Guidelines.

6

Integrating Competitive Dominance into the Baldrige Template

We have described the concrete principles of Competitive Dominance as one where the disciplines and principles of strategy and quality intersect. We have also discussed how the integrated and balanced practice of both disciplines when injected with the new thinking of Competitive Dominance produces a new powerful synergy in a way that neither practice can provide independently. In this chapter, we demonstrate that this is also true when interpreting the Baldrige guidelines. The application of Competitive Dominance principles changes the way in which one interprets the Baldrige criteria in the following ways:

• It gives the criteria new and richer meaning.

- It tightens up the links among the categories in a way that accelerates the achievement of business goals.
- It improves the effectiveness of deployment by consistent and balanced alignment of strategic and quality imperatives.
- It provides a continuous and systematic approach to forward looking processes, which projects into the future and which rejects the tyranny of the rear-view mirror.

A central thesis of this book is that management principles must be deployed and acted on to produce business results. We have also discussed that deployment needs an integrated framework that permits the application of the Competitive Dominance principles in a systematic manner. We have discussed in Chapter 3 why we believe that Baldrige provides that integrating framework. The fundamental reason is that Baldrige addresses the key issues that every enterprise has to deal with: leadership, information, planning, human resources, business processes, operations, and customers. In this chapter we show how the Competitive Dominance principles are integrated in a very specific and focused way in the Baldrige quality template. We use the Baldrige application criteria as a foundation to describe how this is done. By integrating the Competitive Dominance principles into Baldrige we demonstrate in this chapter that the Baldrige framework can be viewed through a different lens; that by applying Competitive Dominance thinking, the Baldrige principles are in fact extended in a way that gives the criteria new meaning and new levels of managerial effectiveness. The combined effect of new meaning and new ways to think about Baldrige, from our experience in strategy and quality, gives businesses a fresh approach to achieve unique, differentiated levels of competitive effectiveness.

The improvements to the 1995 Baldrige guidelines take a step in the direction of Competitive Dominance, with more focus on the key business drivers and better integration of overall performance with business strategy. But they also reduced point values on the Strategy Category, once again increasing the risk that organizations will de-emphasize the importance of an integrated approach between quality and strategy.

In this chapter, we highlight, in bold text, those areas that must be addressed to effectively apply the principles of Competitive Dominance, and we discuss how they should be interpreted within the context of the Baldrige.

1995 AWARD EXAMINATION CRITERIA— ITEM LISTING

1995 Examination Categories/Items	Point Values
1.0 Leadership	**90**
1.1 Senior Executive Leadership	45
1.2 Leadership System and Organization	25
1.3 Public Responsibility and Corporate Citizenship	20
2.0 Information and Analysis	**75**
2.1 Management of Information and Data	20
2.2 Competitive Comparisons and Benchmarking	15
2.3 Analysis and Uses of Company-Level Data	40
3.0 Strategic Planning	**55**
3.1 Strategy Development	35
3.2 Strategy Deployment	20

4.0	**Human Resource Development and Management**		**140**
	4.1	Human Resources Planning and Evaluation	20
	4.2	High Performance Work Systems	45
	4.3	Employee Education, Training, and Development	50
	4.4	Employee Well-Being and Satisfaction	25
5.0	**Process Management**		**140**
	5.1	Design and Introduction of Products and Services	40
	5.2	Process Management: Product and Service Production and Delivery	40
	5.3	Process Management: Support Service	30
	5.4	Management of Supplier Performance	30
6.0	**Quality and Operational Results**		**250**
	6.1	Product and Service Quality Results	75
	6.2	Company Operational and Financial Results	130
	6.3	Supplier Performance Results	45
7.0	**Customer Focus and Satisfaction**		**250**
	7.1	Customer and Market Knowledge	30
	7.2	Customer Relationship Management	30
	7.3	Customer Satisfaction Determination	30
	7.4	Customer Satisfaction Results	100
	7.5	Customer Satisfaction Comparisons	60
	TOTAL POINTS		**1000**

1.0 LEADERSHIP *(90 points)*

The *Leadership* Category examines senior executives' personal leadership and involvement in creating and sustaining a customer focus, clear values, and expectations. This category also looks for a leadership system that promotes performance excellence. Also examined is how the values and expectations are integrated into the company's management system, including how the company addresses its public responsibilities and corporate citizenship.

At each stage of quality/strategy maturity grid, there is an increasing progression in the sophistication of leadership. Leadership at the Competitive Dominance stage must recognize possibilities others do not. From this they must articulate a vision—a picture painted in bold strokes, what the organization ought to be and where it should go, thereby inspiring people to perform beyond their capabilities.

The leadership emphasis is simultaneously focused internally and externally. The internal focus is on organizational transformation. Leaders knows that, in order to be successful, their management role must extend beyond company boundaries to include other participants in providing value to the market. A company cannot be successful if any part of the whole fails. The transformation imperative must include all stakeholders. It is up to the leader to inspire those within company walls as well as those outside the walls who provide added value.

Leadership skill is another important internal element and a key tool for success as described in Chapter 7. Traditional leadership development programs assess either a manager's operational skill or a manager's strategic skill. Leaders of the future must have finely honed skills in both. They must have capability to be excellent operational managers, yet have a sense for future market dynamics and business opportunities. They must have the intuition required to understand market forces and their implications on the company's future. They must also have the ability to deploy, with excellence, the changes required to respond.

The external focus is on Competitive Dominance. Successful leaders recognize that they cannot achieve Competitive Dominance without an integrated approach of strategy and quality and that conventional organizational paradigms are not effective for world-class results. They must conclude that to create substantial competitive advantage, they must simultaneously transform the organization, its structure, its processes, and its value system. They must know that the best measure of world-class quality and high operational effectiveness is not only customer satisfaction but market-share and revenue growth in new opportunities, which can only be demonstrated convincingly through Competitive Dominance.

Public policy, which has not drawn a lot of attention, is another important and differentiating aspect of Competitive Dominance leadership. It is no longer sufficient to act with public responsibility; it is now necessary also to act as an advocate to raise the standards in health, safety, environmental protection, and ethics. Leaders have a responsibility to address emerging important public issues and to teach and increase awareness. In Competitive Dominance, leadership and statesmanship must be synonymous.

1.1 Senior Executive Leadership *(45 points)*

Describe the senior executives' leadership and personal involvement in setting directions and in developing and maintaining a leadership system for performance excellence.

Areas to Address

a. How senior executives' provide effective leadership and direction in building and improving company competitiveness, performance, and capabilities. Describe executives' roles in: (1) creating and reinforcing values and expectations throughout the company's leadership system; (2) setting expectations and performance excellence goals **aligned to** strategic and business planning **for future opportunity;** and (3) reviewing overall company performance, including customer-related and operational performance, **and future opportunity.**

b.   How senior executives evaluate and improve **their leadership skills** and the effectiveness of the company's leadership system and organization to pursue performance excellence goals.

Notes
1.   "Senior executives" means the applicant's highest-ranking official and those reporting directly to that official.

2.   Values and expectations [1.1a(1)] should take into account all stakeholders—customers, employees, stockholders, suppliers and partners, the community, and the public.

3.   Activities of senior executives appropriate for inclusion in 1.1.a might also include customer, employee, supplier, **and other stakeholder** *interactions, mentoring other executives, benchmarking, and employee recognition.*

4.   Review of company performance is addressed in 1.2c. Responses to 1.1a(3) should reflect senior executives' personal leadership of and involvement in such reviews, and their use of the reviews to focus on key business objectives.

5.   Evaluation of the company's leadership system might include assessment of executives by peers, direct reports, or a board of directors. It might also include results of surveys of company employees.

*6.   **Future opportunity means that senior executives develop vision, goals, and a management system to assess*** *and understand the marketplace and environment in which the company will be competing in the future. It should have a direct link to Category 3.*

7.   Alignment implies that required initiatives are prioritized to achieve future goals based on strengths and weaknesses of current capabilities and resources.

8.   Leadership skills should describe the key personal characteristics important to the success of the business. For example:

- *the ability to synthesize information to identify differentiated value;*
- *the ability to deploy priority initiatives; and*
- *the ability to energize the organization to achieve breakthrough.*

There are three key senior executive characteristics that represent the highly integrated strategy and quality approach characterized by Competitive Dominance.

1.   Senior executive leadership and involvement in organizational transformation.

2.   The senior executive leadership and involvement in developing long term goals and supporting values based on understanding of the future marketplace, industry structure, and emerging environment.

3.   The senior executive leadership and involvement in the successful deployment of priority initiatives that support moving company capabilities, skills, and resources from the current position to the future preferred position.

The leadership imperative is to ensure that the company creates and sustains long term advantage by positioning its quality values and customer orientation in a future context. It means that executives must balance their management time and attention between reviewing current operational progress and historical performance and a focus on the future position of the organization. Figure 6-1 illustrates this concept. Too often, quality initiatives are only implemented to address cost or expense deployment in an effort to improve efficiency and effectiveness. While these initiatives can be used effectively to solve current company problems, they are most effective when directed at the opportunity. The future opportunity and policy may dictate a different set of initiatives for efficient and effective deployment than the current problems of the day.

This requires senior executives to transform intuition and "gut" about the future into processes that continuously scan the environment and adapt to changes in support of the vision they see for their business. Examples of actions that meet Competitive Dominance practice are

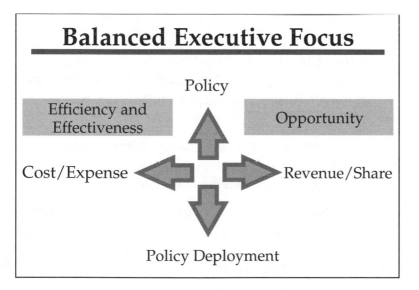

Figure 6-1 Ensuring a Balanced Leadership System.

- An executive level continuous environmental scanning process.
- A change road map that identifies the journey from current to future preferred position—competitive, leadership, or dominance.
- A matrix that identifies current strengths and weaknesses of the company and aligns prioritized initiatives to support the future quality values and goals.
- Executive skill development. Training in **both** the ability to understand the future environment and marketplace (visionary skills), and ability to implement the strategy most effectively and efficiently (operational skills).

1.2 Leadership System and Organization (*25 points*)

Describe how the company's **long term focus**, customer **orientation**, and performance expectations are integrated into the company's leadership system and organization.

Areas to Address

a. How the company's leadership system, **long term** management **focus**, and organization focus on customers and high performance objectives.

b. How the company effectively communicates and reinforces its values, expectations, and directions throughout the entire **extended enterprise** workforce.

c. How overall company **progress in its journey toward the future**, and work unit performance are reviewed. Describe the types, frequency, and content of reviews and who conducts them.

Notes

1. Reviews described in 1.2c should use information from business and customer-related results Items—6.1, 6.2, 6.3, 7.4, and 7.5—and also may draw upon evaluations described in other Items and upon analysis (Item 2.3). The descriptions should address key measures and/or indicators used to track performance, including performance related to the company's public responsibilities. Reviews could also incorporate results of process assessments and address regulatory, contractual, or other requirements, including review of required documentation.

*2. **Reinforcing with the extended enterprise workforce means engaging all stakeholders critical to success to specifically articulate their role in success, what is the benefit for them, and how progress and milestones are communicated.***

3. Progress in its journey toward the future implies that the company not only reviews work unit performance but also reviews key indicators that determine progress and success of management actions to change to a future preferred state.

The Competitive Dominance action in Item 1.2 is to deploy the future based strategy throughout all company units. The company communicates and reinforces initiatives, responsibilities, and timeline to transform the organization from its current state to the future preferred position. This definition of the transformational road map developed by the senior executive team is addressed in Item 1.1. It identifies the work unit's role in success, and the value to them. These *work units must include all stakeholders* in the extended enterprise that are critical to overall company success (see Item 5.1).

Item 1.2b emphasizes the importance of leadership skills in all managers, supervisors, and **team leaders**.

They are the key agents in the *implementation of change and continuous improvement*. A company must assess the acceptance of change and the implementation success of these group of transformational agents. Employee attitude surveys and management and team leader meetings are two ways to evaluate effectiveness. Enhanced communication and leadership training are improvement methods for managers and supervisors. The company should pattern leadership training along the same lines as those used for executives, with emphasis *beyond operational excellence which includes future strategy considerations.* To improve organizational effectiveness of team leaders, the company must continue to reinforce the importance of their role, and to develop team leader interpersonal relationship skill.

Some actions to meet better meet the intent of Competitive Dominance theory might be

- More supporting detail from the change road map such as key checkpoints and milestones, key roles and responsibilities of participants, and a timeline of events.
- A defined set of communication actions and reviews that enable the company to assess progress on its change journey and on its improvement journey.
- A process to assess the acceptance by the entire work forces of change by critical skill categories (see Item 4.1).
- A process to develop leadership skills in managers, supervisors, and team leaders.

In Item 1.2c, Competitive Dominance theory requires that the company not only demonstrate its review system for quality and operational performance, it must also demonstrate a management system to review and communicate progress on its journey to the future.

1.3 Public Responsibility and Corporate Citizenship *(20 points)*

Describe how the company includes its responsibilities to the public in its performance improvement practices. Describe also how the company leads and contributes as a corporate citizen in its key communities.

Areas to Address

a. How the company integrates its public responsibilities into its performance improvement efforts. Describe: (1) the risks and regulatory and other legal requirements addressed in planning and in setting operational requirements and targets; (2) how the company looks ahead to anticipate public concerns and to assess possible impacts on society of its products, services, and operations; and (3) how the company promotes legal and ethical conduct in all that it does.

b. How the company leads as a corporate citizen **and proactively shapes policy** in its key communities. Include a brief summary of the types of leadership and involvement the company emphasizes.

Notes

1. The public responsibility issues addressed in 1.3 relate to the company's impacts and possible impacts on society associated with its products, services, and company operations. They include environment, health, safety, and emergency preparedness as they relate to any aspect of risk or adverse effect, whether or not these are covered under law or regulation. Health and safety of employees are not included in Item 1.3. Employee health and safety are covered in Item 4.4.

2. Major public responsibility or impact areas should be addressed in planning (Item 3.1) and in the appropriate process management Items of Category 5.0. Key results, such as environmental improvements, should be reported in Item 6.2.

3. *If the company has received sanctions under law, regulation, or contract during the past three years, briefly describe the incidents(s) and their current status. If settlements have been negotiated in lieu of potential sanctions, give explanation. If no sanctions have been received, so indicate.*

4. *The corporate citizenship issues appropriate for inclusion in 1.3b relate to efforts by the company to strengthen community services, education, health care, environment, and practices of trade or business associations. Such leadership and involvement depend upon the company's size and resources. However, smaller companies might take part in cooperative activities with other organizations.*

The company should describe social, environmental, and political forces affecting it. These forces are fundamental to the future of most companies and must be part of any effective environmental scanning process (refer to Category 3 and Item 1.1). These forces are generally outside the company's ability to control, yet may have significant impact on its success. The criteria in Item 1.3a(2) is an example of the essence of Competitive Dominance theory.

The criteria requires the company to describe how it *"looks ahead to anticipate"* and *"assess possible impacts on society."* More importantly, Competitive Dominance requires that the company proactively establish initiatives to *shape* new, innovative *policies* that *lead* industry, and government, and to improve the well-being of society in general. For instance, Thomas Watson, Jr. recognized the need for security in computer systems and drove actions to make computers secure long before public attention and concern required governmental regulation.

In describing *"how this assessment is used in planning,"* the company should also identify the possible impact on its organization and business. Any significant actions should be part of the alignment initiatives. Key indicator trends should align to the important social, environmental, and political factors for future success. For example, a company that develops or uses chemical products is under increasing governmental regulation, liability, and societal pressure. An indicator of past excellence may be the reduced number of sanctions or incidences of problems. The fact that it uses or produces chemicals at all may become a societal problem in the future. So future initiatives might include indicators and goals such as: reduction in use to zero chemicals over time, improvements in control and reporting, and/or development of environmentally acceptable alternatives.

2.0 INFORMATION AND ANALYSIS
(75 points)

The *Information and Analysis* Category examines the management and effectiveness of the use of data and information to support customer-driven performance excellence and marketplace success.

Competitive Dominance theory departs sharply from traditional thinking in the way the company develops and uses information. Traditional factual and quantitative analysis is most frequently based on trends of historical information. Competitive Dominance not only requires this kind of analysis, but it also demands that decision making be based on opportunity analysis and predictive analytic models. For example, in a highly integrated and aligned approach to quality and strategy, sophisticated managers develop analytic models of the market, its constituent segments, and their dynamic behavior. They select, very intelligently, the target markets based on models that can forecast market growth, new opportunities, profitability, and future customer requirements. IBM Rochester developed sophisticated models that identified market segments that best matched our business goals. Then it extended the model to select and prioritize product and service features that best met the needs of those segments. It also used advanced multivariate statistical tools to identify the most useful product features and functions, which would not only satisfy customers' expectations, but which would also exceed them, delight them and chagrin the competition.

The IBM Rochester engineers and programmers invented a mechanism that would cause a computer in use anywhere in the world to send early warning symptoms of potential failure to a centralized service center. A technician could be dispatched before an actual failure occurred (Bauer, Collar, Tang 1992). IBM Santa Teresa developed sophisticated statistical reliability models to predict potential software failure rates, by type of error and by stage of life cycle, to assure they could meet customers' quality expectations (Kaplan, Clark, Tang 1995). In still another high-tech "Fortune 25" company, management decision models were used to determine systematically the best portfolio alternatives based on the company future goals and vision. Analytic models used for decision making enable organizational learning and record the cumulative judgments of the organization. As such, models also serve as the repository for institutional memory. In this way, management has made the progression from data, to information, to the development of organizational knowledge.

The use of analytical tools and models requires timely and accurate information sources. A Competitive Dominance extension to Information and Analysis is the addition of market and industry information sources and the principal role(s) of this information. Also included is how market and industry data are analyzed and used to identify risks, opportunities, and market shifts. Similar models using these data can be used to set company priorities.

Benchmarking continues to be a practice among leadership organizations and enterprises. Competitive Dominance and sharing of best practices are not orthogonal or inconsistent. Leaders recognize that "the rising tide raises all boats." Namely, that if all the participants in the industry improve, customer satisfaction improves for all, and industry innovation accelerates, resulting in increased demand. This increased demand creates market growth that benefits all. Competitive Dominance requires that the criteria to select benchmarking candidates be aligned with the future competitive position.

2.1 Management of Information and Data (*20 points*)

Describe the company's selection and management of information and data used for planning, management, and evaluation of overall performance.

Areas to Address

a. How information and data needed to drive improvement of overall company performance are selected and managed. Describe: (1) the main types of data and information and how each type is related to the key business drivers, **current and future**; and (2) how key requirements such as reliability, rapid access, and rapid update are derived from user needs.

b. How the company evaluates and improves the selection, analysis, and integration of information and data, aligning them with the company's business priorities. Describe how the evaluation considers: (1) scope of information and data; (2) use and analysis of information and data to support process management and performance improvement; and (3) feedback from users of information and data.

Notes

1.   Reliability (2.1a(2)) includes software used in the information systems.

2.   User needs (2.1a(2)) should consider knowledge accumulation, such as knowledge about specific customers or customer segments. User needs should also take into account changing patterns of communications associated with changes in process management and/or in job design.

*3.   Scope of information and data (2.1b(1)) should focus primarily on key business drivers **and include requirements for all Stakeholders (defined as any work unit within or outside the company that is involved in producing, delivering, or servicing the company's goods and in providing value to its customers (See Item 5.1)).***

4.   Feedback from users (2.1b(3)) might entail formal or informal surveys, focus groups, teams, etc. However, evaluations should take into account patterns of communications and information use, as users themselves might not be utilizing the information and data available well. Even though the information and data system should be user friendly, the system should drive better practice. This might require training of users.

*5.   **Scope should also address broadening the scope of historical and forecast data.***

Market and industry data are the basis for Competitive Dominance. The Malcolm Baldrige guidelines do not specify this type of data in either the past or current versions. The 1995 guidelines are less prescriptive than in previous years, requesting information and data related to "key business drivers." In Competitive Dominance, these "key business drivers" must be current *and* future drivers. Market and industry data are the basis for factual understanding of the future. Along with customer data, market and industry data are the only data that drive the company to externalize its goals and actions.

It is also important that the **scope** of the data for Competitive Dominance includes forecast data in addition to historical data to permit future based planning. In our assessment experience with many companies, market and industry data are overlooked as the critical link between quality improvement and business performance improvement. Progressive companies have finally started to see the relationship and importance of having a future view of their business. Unfortunately many discover that their market and industry data are lacking in depth and scope and are disconnected with the operational side of the business. Some examples of market and industry data are

- economic forecasts;
- market growth forecasts;
- market research reports;
- market penetration information;
- industry trends from trade press;
- industry trends from consultant reports;
- competitor analysis of investment and market strategies;
- competitive analysis of competitor products and services; and
- profitability analysis of market segments.

2.2 Competitive Comparisons and Benchmarking (*15 points*)

Describe the company's processes and uses of comparative information and data to support improvement of overall performance.

Areas to Address

a. How competitive comparisons and benchmarking information and data are selected and used to help drive improvement of overall company performance. Describe: (1) how needs and priorities are determined; and (2) criteria for seeking appropriate information and data—from within and outside the company's industry; (3) how the information and data are used within the company to improve understanding of processes and process performance; and (4) how the information and data are used to set stretch targets and/or encourage breakthrough approaches **aligned to the future competitive position.**

b. How the company evaluates and improves its overall processes for selecting and using competitive comparisons and benchmarking information and data to improve planning and company performance.

Notes

1. Benchmarking information and data refer to processes and results that represent best practices and performance.

*2. Needs and priorities (2.2a(1)) should show clear link to the company's key business drivers **of opportunity.***

3. Use of benchmarking information and data within the company (2.2a(3)) might include the expectation that company units maintain awareness of related best-in-class performance to help drive improvement. This could entail education and training efforts to build capabilities.

4. *Sources of competitive comparisons and benchmarking information might include: (a) information obtained from other organizations such as customers or suppliers through sharing; (b) information obtained from open literature; (c) testing and evaluation by the company itself; and (d) testing and evaluation by independent organizations.*

5. *The evaluation (2.2b) may address a variety of factors such as the effectiveness of use of the information, adequacy of information, training in acquisition and use of information, improvement potential in company operations, and estimated rates of improvement by other organizations.*

Benchmarking is a method of market and industry scanning, but market and industry processes themselves are important to successful implementation of Competitive Dominance theory. Few companies have demonstrated the breadth, depth, and scope in this area to maintain leadership and become dominant. Some potential areas to benchmark are

- market research;
- strategic planning;
- competitor analysis;
- portfolio analysis;
- distribution methodologies;
- product development processes; and
- warranty processes.

In Item 2.2a(4), Competitive Dominance theory is more specific about aligning stretch goals or breakthrough approaches to the important priorities of the future. It takes time to make change and when a company achieves a stretch goal, it must ensure that the market or business has not moved beyond them, making the company achievement meaningless.

2.3 Analysis and Use of Company-Level Data (*40 points*)

Describe how data related to quality, **market**, customers and operational performance, together with relevant financial data, are analyzed to support company-level review, action and planning.

Areas to Address
a.   How information and data from all parts of the company are integrated and analyzed to support reviews, business decisions, and planning. Describe how analysis is used to gain **actionable** understanding of: (1) customers and markets; (2) operational performance and company capabilities; and (3) competitive performance.

b.   How the company relates customer and market data, improvements in product/service quality, and improvements in operational performance to changes in financial and/or market indicators of performance. Describe how this information is used to set priorities for improvement actions.

Notes
1. Item 2.3 focuses primarily on analysis for company-level purposes such as reviews (1.2c) and strategic planning (Item 3.1). Data for such analysis come from all parts of the company and include results reported in Items 6.1, 6.2, 6.3, 7.4, and 7.5. Other Items call for analyses of specific sets of data for special purposes. For example, the Items of Category 4.0 require analyses to determine effectiveness of training and other human re-

source actions. Such special-purpose analyses should be part of the overall information base available for use in Item 2.3.

2. *Analysis includes trends, projections, cause-effect correlations, and the search for deeper understanding needed to set priorities to use resources more effectively to serve overall business objectives.*

3. *Examples for analysis appropriate for inclusion in 2.3a(1) are **for customer information and data:***

- *how the company's product and service quality improvement correlates with key customer indicators such as customer satisfaction, customer retention, and market share; and*
- *cost/revenue implications of customer-related problems and problem resolution effectiveness;*

For Market information and data:

- *identification of key forces that will affect the company's future and the development of alternative initiatives to address potential changes;*
- *demand and supply analysis;*
- *rates of market growth and future opportunity by segments and targeting the opportunity segments;*
- *establishing investment priorities based on segment attractiveness and product or service fit;*
- *use of forecasting data in the development of predictive analytic models which consider many variables systematically.*

4. *"Actionable" means that the analysis provides information that can be used for priorities and decisions leading to allocation of resources.*

5. *Examples of analysis appropriate for inclusion in 2.3a(2) are*

- *trends in improvement in key operational indicators such as productivity, cycle time, waste reduction, new product introduction, and defect levels;*
- *financial benefits from improved employee safety, absentee-ism, and turnover;*
- *How the company's ability to identify and meet employee requirements correlates with employee retention, motiva-tion, and productivity; and*
- *cost/revenue implications of employee-related problems and problem resolution effectiveness.*

6. *Examples of analysis appropriate for inclusion in 2.3a(3) are*

- *performance trends relative to competitors on key quality attributes; and*
- *productivity and cost trends relative to competitors.*

7. *Examples of analysis appropriate for inclusion in 2.3b are*

- *relationships between product/service quality and opera-tional performance indicators and overall company finan-cial performance trends as reflected in indicators such as operating costs, revenues, asset utilization, and value add-ed per employee;*
- *allocation of resources among alternative improvement projects based on cost/revenue implications and improve-ment potential;*
- *net earnings derived from quality/operational/human re-source performance improvements;*
- *comparisons among business units showing how quality and operational performance improvement affect financial performance;*
- *Contributions of improvement activities to cash flow and/ or shareholder value;*
- *trends in quality versus market indicators;*
- *profit impacts of customer retention; and*
- *market share versus profits.*

Competitive Dominance theory places additional emphasis on the analysis and uses of market and industry data. Markets are a company's potential future customers. To ensure long term growth and success, the company must understand the difference between markets and customers. A company's current customer base is in its current market. Its future market may include its current customers and a set of new customers, as shown in Figure 6-2. Then again, the company's future market might contain an entirely different set of customers, depending upon the market forces affecting the business. This is specially true in declining businesses. An example is the tobacco companies. With tobacco-based product demand decreasing, the only way for these companies to grow is to diversify into different market opportunities. This has a profound effect on their current products and services, and may lead to a future customer base that is entirely different than the current install base.

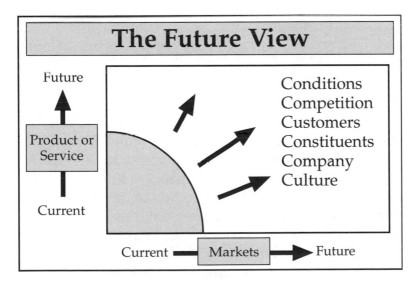

Figure 6-2 Factors Affecting the Future View.

Similarly, a company with very impressive trends in customer satisfaction and operational indicators for current products and services may have financial problems from poor sales because it does not recognize changes in market structure, consumer buying habits, or customer expectations. *"Defect free" products and services in a mis-targeted marketplace will fail.* By the same token, "defect free" products in a diminishing market is not an effective management practice.

The Competitive Dominance extension to Item 2.3a is to determine the degree to which the analysis of company information is limited to historical trends which may have reached an inflection point where a large scale shift is now taking place. The objective of this analysis is to determine whether the company is *alert to shifts.* An example of an effective Competitive Dominance approach examines how the company uses predictive analytic models which consider many variables systematically, not just one at a time in stand alone manner. How market and industry related data are aggregated with other key data and analyzed to

1. identify potential risks and opportunities;

2. predict potential market shifts; and

3. set priorities.

The relationship between the market and industry-related data is the key Competitive Dominance focus of Item 2.3. For example, in the telecommunications industry, one must consider the regulatory environment, customer demographics, the economics of new technology, distribution costs, etc. It departs from conventional practice of "rear view" or straight-line planning which omits the analysis of the impacts of forces or shifts.

Item 2.3a(1) criteria require the same level of fact based analysis of future market dynamics and industry structure as is required for customer (Item 2.3a(1)) and operational (Item 2.3a(2)) quality. Anecdotal evidence for customer and operational quality results is unacceptable as a measure of current progress, therefore, anecdotal evidence and "gut" is unacceptable as a measure of future potential business opportunities. Market and industry analysis enables the company to anticipate the future based on facts and supporting evidence and is the most effective way to prevent future business problems. The market analysis in Item 2.3a(1) is fundamental to Item 7.1 and Category 3.

3.0 STRATEGIC PLANNING *(55 points)*

The *Strategic Planning* Category examines the company sets strategic directions, and how it determines key plan requirements. Also examined is how the plan requirements are translated into an effective performance management system.

Quality planning takes on a long range and strategic perspective in Competitive Dominance. Quality management merges seamlessly with the other planning disciplines within the organization. The planning disciplines of strategic planning, business planning, product/service planning, and financial planning fully integrate and embrace quality as part of their discipline. For example, product planning now includes customer satisfaction as an integral element of its processes. In addition to concentrating on the satisfaction of existing customers, it begins to place an equal emphasis on future requirements. These are the requirements of potential customers, and potential new markets that the business must capture for future growth.

Planning is no longer based on historical trends, but rather on predictive analytic models. The management style is not merely one of analysis and reporting, but also of creating the instruments for organizational learning and institutional memory to continuously improve strategically. The organization develops the capability to anticipate market and industry dynamics and respond fluidly to the changes. An **external future view** drives company goals and initiatives for market leadership and dominance. The company deploys strategy and plans throughout the organization to synchronize and align resources to achieve these goals. Organizational transformation initiatives have a direct link to market leadership objectives. Time to market goals replace cycle time reduction goals. Industry and value chain analyses expand traditional competitive analyses.

Strategy initiatives now deploy quality initiatives to gain competitive advantages. Strategic planning includes quality as a key business initiative. The company deploys quality as a market differentiator and demand generator, as well as a means to improve operational effectiveness, raise employee morale, and increase productivity.

The planning process expands to include all important stakeholder in success—inside and outside the company. For example, IBM Rochester used the stakeholder integration process (See Item 5.1) to assure that the product would meet its customers' expectations. It also used this process to train business partners, and to prepare its channels to distribute and service the product.

3.1 Strategy Development *(35 points)*

Describe the company's strategic planning process for overall performance and competitive leadership for the short term and the longer term Describe also how this process leads to the development of key business drivers to serve as the basis for deploying plan requirements throughout the company **and with all stakeholders.**

Areas to Address

a. How the company develops strategies and business plans to strengthen its **market position**, customer-related, operational, and financial performance and its competitive position. Describe how strategy development considers: **(1) Market opportunity segmentation;** (2) customer requirements and expectations, and their expected changes; (3) the competitive environment **both current and future**; (4) risks: financial, market, technological, and societal; (5) company capabilities - human resource, technology, research and development and business processes—to seek new market leadership opportunities and/or to prepare for key new requirements; and (6) supplier and/or partner **(stakeholder)** capabilities.

b. How strategies and plans are translated into actionable key business drivers which serve as the basis for **aligning the extended enterprise resources and** deploying plan requirements, addressed in Item 3.2.

c. How the company evaluates and improves its strategic planning and plan deployment processes.

Notes

1. Item 3.1 addresses overall company strategies and business plans, not specific product and service designs.

2. The sub-parts of 3.1a are intended to serve as an outline of key factors involved in developing a view of the future as a context for strategic planning. Strategy and planning refer to a future-oriented basis for major business decisions, resource allocations, and company-wide management. "Strategy and planning" addresses both revenue growth thrusts as well as thrusts related to improving operational performance.

3.   Strategies for future market position may require significant change to current processes and management systems, requiring major reengineering.

4. *Customer requirements and their expected changes (3.1a(1)) might include pricing factors. That is, market success may depend upon achieving cost levels dictated by anticipated price levels rather than setting prices to cover costs.*

5. *The purposes of projecting the competitive environment (3.1a(2)) are to detect and reduce competitive threats, to improve reaction time, and to identify opportunities. If the company uses modeling, scenario, or other techniques to project the competitive environment, such techniques should be briefly outlined in 3.1a(2)* **and addressed in Item 2.3.**

6. *Key business drivers are the areas of performance most critical to the company's success. They include customer-driven quality requirements and operational requirements such as productivity, cycle time* **(or time to market),** *deployment of new technology, strategic alliances, supplier development, employee productivity and development, and research and development. Deployment of plans should include how progress will be tracked such as through the use of key measures.*

7.   Time to market is cycle time defined by customer need or to meet a "window of opportunity" in the market.

8. *Examples of strategy and business plans that might be the starting points for the development of key business drivers are*

- *new product/service lines;*
- *entry into new markets or segments;*
- *new manufacturing and/or service delivery approaches such as customization;*

- *new or modified competitive thrusts;*
- *launch of joint ventures and/or partnerships;*
- *new R&D thrusts;*
- *new product and/or process technologies; and*
- **new alliances or partnerships that expand market opportunity.**

9. Stakeholders are defined as any work unit within or outside the company that is involved in producing, delivering, or servicing the company's goods and in providing value to its customers (see Item 5.1). For success, key business drivers must be deployed to all stakeholders.

The important Competitive Dominance themes in Item 3.1 are

1. market leadership as well as customer leadership based on market opportunity analysis in Item 2.3 and 7.1;

2. considering supply side economics related to competition, both current and future;

3. use of predictive analytic models for quality and future planning

4. time to market as a key indicator of competitiveness;

5. integration of all constituencies (stakeholders) important to success in the process;

6. deployment of strategy as well as plans.

Customer satisfaction leadership and customer loyalty are strong factors to ensure continued growth. Studies done at IBM Rochester indicate that for every one point (on a scale of 1-5) of customer satisfaction improvement, the business could gain an additional two hundred fifty million dollars in revenue. Also, the longer a company retained customers, the more revenue per customer it generated from additional sales.

But the customer satisfaction bar raises each year because customer expectations change. Customers become more demanding with the passage of time. *Companies that lead in customer satisfaction but do not continue to offer progressive new products and services will find that they become a lost leader.* Another study at IBM Rochester determined that each year customer expectation rises by one point of satisfaction. In other words, satisfaction will go down year to year if a company does nothing to improve.

While customer requirements and the expected evolution of these requirements are important to customer satisfaction leadership, it is not sufficient to ensure market leadership. Changing environmental conditions, customer buying habits, competition, innovative new products and services and technology are just some of the dynamics that affect business growth. Let's just explore two areas using real life case studies:

Assume a company's products and services result in industry leading customer satisfaction for the last three to five years. Then a competitor, or an entirely new company introduces technology that provides significant price and performance improvement over the product. Many customers flock to the new product and those that remain loyal demand the same level of capability. The first company's sales drop off, and customer satisfaction drops off rapidly until the company reacts to the change. The company quickly drops from leader to survivor because it did not anticipate market and industry dynamics.

Let us consider another example. This company continues to show leadership customer satisfaction, revenue, and profit growth over a five to ten year period. Its customer base is also growing each year. The strategic planning focus of this company is on customer requirements.

Historical trends determine the company's growth pro-jections. This company's situation looks strong, on the surface. Then the company decides to analyze future market opportunities and to identify growth segments. When it maps its current customer base into the segment-ed opportunity, it finds its customer base well positioned in non-growth market segments. As the company analyz-es its market share, it finds that it is loosing one to two points of share each year because the growth rate of its segments are slower than the growth rates of the market as a whole. This company was heading for disaster.

When assessing competition, or those suppliers of competi-tive products and services, a company must consider that cur-rent competition may change in future markets. In fact, competition is becoming less institutional and more situ-ational. To respond swiftly to the market, strategies may dictate that it becomes a partner with a current major competitor on a technology investment or product devel-opment. Future market opportunity may dictate that the company should expand into new products and services where it will compete with nontraditional competitors.

Cycle time reduction is a key element of business re-sponsiveness and competitiveness. Most companies es-tablish cycle time objectives with an internal bias. Short cycle manufacturing or reduced development cycle times are internal company capabilities and objectives. Time to market is cycle time based on external criteria—when the customer needs it, when the timing is best for optimum market acceptance, or to preempt competitors. A compa-ny may achieve internal cycle times that enable them to introduce products faster than the customer or market can absorb them. Negative backlash can occur when a company introduces a new and improved product at the same time that a customer is just getting the current one installed and operational. The personal computer marketplace is a good example of this. Knowing the right time to market enables the company to prioritize and optimize internal cycle time.

Item 3.1a addresses two Competitive Dominance considerations. The first is stakeholders. Stakeholders are those work units within and outside a company that are fundamental to the company's success. Stakeholders are fundamental because they participate at specific stages of the value chain by adding value to the product or service offering. They implement part of the process of producing, delivering, or servicing your customers. Stakeholders can be suppliers, distributors, value added remarketers, alliances, or customer partnerships. The simplest way to identify these stakeholders is to consider the process in the broadest scope—from source to customer and back. Then identify everyone involved in that process. Any process improvement or reengineering must consider this process scope and the stakeholders. The term "work units" in Competitive Dominance terminology means teams of stakeholders (See Item 5.1).

Stakeholders are important to strategy and plan alignment and deployment—this is the second consideration. It is not sufficient for business success to deploy operating plans. Companies must deploy strategy which provide context to the operating plans, otherwise there is disconnect between the plans and strategy. Figure 6-3 illustrates this with the example of a company that identified six key strategic initiatives important to its future. This company has a well-defined and deployed operational plan yielding excellent results, but when the company mapped the amount of resources it applied to each of the six strategic initiatives, it found that only four of the six initiatives had any resources aligned to achieve the opportunity. The operational management systems also had no structure in place to guide the implementation of strategic initiatives. The company was not deploying the

Strategic Initiatives (Key Business Drivers)	Current Resources	Redeployed Resources
Meet the new product introduction objectives	80%	50%
Implement advanced application solutions	10%	20%
Focus on high growth industries	0%	10%
Alliances and partnerships	5%	5%
Address world wide business opportunity	0%	5%
Improve alternate channel effectiveness	5%	10%

Figure 6-3 Deploying Strategic Initiatives.

strategy with operational plans that were consistent with its intent.

The "Current Resources" column shows the deployment of resources as they are applied in actuality. The "Redeployed Resources" column shows how the resources were redistributed to align the operational plans with the strategic direction. Note that the two initiatives in Current Resources, which were uncovered with resources, are now deployed with resource commitments

3.2 Strategy Deployment *(20 points)*

Summarize the company's key business drivers and how they are deployed. Show how the company's performance projects into the future relative to competitors and key benchmarks.

Areas to Address

a. Summary of the specific key business drivers derived from the company's strategic directions and how these drivers are translated into an action plan. Describe: (1) key performance requirements and associated operational performance measures and/or indicators and how they are deployed; (2) how the company aligns work unit and supplier and/or partner **(stakeholders)** plans and targets; (3) how productivity and cycle time improvement and reduction in waste are included in plans and targets; and (4) the principal resources committed to the accomplishment of plans. Note any important distinctions between short-term plans and longer-term plans.

b. Two-to-five-year projection of key measures and/or indicators of the company's **market,** customer-related, and operational performance. Describe how product and/or service quality and operational performance might be expected to compare with key competitors and key benchmarks over this time period. Briefly explain the comparisons, **and how the drivers and projections will sustain long term leadership** including any estimates or assumptions made regarding **market shifts** and the projected quality, operational, **and market** performance of competitors or changes in benchmarks.

Notes

*1. The focus in Item 3.2 is on the translation of the company's strategic plans, resulting from the planning process described in Item 3.1, to requirements for work units and **stakeholders**. The main intent of Item 3.2 is alignment of short- and long-term operations with strategic directions. Although the deployment of these plans will affect products and services, design of products and services is not the focus of Item 3.2. Such design is addressed in Item 5.1*

2. *Productivity and cycle time improvement and waste reduction (3.2a(3)) might address factors such as inventories, work-in-process, inspection, downtime, change over time, set-up time, and other examples of utilization of resources—materials, equipment, energy, capital, and labor.*

3. *Area 3.2d addresses projected progress in improving performance and in gaining advantage relative to **current or future** competitors. **Explain how market share is going to be improved and the basis for the forecast. (See Item 7.5).** This projection may draw upon analysis (Item 2.3) and data reported in results Items (Category 6.0 and Items 7.4 and 7.5). Such projections are intended to support reviews (1.2c), evaluation of plans (3.1c), and other Items. Another purpose is to take account of the fact that competitors and benchmarks may also be improving over the time period of the projection.*

Item 3.2a adds the perspective of "planned markets" to cover the requirements of Competitive Dominance. It differentiates the criteria for customers and markets, as they may require different approaches. Quality requirements may differ based on distinct market segments. For example, a key quality requirement for large customers might be to operate twenty-four hours a day seven days a week; for small customers, cost may be the key requirement. These two requirements might be conflicting, so the company must balance and prioritize its operational plan based on revenue, profit, or market share objectives of the market segments it intends to target. In Competitive Dominance, leadership companies determine the requirements to achieve the next strategic plateau. They are not merely satisfied with maintaining the status quo. Our experience has demonstrated that maintaining the status quo leads to long term erosion of industry and market position. This is natural because nimble, creative, and aggressive competitors are always seeking to dislodge the incumbent leader.

In item 3.2b, two-to-five-year projections must consider market shifts and market share growth. This is necessary because the market, the industry, the competition, and the environment are in continual change. The company must anticipate these dynamics and consider alternative actions in advance of change in order to keep out of reaction mode.

The criterion in note (1) reinforces the notion of "stakeholder." The criteria in note (2) change to focus on current and future competition. Both of these items were discussed in Item 3.1

Category 3 is pivotal to successful Competitive Dominance implementation. In the current Baldrige scale, this category is the least significant in terms of point weighting, and it was reduced from 1994 to 1995. Yet weakness in this area spells long term problems. To achieve the integration of strategy and quality that determines Competitive Dominance, the attention on Category 3 should be inversely proportional to the weight of the Baldrige points.

4.0 HUMAN RESOURCE DEVELOPMENT AND MANAGEMENT *(140 points)*

The *Human Resource Development and Management* Category examines how the work force is enabled to develop and utilize its full potential, aligned with the company's performance objectives. Also examined are the company's efforts to build and maintain an environment conducive to performance excellence, full participation, and personal and organizational growth.

At the Competitive Dominance stage of the strategy/ quality maturity grid, employee morale and well-being are a given. They are prerequisites in Competitive Dominance because organizational transformation and cultural change are the prime drivers of Human Resource Development and Management. Fundamental to transforming an organization is understanding the skill requirements that employees and managers will need for future success. Competitive Dominance emphasizes the importance of identifying these skill needs and the requirements to develop human resource plans to acquire the new skills to compete in the future. Fundamental to changing culture is the awareness of the strengths and weaknesses of the organization and human resources of the company. In order to change culture, a company must capitalize on its human resource strengths and implement initiatives to attack its weaknesses. Critical to this change are education, tools, and an empowered environment that is consistent with the strategic direction of the company.

Every employee must become an agent of change to achieve Competitive Dominance. They participate not only in actions to improve product and service quality; they are actively engaged in the company and organizational initiatives that create change. A key element of a highly refined strategy/quality approach is a customer-centric culture. Systematic processes that involve employees with customers and stakeholders on a regular basis develop an external customer bias to employee actions. Traditional bias and methods of operation fall by the wayside as employees move away from their internal view of the world.

The education and training plans expand from a short term perspective that address current problems and needs to a longer term perspective that focus on developmental actions in support of future skill categories. Education and training plans will have a direct tie back to the company revenue growth and market growth objectives. Competitive Dominance has a focus on the development of selected leaders with skills honed in strategic perspective, operational excellence, and organizational transformation. The selection criteria for future leaders go beyond their ability to manage "the business" (revenue, profit, expense). These new leaders must also have skills in internal and external environmental scanning, organizational transformation, and market growth strategies, in addition to operational management.

The high performance work system, recognition and reward systems are based on achieving progress and milestones in the journey toward a future vision. The company uses these systems to establish the benchmark of expected excellence and to create organizational energy and enthusiasm for company progress toward its future goals. A natural outgrowth of this "organizational energetics" is higher morale. "Listening posts" that keep a constant pulse on employee attitudes reinforce traditional annual employee satisfaction surveys. These listening post processes rapidly consolidate employee attitudinal information throughout the organization and initiate closed-loop responses to address issues, improve communications, and keep everyone informed of progress.

4.1 Human Resource Planning and Evaluation *(20 points)*

Describe how the company's human resource planning and evaluation are aligned with its strategic and business plans and address the development and well-being of the entire work force.

Areas to Address
a.   How the company translates overall requirements from strategic and business planning (Category 2.0) to specific human resource plans. Summarize key human resource plans in the following areas: (1) changes in work

design to improve flexibility, innovation, and rapid response; (2) **Key current and future, critical skill categories and their** development, education, and training; (3) changes in **morale**, compensation, recognition, and benefits; (4) recruitment, including expected or planned changes in demographics of the work force; and **(5) cultural strengths and weaknesses**. Distinguish between the short term and the longer term, as appropriate

b. How the company evaluates and improves its human resource planning and practices and the alignment of the plans and practices with the company's strategic and business directions. Include how employee-related data and company performance data are analyzed and used: (1) to assess the development and well-being of all categories and types of employees; (2) to assess the link of the human resource practices to key business results; and (3) to ensure that reliable and complete human resource information is available for company strategic and business planning.

Notes
1. Human resource planning addresses all aspects of designing and managing human systems to meet the needs of both the company and the employees. This Item calls for information on human resource plans. This does not imply that such planning is separate from overall business planning. Examples of human resource plan elements or plan thrusts (4.1.a) that might be part(s) of a comprehensive plan are

- *redesign of work organizations and/or jobs to increase employee responsibility and decision making;*
- *initiatives to promote labor-management cooperation, such as partnerships with unions;*
- *creation or modification of compensation and recognition systems based on building shareholder value, customer satisfaction, **and/or market share;***

- *creation or redesign of employee surveys* **or establishment of listening posts** *to better assess the factors in the work climate that contribute to or inhibit high performance or* **acceptance of change;**
- *Prioritization of employee problems based upon potential impact on productivity;*
- *development of hiring criteria;*
- *creation of opportunities for employees to learn and use skills that go beyond current job assignments through redesign of processes or organizations;*
- *education and training initiatives, including those that involve developmental assignments;*
- *forming partnerships with educational institutions to develop employees or to help ensure the future supply of well-prepared employees*
- *establishment of partnerships with other companies and/or networks to share training and/or spread job opportunities;*
- *introduction of distance learning or other technology-based learning approaches; and*
- *integration of customer and employee surveys* **and/or listening posts.**

2. *"employee-related data" (4.1b) refers to data contained in personnel records as well as data described in Items 4.2, 4.3, and 4.4. This might include employee satisfaction data and data on turnover, absenteeism, safety, grievances, involvement, recognition, training, and information from exit interviews.*

3. *"Categories of employees"* **(4.1a(2))** *and (4.1b(1)) refers to the company's classification system used in its human resource practices and/or work assignments. It also includes factors such as union or bargaining unit membership. "Types of employees" takes into account other factors, such as work force diversity or demographic makeup. This includes gender, age, minorities, and the disabled.*

4. *The evaluation in 4.1b might be supported by employee-related data such as satisfaction factors (Item 4.4), absenteeism,* turnover, and accidents. It might also be supported by employee feedback and information from exit interviews. Evaluations might also be supported by comparative or benchmarking information.

Evaluation should take into account factors such as employee problem resolution effectiveness, and the extent of deployment of education and training throughout the company.

5. *Human resource information for company strategic and business planning might include an overall profile of strengths and weaknesses that could affect the company's abilities to fulfill plan requirements. This could result in the identification of specific needs requiring resources or new approaches.*

Cultural strengths and weaknesses are those organizational elements that have historic benefits or inhibit change. Some strengths may be customer orientation, technical skill base, or work ethic. Some weaknesses may be internal focus, functionalization, or hierarchical structure.

The emphasis on Item 4.1, Human Resource Planning and Management, are in four areas:

1. management of critical skill categories for future company success;

2. understanding cultural and organizational strengths and weaknesses and the initiatives to address them;

3. understanding and improving morale throughout the change; and

4. valuing diversity, not merely tolerating it.

A common weakness in Baldrige applications is the lack of human resource initiatives and indicators specific to skill categories. While this is a basic Stage 3 requirement to ensure a comprehensive TQM approach, Competitive Dominance goes further. It requires that the company understands its current skill categories and defines its future skill requirements in support of strategic alignment. Item 4.1 should clearly define current and future skill categories and reference these categories throughout the remainder of Category 4. A Stage 4 assessment would evaluate company actions to move the current skill categories to meet the needs of the future. Item 3.2 should broadly articulate the human resource strategy and Item 4.1 should identify specific actions. Figure 6-4 illustrates an example of a sales organization that anticipates the need for future skill set within the next three to five years.

The company's historical trends and processes are based on the current skill set. A Competitive Dominance assessment would evaluate the process changes, initiatives, indicators, and goals in place for the transformation journey to the future. As part of this assessment, a company must identify its cultural and organizational strengths

Current skill set	%	Future skill set needed	%
Sales	25	Technical sales support	10
Marketing	10	Marketing	10
Service	25	Service	15
Systems engineers	15	Systems engineers	5
Account		Account representatives	0
Representatives	5	Administration	5
Administration	10	Management	5
Management	10	Information Technology	
		consultant	30
		Account relationship	
		manager	20

Figure 6-4 Current and Future Skill Set Required.

and weaknesses, and the actions it will take to overcome weaknesses and build on strengths. Strengths are organizational characteristics that are an aid to achievement of new initiatives. Weaknesses are inhibitors to progress. Note (5) has been expanded to describe examples of these strengths and weaknesses.

In Item 4.1a(3), morale was added as an important element of human resource plans. Morale management is critical because change has the most impact on human resource systems. Moving on a journey from a current set of skills, organization structure, and management systems to a future set requires processes to continuously monitor attitude. The company must continually assess, by skill category, satisfaction with change, acceptance of change, employee feelings about the company and management, and feelings about the adequacy of skills to accomplish tasks. Listening posts are describe further in Item 4.4.

One other emphasis just added as a note to the 1995 Baldrige criteria, is diversity. A Competitive Dominance assessment would evaluate company actions to pro-actively leverage people of diverse ethnic and cultural backgrounds. For example, tolerance is strictly a Stage 3 strategy/quality concept. On the other hand, valuing diversity is a Stage 4 concept. Minimally, if a company was global, Competitive Dominance theory would expect to see an extremely diverse set of skills in the strategic planning organization and a recruiting process for that organization that identified the need for specific diverse skills. If the company is U.S.-based, but half of its customer presence is in Europe, and more than half the future opportunity is in Europe, wouldn't it expect that key organizational positions would be staffed with Europeans? A good test of diversity is to take the company's organization chart and perform that type of analysis. No cheating or rationalizing is allowed.

4.2 High Performance Work Systems *(45 points)*

Describe how the company's work and job design and compensation and recognition approaches enable and encourage all employees to contribute effectively to achieve high performance objectives.

Areas to Address

a.   How the company's work and job design promote high performance. Describe how work and job design: (1) create opportunities for initiative and self-directed responsibility; (2) foster flexibility and rapid responses to changing requirements; and (3) ensure effective communications across functions or units that need to work together to meet customer and/or operational requirements.

b.   How the company creates a customer centered culture. Include how the company involves all employees and groups with customers and/or stakeholders to improve results.

c.   How the company's compensation and recognition approaches for individuals and groups, including managers, reinforce the effectiveness of the work and job design.

Notes

*1.   Work and job design refers to how employees are organized and/or organize themselves in formal and informal, temporary or longer-term units. This may include work teams, problem-solving teams, functional units, departments, self-managed or managed by supervisors, **and including all stakeholders important to accomplishing the initiative**. In some cases, teams might involve individuals in different locations linked via computers or conferencing technology.*

2. *Examples of approaches to create flexibility in work design to enhance performance might include simplification of job classifications, cross training, job rotation, work layout, and work locations. It might also entail use of technology and changed flow of information to support local decision making.*

3. *Item 4.2b assesses the company's approach to develop an external focus in it work and job design.*

4. *Compensation and recognition refer to all aspects of pay and reward, including promotion and bonuses. The company might use a variety of reward and recognition approaches— monetary and non-monetary, formal and informal, and individual and group.*

*Compensation and recognition approaches could include profit sharing and compensation based on skill building, use of new skills, and demonstrations of self learning. The approaches could take into account the link to customer retention or other performance objectives. **Item 4.2c should address the transition to the future skill set (see Item 4.1).***

5. *Employee evaluations and reward and recognition approaches might include peer evaluations, including peers in teams and networks.*

Competitive Dominance extends the customer based concepts of stage 3 to create a customer-centric culture. This means creating a high performance work system where the customer perspective has primacy in the priorities of the organization and where all people can interact regularly with customers and stakeholders to develop this critical external focus. This broad-based involvement of all groups and skill categories helps develop a service attitude in all people and brings into focus how each person's task ultimately affects the customer. Our experience shows that customer involvement also improves morale. Recognition and feedback directly from customers and stakeholders creates an environment of energy and enthusiasm in each individual. It creates a renewed commitment toward excellence in their tasks because of the personal relationship that develops. Some methods to gain broad based customer and stakeholder involvement are

- involving customers and stakeholders as partners in the product development process;
- involving manufacturing employees on customer calls or installations;
- bringing customers into the location for small group meetings;
- working on process improvement teams that include other non-company stakeholders; and
- involving employees in telemarketing activity.

A Competitive Dominance high performance work system includes all stakeholders important to accomplishing the initiative at hand. For instance, to improve delivery time, work units or individuals from distributors would be involved in the process improvement team, and information flow to and from distributors would be a key element of fact based management and evaluation of the process improvements.

Recognition for progress and success toward a future vision is as important as recognition for operational achievement. In the development of a transformation road map (Category 1), the company identifies checkpoints and milestones that constitute progress along the journey to success (goal(s) achievement). The achievement of these milestones are excellent opportunities to recognize contributions that identify role models for success—the benchmark of expected excellence. This type of recognition is important because it renders explicit the new standards that are valued in the organization. Organization excitement builds as the company progressively achieves these checkpoints and milestones. The pony has left the corral, and everyone will want to ride it. The company can demonstrate factually that it is progressing along a planned journey. Those who have not accepted change will find it increasingly more difficult to pose credible arguments against the change. A Competitive Dominance assessment would evaluate the company for a recognition and communication plan that supports the transformation road map.

Recognition should not be limited to within the company. The company should address industry wide and even global recognition, where appropriate. Examples of this are nominating employees to become IEEE Fellows or on advisory boards in universities, etc. The added element of note (4) is to ensure that the recognition and compensation approaches address future skill groups as part of increasing empowerment, responsibility, and innovation.

4.3 Employee Education, Training, and Development *(50 points)*

Describe how the company's education and training address company **strategies and** plans, including building company capabilities and contributing to employee motivation, progression, and development.

Areas to Address
a.   How the company's education and training serve as a key vehicle in building company and employee capabilities **that support the key business drivers**. Describe how education and training address: (1) key performance objectives, including those related to enhancing high performance work units; and (2) progression and

development of all employees **and managers taking into account critical future skill categories.**

b. How education and training are designed, delivered, reinforced, and evaluated. Include: (1) how employees and line managers contribute to or are involved in determining specific education and training needs and designing education and training; (2) how education and training are delivered; (3) how knowledge and skills are reinforced through on-the-job application; and (4) how education and training are evaluated and improved.

Notes

1. *Education and training address the knowledge and skills employees need to meet their overall work objectives **in support of the key business factors defined in Item 3.2.** Education and training might include leadership skills, communications, teamwork, problem solving, interpreting and using data, **strategy development,** meeting customer requirements, process analysis, process simplification, waste reduction, cycle time reduction, error-proofing, priority setting based upon cost and benefit data, and other training that affects employee effectiveness, efficiency and safety. This might include job enrichment and job rotation to enhance employees' career opportunities and employability. It might also include basic skills such as reading, writing, language, and arithmetic.*

2. *Training for customer-contact (front-line) employees should address: (a) key knowledge and skills, including knowledge of products and services; (b) listening to customers; (c) soliciting comments from customers; (d) how to anticipate and handle problems or failures ("recovery"); (e) skills in customer retention; and (f) how to manage expectations.*

3. *Education and training for managers should address the development of future leadership skills. These may include skills in environmental scanning, visioning, abil-*

ity to understand market and industry forces and how to position the business within context of these forces, organizational transformation, and strategy deployment.

4. *Determining specific education and training needs (4.3b(1)) might include use of company assessment or employee self-assessment to determine and/or compare skill levels for progression within the company or else-where. Needs determination should take into account job analysis—the types and levels of skills required—and the timeliness of training.*

5. *Education and training delivery might occur inside or outside the company and involve on-the-job classroom, or other types of delivery. This includes the use of developmental assignment within or outside the company.*

6. *How education and training are evaluated (4.3b(4)) could address: effectiveness of delivery of education and training; impact on work unit performance; and cost effectiveness of education and training alternatives.*

The Competitive Dominance emphasis in Item 4.3 is in two areas:

1. Identification of education and training of future critical skills to support the key business drivers identified in Item 3.2, and;

2. The development of leadership and transformational skills in managers to support business strategy development and deployment.

A Competitive Dominance assessment would evaluate the development and deployment of education and training in support of skills required to compete in the future. This would be specific to the changes from current to future skill categories (Item 4.1), and it would include employee development, changes in current skills, and the recruitment of new skills. Education and training imperatives should have a direct relationship to the key business drivers as identified in Strategy Deployment (Item 3.2) as a way to determine alignment.

A key element of successful change in a company is the ability to continuously revitalize and refresh its skill base. Another Competitive Dominance consideration would assess the company's pro-active programs to develop and encourage innovation and continuous technical vitality. Sustained leadership is achieved by capitalizing on the skills and experiences of the employee base while continuing to enhance its existing skill base directed at future needs.

Traditional management practices no longer apply. New organization structures are emerging, global market dynamics require companies to respond more rapidly and continuously to change, and computers and communications are changing the nature of how work is done. Management and executive development programs must develop new leadership skills for the twenty-first century. Company executive and management development programs must balance skills in operational excellence with skills in environmental scanning and organizational change. Companies must develop the full potential of the work force. People currently entering the work force have had far more access to information and more awareness of the global environment than those entering the workforce before them. Because of this access and awareness, they have more talent and capability to know where and how to get information to make correct decisions. Yet the management system and methods of operation within companies have not kept up with these new capabilities of people. Therefore, businesses have constrained the inherent capabilities of their most valuable resource. Most executive development programs were designed ten to twenty years ago and are still structured with the same old "in-basket" exercises and management situations that support archaic structures of the past.

4.4 Employee Well-Being and Satisfaction (*25 points*)

Describe how the company maintains a work environment and a work climate conducive to the well-being and development of all employees **as well as to the business.**

Areas to Address

a. How the company maintains a safe and healthful work environment. Include: (1) how employee well-being factors such as health, safety, and ergonomics are included in quality improvement activities; and (2) principal improvement requirements, measures and/or indicators, and targets for each factor relevant and important to the work environment of the company's employees. Note any significant differences based upon differences in work environments among employees or employee groups.

b. What services, facilities, activities, and opportunities the company makes available to employees to support their overall well-being and satisfaction and/or to enhance their work experience and development potential.

c. How the company determines employee satisfaction, well-being, and motivation. Include a brief description of methods, frequency, the specific factors used in this determination, and how the information is used to improve satisfaction, well-being, and motivation. Note any important differences in methods or factors used for different categories or types of employees, as appropriate.

Notes

1.   Examples of services, facilities, activities, and opportunities (4.5b) are: personal and career counseling; career development and employability services; recreational or cultural activities; non-work related education; day care; special leave for family responsibilities and/or for community service; safety off the job; flexible work hours; and out placement. These services also might include career enhancement activities such as skill assessment, helping employees develop learning objectives and plans, and employability assessment.

2.   Examples of specific factors which might affect satisfaction, well-being, and motivation are: effective employee problem or grievance resolution; safety; employee views of leadership and management; employee development and career opportunities; employee preparation for changes in technology or work organization; work environment; workload; cooperation and teamwork; recognition; benefits; communications; job security; compensation; equality of opportunity; and capability to provide required services to customers. An effective determination is one that provides the company with actionable information for use in improvement **initiatives that support key business drivers.**

3.   Measures or indicators of satisfaction, well-being and motivation (4.4c) might include safety, absenteeism, turnover, turnover rate for customer-contact employees, grievances, strikes, worker compensation, as well as results of surveys.

4.   Item 4.4c should address feedback methods the company uses to continually understand employee opinion and attitude (listening posts) and adjust as required to maintain organizational energy.

Competitive Dominance Theory expands practice in Item 4.5c to include processes and methods beyond satisfaction determination. The emphasis is on listening posts to obtain continuous employee feedback. Listening posts are closed-loop processes that continuously collect, aggregate, and analyze employee information to identify problems and opportunities. The process also addresses these problems or opportunities through communications, changes in practices or procedures, or involving employees in the solution. Most companies monitor employee satisfaction quarterly or yearly. Competitive Dominance deployment demands faster cycles of information flow. As companies manage through the change journey, they need to continually keep a pulse on attitudes, activities, ideas, and issues. They need to be able to respond swiftly to seize opportunity or neutralize problems. Examples of listening posts are

- employee round tables;
- employee speak-up programs;
- step-level interviews;
- all employee meetings;
- one-on-ones between manager and employee; and
- management by walking around.

The important aspect of all these listening posts is that the *organization consolidates information quickly to a central point and takes action as a result of analysis.* Just as a company needs to consolidate customer complaints in order to prevent pervasive problems, it needs to consolidate feedback from employee listening posts.

5.0 PROCESS MANAGEMENT *(140 points)*

The *Process Management* Category examines the key aspects of process management, including customer-focused design, product and service delivery processes, support services, and supply management involving all work units *and stakeholders,* including research and development. The Category examines how key processes are designed, effectively managed, and improved to achieve higher performance.

A direct result of business transformation is process reengineering. Competitive Dominance places its closed-loop focus on the scope of the process to encompass the length and breadth of the value chain. A key differentiator of maturity toward a Competitive Dominance position is the use of the term "stakeholder" in place of supplier. Supplier implies another company at the front-end of the process. Stakeholder defines any group, upstream or downstream within or outside the company, that provides value to the market(s) that the company serves. Stakeholders can be companies providing products or services to the company, or providing value-added support to its customers. Some examples of stakeholders are distributors, service providers, and value-added product providers. The key is it that they have the ability to positively or negatively affect customers in the markets you serve.

Failure of one stakeholder in the value chain will likely mean problems for everyone else. So in Competitive Dominance, management now invites all stakeholders, not only to participate in the value-chain activities, but to redesign and optimize the structure or process of the value chain. In this way, Competitive Dominance creates not only a "horizontal organization," which includes external stakeholders, but one where external stakeholders are participants in the reengineering process. Traditional management systems change to integrate stakeholders in business reviews. Systems and procedures to audit, monitor, and control processes take on new forms to support the broader scope.

Distinguishing criteria of Competitive Dominance are the intensity of functional integration and the degree of synchronization of all stakeholders. In traditional TQM, suppliers, product development, and manufacturing teams work as partners to provide high quality products and services to customers. In a Competitive Dominance strategy and quality system, suppliers, product development, manufacturing, support services, sales, service, distributors, and customers all have common goals. Product image, product development and introduction, and follow-on support processes must all be developed concurrently. Yet Competitive Dominance goes beyond "concurrent engineering" and expands to "concurrent product cycle." Product introduction is not an event that happens at the end of a product development cycle. It is a continuous process that begins at the start of product development and continues on after the product launch, and involves all the stakeholders (Tang, Collar 1992). Exploratory development projects with leading edge customers provide the company with more accurate requirements and early market presence, and provide customers with innovative solutions to their problems or opportunities.

Another characteristic of Competitive Dominance is the importance of the flow of information through the total process. The design of information flow and the use of information technology are critical elements to leadership. Information is a competitive advantage. It is a basic requirement for strategy, quality improvement, cycle-time responsiveness, and basic to closed-loop process management. In business, leaders practicing Competitive Dominance theory realize that their processes cannot function with the agility and accuracy that Competitive Dominance requires unless they align computer networks and supporting information systems with these new processes (Henderson, Ventrakaman 1993).

In Competitive Dominance, business and support service processes demand the same rigor as production and service processes. More and more companies are using "vendors" to provide support services, and they must integrate these stakeholders into the improvement process. Business and support service process reengineering must consider how it supports and enhances the organization's transformation to the future.

5.1 Design and Introduction of Products and Services *(40 points)*

Describe how new and/or modified products and services are designed and introduced and how key production/delivery processes are designed to meet **market opportunity** requirements and company operational performance requirements.

Areas to Address
a. How products, services, and production/delivery processes are designed Describe: (1) how **market and** customer requirements are translated into product and service design requirements, **for both short term and long term needs**; (2) how product and service design requirements are translated into efficient and effective production/delivery processes, including an appropriate measurement plan; (3) how all requirements associated with products, services, and production/delivery processes are addressed early in design process by all appropriate company units, suppliers, and partners **(stakeholders)** to ensure integration, coordination, and capability; and **(4) how designs take into account current and projected capabilities of competition.**

b.   How product, services, and production/delivery process designs are reviewed and/or tested in detail to ensure trouble-free launch.

c.   How designs and design processes are evaluated and improved so that introductions of new or modified products and services progressively improve in quality and **time to market**.

Notes

1. Meeting market opportunity requirements implies that key product and service requirements achieve rapid market acceptance. Product and service requirements are an internal translation; market requirements are the external customer needs and wants to be satisfied.

2.   *Design and introduction might address:*

- *modifications and variants of existing products and services;*
- *new products and services emerging from research and development or other product/service concept development*
- *new/modified facilities to meet operational performance and/or product and service requirements; and*
- *significant redesigns of processes to improve customer focus, productivity, or both.*

Design approaches could differ appreciably depending upon the nature of the products/services—entirely new, variants, major or minor process changes, etc. if many design projects are carried out in parallel, responses to Item 5.1 should reflect how coordination of resources among projects is carried out.

3.   *Applicants' responses should reflect the key requirements for their products and services. Factors that might need to be considered in design include: health; safety; long-term performance; environment; measurement capability; process capability; manufacturability; maintainability; supplier capability; and documentation.*

4. *Service and manufacturing businesses should interpret product and service design requirements to include all product- and service-related requirements at all stages of production, delivery, and use.*

5. *A measurement plan (5.1a(2)) should spell out what is to be measured, how and when measurements are to be made, and performance levels or standards to ensure that the results of measurements provide information to guide, monitor, control, or improve the process. This may include service standards used in customer-contact processes. The term "measurement plan," may also include decisions about key information to collect from customers and/or employees from service encounters, transactions, etc. The actual measurement plan should not be described in Item 5.1. Such information is requested in Item 5.2.*

6. *"All appropriate company units" means those units and/or individuals who will take part in production/delivery and whose performance materially affects overall process outcome* **whether they are within the company or in another company providing added value to your customers.**

7. **Integration and coordination in 5.1a(2) includes how critical information flows and is used for rapid communication, competitive advantage, and market share growth.**

8. **Item 5.1a(4) evaluates customer and market requirement compared to current and projected competitor capabilities.**

9. **Time to market is cycle time defined by customer need or to meet a "window of opportunity" in the market.**

The Competitive Dominance criteria enhance the company focus on processes to meet market demand and develop competitive advantage. Note (1) points the company focus to the external need versus the internal interpretation, for product, service, and process. Note (7) includes information flow as a key process management assessment item. Four areas identify the major difference between TQM and Competitive Dominance:

1.   The breadth and scope of the process;

2.   the integration of all stakeholders in the product development and introduction process;

3.   the importance of information flow as a competitive advantage; and

4.   the current and projected competitive capabilities.

When a company begins process management or re-engineering, it typically approaches the activity with an internal perspective that is functional or cross-functional. It identifies internal customer and supplier relationships and identifies areas for improved operational efficiency. While opportunities exist to improve in all functions, most of the real improvement and potential for break-throughs are in cross-functional areas. When companies include other non-company participants in the process (such as suppliers and distributors), the breakthrough opportunities are even more numerous. When companies define the scope of a process from an external customer perspective, the improvement opportunities accelerate even faster. Category 5 Competitive Dominance is all about taking the broadest possible scope of the process—the extended enterprise scope. In the extended enterprise, market requirements are the basis for defining the scope. Within this extended enterprise scope, the company designs the process flow and identifies the value providing stakeholders that meet market requirements (see Item 7.1 and Chapter 8 for definition of natural market and investment market).

The company and its stakeholders provide different value at different segments within the total value chain. The value and significance of stakeholders are that they can contribute to the level of competitiveness and timeliness in which the offering is introduced, beyond what the company can do alone. The product, service, and support offering is as weak as the weakest link in the value chain. If one important stakeholder fails, the process and the quality of the deliverable suffers. Smart companies find weaknesses in their competitor's value chain and develop strategies to achieve advantage by exploiting those weaknesses. For example, the company may produce a computer system, but it procures integrated circuit technology from a supplier. The company, in turn, sells the computer system to an application software company who adds their value by installing software on the computer. The software company then sells the product to a customer. The computer company and the software company both provide value in service and support. The value chain across that process would look as illustrated in Figure 6-5.

If the computer company only considers its value in attempting to meet market requirements, it will fall short of customer expectations. Who is responsible for customer satisfaction if the technology fails or the application software lacks function? Typically the first point of dissatisfaction is with the computer company, yet it may take all three stakeholders to solve a problem—or create an opportunity. That is why it is important to consider the market requirement and the structure of the value chain when defining Competitive Dominance processes. It is equally as important to involve all stakeholders in the value chain as participants in process improvement teams. In Competitive Dominance practice, Item 5.1 of the Baldrige Criteria assesses the scope of the process and

Value Added Chain	Computer Company	Technology Stakeholder	Software Stakeholder
Integrated Circuits		X	
Systems design	X		
Systems software	X		
Systems manufacturing	X		
Application software			X
Systems installation	X		X
Systems service/ support	X		
App. software support			X

Figure 6-5 Value Chain Example.

its consideration for involving all stakeholders in the value chain.

Figure 6-6 graphically illustrates the process scope of Competitive Dominance. The concept of cross-functional teams or work groups expands to mean all stakeholders involved in process improvement (cross-enterprise teams). Traditional, inwardly-focused hierarchical organization structures must give way to flatter, more dynamic structures that span across the process, beyond the company.

Involving all stakeholders in the process means that process ownership requires executive level perspective and management system changes (the traditional way a company manages its day to day operations). To be effective, stakeholder involvement should be throughout the process from planning to product design, development, production, delivery, installation, and after sales support as illustrated by Figure 6-7.

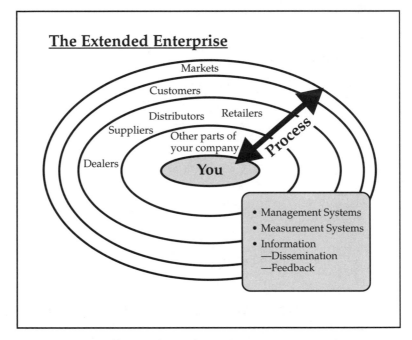

- Processes typically span beyond your company boundaries.
- Stakeholders are other parts of your company, dealers, distributors, suppliers, and retailers.
- Stakeholders are fundamental to delivering a product or service value and ensuring business success.
- Stakeholders many times represent your product or service to a customer.

- A customer transaction may involve different stakeholders than a market transaction.
- Management systems (the methods used to manage day to day operations) and measurement systems will change with the process scope.
- Information flow is as important as process flow for closed-loop responsive systems.

Figure 6-6 Process Scope and Stakeholders in the Extended Enterprise.

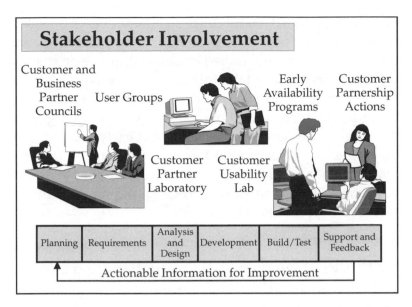

Figure 6-7 Stakeholders Involved Throughout the Product Cycle.

Information flow becomes an increasingly important element to maintain communication, control, and responsiveness throughout the value chain. Information flow from source to market and back is a key Competitive Dominance evaluation criteria. Product and service process flow and information flow generally are not the same, yet one cannot achieve successful process reengineering without considering both. Information must flow across company boundaries and throughout all stakeholders to customers and back. The design of information flow and use of information technology is as critical to Competitive Dominance as the design of process flow. Timely update, rapid access, ease of use and analysis, and integrity of the information is a competitive advantage in Competitive Dominance theory.

One of the key areas where Competitive Dominance parts company from traditional quality approaches is the importance of *competitive* quality products and services.

The offering must show improvement over historical trends and must also be increasingly more competitive in the industry. In Competitive Dominance, all the processes and evaluations must take this factor into account.

Product introduction becomes a process, not an event. It begins at the planning stages and continues throughout the product design, development, and early production, involving all stakeholders. In certain cases, a company may initiate exploratory development partnerships where customers and stakeholders jointly develop innovative new products and services.

5.2 Process Management: Product and Service Production and Delivery *(40 points)*

Describe how the company's key product and service production/delivery processes are managed to ensure that design requirements are met and that both quality and operational performance are continuously improved.

Areas to Address

a. How the company maintains the performance of its key production/delivery processes to ensure that such processes meet design requirements addressed in Item 5.1. Describe: (1) the key processes, **their tie to key business drivers**, and their principal requirements; and (2) the measurement plan and how measurements and/or observations are used to maintain process performance.

b. How processes are evaluated and improved to achieve better operational performance, including cycle time. Describe how each of the following is used or considered: (1) process analysis and research; (2) benchmarking; (3) use of alternative technology; and (4) information **and information flow** from customers of the processes—within and outside the company.

Notes

1.   Key production/delivery processes are those most directly **link to the key business drivers as defined in Item 3.2 and** *are involved in fulfilling the principal requirements of customers* **and/or market opportunity**—*those that define the products and services.*

2.   Measurement plan (5.2a(2)) is defined in Item 5.1, Note (5). Companies with specialized measurement requirements should describe how they assure measurement effectiveness. For physical, chemical, and engineering measurements, describe briefly how measurements are made traceable to national standards.

3.   The focus of 5.2a is on maintenance *of process performance using measurements and/or observations to decide whether or not corrective actions is needed. The nature of the corrective actions depends on the process characteristics and the type of variation observed. Responses should reflect the type of process and the type of variation observed. A description should be given of how basic (root) causes of variation are determined and how corrections are made at the earliest points(s) in processes. Such correction should then minimize the likelihood of recurrence of this type of variation anywhere in the company.*

4.   Process improvement methods (5.2b) might utilize financial data to evaluate alternatives and to set priorities.

5.   Process analysis and research (5.2b(1)) refers to a wide range of possible approaches to improving processes. Examples include process mapping, optimization experiments, basic and applied research, error proofing, and reviewing critical encounters between employees and customers from the point of view of customers and employees.

6. *Information from customers (5.2b(4)) might include information developed as described in Items 7.2, 7.3, and 2.3.*

7. *Results of improvements in product and service delivery processes should be reported in Items 6.1 and 6.2, as appropriate.*

Item 5.2 should be answered in the context of the extended enterprise as defined in Item 5.1 to meet Competitive Dominance theory criteria. Key considerations in this item are

1. involvement of all stakeholders in tracking, reviewing, and maintaining performance

2. information flow across the process, and its use in in-process measures and end-of-process measures, root cause determination, and identification of improvement actions

3. how information flow improves cycle time response, communicates with all involved, and provides closed-loop feedback.

5.3 Process Management: Support Services *(30 points)*

Describe how the company's key support service processes are designed and managed so that current *and future* requirements are met and that operational performance is continuously improved.

Areas to Address
a. How key support service processes are **selected and** designed. Include: (1) how key requirements are determined or set; (2) how these requirements are translated into efficient and effective processes, including opera-

tional requirements and an appropriate measurement plan; and (3) how all requirements are addressed early in design by all appropriate company units **and important stakeholders** to ensure integration, coordination, and capability.

b.   How the company maintains the performance of key support service processes. to ensure that such processes meet design requirements. Describe: (1) the key processes and their principal requirements; and (2) the measurement plan and how measurements are used to maintain process performance.

c.   How processes are evaluated and improved to achieve better operational performance, including cycle time. Describe how each of the following is used or considered: (1) process analysis and research; (2) benchmarking; (3) use of alternative technology; and (4) information **and information flow** from customers of the processes—within and outside the company.

Notes
1.   Support services are those which support the company's product and/or service delivery but which are not usually designed in detail with the products and services themselves because their requirements do not usually depend a great deal upon product and service characteristics. Support service design requirements usually depend significantly upon internal requirements. Support Services might address finance and accounting, software services, sales, marketing, public relations, information services, purchasing, personnel, legal services, plant and facilities management, basic research and development, and secretarial and other administrative services. **The descriptions should include, if applicable, how stakeholder processes are synergistic with the company's processes.**

2.   The purpose of Item 5.3 is to permit applicants to highlight separately the improvement activities for processes that support the product and service design, production, and delivery processes addressed in Items 5.1 and 5.2. The support services and business processes included in Item 5.3 depend on the applicant's type of business and other factors. Thus, this selection should be made by the applicant. **Key support services are those which the key business drivers have greatest dependency on.** *Together, Items 5.1, 5.2, 5.3, and 5.4 should cover all operations, processes and activities of all work units.*

3. *Process improvement methods (5.3c) might utilize financial data to evaluate alternatives and to set priorities.*

4. *Process analysis and research (5.3c(1)) refers to a wide range of possible approaches to improving processes. See Item 5.2, Note (5)*

5. *Information from customers (5.3c(4)) might include information developed as described in Items 7.2, 7.3, and 2.3. However, most of the information for improvement (5.3c(4)) is likely to come from "internal customers"—those within the company who use the support services.*

6. *Results of improvements in support services should be reported in Item 6.2.*

In Competitive Dominance practice, support service processes have the same design parameters as production and delivery processes. An emerging trend is the use of non-company resources to provide traditional support services defined in note (1). These "vendors" are stakeholders in the process and must be partners in all key improvement initiatives. The process scope requires stakeholder involvement in tracking, reviewing, maintaining, and improving processes.

In any process management or reengineering action, a company must develop its design based upon both current and future requirements. It takes hard work and time to achieve breakthroughs or stretch goals through process reengineering. If a company only considers current requirements, these requirements may be obsolete by the time the process improvements take effect.

Information flow in support processes is as critical as in production processes because it flows within the company and between other companies. When companies have highly-integrated production and support processes, information flow will typically pass between both processes. There is significant opportunity to simplify and optimize the integration of production and support processes by analyzing the information requirements and flow before analyzing the process flow.

5.4 Management of *Stakeholder* Performance (*30 points*)

Describe how the company assures that materials, components, and services furnished by other businesses meet the company's performance requirements. Describe also the company's actions and plans to improve *stakeholder* relationships and performance.

Areas to Address

a. Summary of the company's requirements **in support of the key business drivers,** and how they are communicated to **stakeholders.** Include a brief summary of: (1) the principal requirements for key **stakeholders, both short term and long term,** the measures and/or indicators associated with these requirements, and the expected performance levels; (2) how the company determines whether or not its requirements are met by **stakeholders;** and (3) how performance information **flows from and to stakeholders.**

b.   How the company evaluates and improves its management of **stakeholder** relationships and performance. Describe current actions and plans: (1) to improve **stakeholders'** abilities to meet requirements **or improve cost, market responsiveness, stakeholder satisfaction and customer satisfaction**; (2) to improve the company's own procurement **and support** processes, including feedback sought from **stakeholders** and from other units within the company ("internal customers") and how such feedback is used; and (3) to minimize costs associated with inspection, test, audit, or other approaches used to verify **stakeholder** performance.

Notes

*1.   The term **"stakeholder"** refers to providers of goods and services **that participate in the value chain (see Item 5.1).** The use of these goods and services may occur at any stage in the **planning,** production, delivery, **distribution, support** and use of the company's products and services. Thus, **stakeholders** include businesses such as distributors, dealers, warranty repair services, contractors, and franchises as well as those that provide materials and components. If the applicant is a unit of a larger company, and other units of that company supply goods/services, this should be included as part of Item 5.4.*

*2.   Key **stakeholders** (5.4a(1)) are those which provide the most important products and/or services, taking into account the criticality and volume of products and/or services **that affect the key business drivers. One would expect to see a link between stakeholder actions and how they support the strategy in Item 3.2 and how they support markets and customers in Item 7.1.***

*3.   "Requirements" refers to the principal factors involved in the purchases **or contracts:** quality, delivery, price, **customer satisfaction, etc.***

4. How requirements are communicated and how performance information is fed back might entail ongoing working relationships or partnerships with key stakeholders. Such relationships and/or partnerships should be briefly described in responses.

*5. Determining how quality requirements are met (5.4a(2)) might include **process control information technology**, audits, process reviews, receiving inspection, certification, testing, rating systems.*

*6. Actions and plans (5.4b) might include one or more of the following: joint planning, rapid information and data exchanges, use of benchmarking and comparative information, customer-supplier **improvement** teams, partnerships, training, long-term agreements, incentives, and recognition, partnership, training, long-term agreements, incentives, and recognition. They might also include changes in **stakeholder** selection **based on future market needs,** or reduction In the number of **stakeholders**.*

*7. Efforts to minimize costs might be backed by analyses comparing **like stakeholders** based on overall cost, taking into account **process and information efficiency and effectiveness,** quality and delivery. Analyses might also address transaction costs associated with alternative approaches to supply management.*

Competitive Dominance theory requires that the context of "supplier" be broadened to "Stakeholder." The term "stakeholder" actually fits the current Baldrige guidelines well in note (1). Most companies address this category in the traditional sense of "front-end" suppliers that provide materials and components. Distributors, retailers, and other service providers at the "back-end" of processes could be considered as customers, but they also provide value-added goods and services that influence end customer purchase intentions and satisfaction.

Therefore, Competitive Dominance considers these participants as suppliers in the value chain described in Item 5.1. Key considerations are

1.   defining the key stakeholders and the requirements important to success in served markets, natural markets, and investment markets (short and long range);

2.   uses of information to maintain expected performance levels and synchronize process operations involving stakeholders;

3.   how the company improves its own processes that involve stakeholders as partners in success.

4.   going beyond inspection, test, and audit methods to pro-active involvement and ownership that improves stakeholder capability to deliver more customer value and improve customer satisfaction.

In Item 5.4a, a Competitive Dominance assessment would evaluate who the key stakeholders are in the value chain and their contribution to customer value and product/service quality. It would evaluate the alignment between those stakeholders and the markets they serve— both current customers, and future investment markets. They may be the same, or entry into new markets may require alliances with new stakeholders.

The important element in Item 5.4a(2) is the company's ability to determine factually if its requirements are being met. How does information flow from and to the stakeholder? What are the timeliness and accuracy of the information? Is the information valuable for responsive decision support to the company and the stakeholder.

The Baldrige criteria in 5.4b assess the company methods to improve its own procurement processes. Competitive Dominance extends the thinking beyond just stakeholder feedback to describe how the company involves stakeholders to optimize the process in each company, and between them. This practice extends further in Item 5.4b(1) and note (7).

Competitive Dominance methods go beyond traditional quality audits and inspections to include stakeholders as work group participants in process improvement, customer satisfaction, and future market success. Another additional element is the consideration of stakeholder satisfaction with the company relationship. A process should be in place to understand, and improve inter-company and intra-company relationships.

Note (2) clarifies important links to other categories. A Competitive Dominance evaluation would expect to see stakeholder involvement in planning in Item 3.1, important stakeholder strategies addressed in Item 3.2. The evaluation would also expect to see what role stakeholders play in supporting natural and investment markets in Item 7.1.

6.0 BUSINESS RESULTS *(250 points)*

The *Business Results* Category examines the company's performance and improvement in key business areas— product and service quality, productivity and operational effectiveness, *stakeholder performance,* and financial performance indicators linked to these areas. Also examined are performance levels relative to competitors.

Traditionally, key measures for quality and operational results have been cost, expense, cycle time, and those elements that are the best determinants of customer satisfaction. These conventional measures are still very important, but they are insufficient where Competitive

Dominance are the quality and strategic objectives. By Competitive Dominance we mean the situation where a company's lead in customer satisfaction is so large that it overwhelms the competition and attracts an increasing number of new customers from their competition and from new market opportunities. We also mean where a company may not be in the lead, but its improvement in customer satisfaction is so dominant that it overshadows the leader. Therefore, the key measure for quality and operational results is Competitive Dominance and the most effective indicators are revenue growth, productivity, and market opportunity captured or share. They are easy to understand and are also useful proxies for customer satisfaction. Revenue growth is important, but it must be accompanied by market share growth. It is possible to grow revenue and lose market share when the revenue growth is slower than the growth of the market. Neither revenue nor market share growth can be achieved if the organization cannot respond to market demand. Today, speed is one of the "buzz-words" on executive lips. Competitive Dominance theory addresses organizational productivity, a part of which is speed.

It is important to measure all three parameters to ensure that they are pointing in the same direction. This focus on revenue growth, productivity, and market share growth is the hallmark of Competitive Dominance. Category 6 addresses revenue growth and productivity; Category 7 addresses market share.

Business Week conducted a simple test recently to validate these concepts (Betting 1993). Quality guru Juran wondered what would be the financial results of investing a $1000 in each of the Baldrige winners. *Business Week* invested a hypothetical $1000 in each of the publicly traded Baldrige winners. Excluding dividends, *Business Week's* portfolio increased by 89.2%, while the Standard and Poor's stock index increased by only 33.1%.

Traditional TQM emphasizes product and service quality results that best represent the most important factors that predict customer satisfaction. Competitive Dominance emphasizes product and service quality results that best represent the most important factors that predict customer satisfaction *and market acceptance*. They may be the same, but it is likely that the product and service results that drive customer expectations may need to be different to drive market demand. For example, a key measure to improve customer satisfaction would be product reliability as measured by mean time to failure. In a major emerging growth market, the demand is for products that never fail. In this case, product availability, as measured by effective customer operational hours, may be the important measure. Inability to demonstrate availability by means of that measure could be a barrier to entry into that market segment.

In Company Operational and Financial Results, the Competitive Dominance focus is on revenue-based measures, such as ratios of revenue to expense, and productivity measures such as time to market and revenue per employee. Another important Competitive Dominance aspect of Item 6.2 is the focus placed on measures of transformation. Those indicators of progress and success in achieving milestones toward the vision or goal. These may be indicators of speed, efficiency, competency development, or win rates in new target markets.

6.1 Product and Service Quality Results
(75 points)

Summarize results of improvement efforts using key measures and/or indicators of product and service quality.

Areas to Address

a.   Current levels and trends in key measures and/or indicators of product and service quality. Graphs and tables should include appropriate comparative data.

Notes

*1.   Results reported in 6.1 should reflect performance relative to specific non-price product and service key quality requirements. Such key quality requirements should relate closely to customer satisfaction and customer retention **and market growth**. These requirements are those described in the Business Overview and addressed in Items 7.1 and 5.1.*

2.   Data appropriate for inclusion are based upon:

- *internal (company) measurements;*
- *field performance;*
- *data collected by the company through follow ups (7.2c) or surveys of customers;*
- *data collected or generated by other organizations; and*
- *data collected by other organizations on behalf of the company.*

3.   Product and service quality measures and/or indicators may address requirements such as accuracy, timeliness, reliability, and behavior. Examples include defect levels, repeat services, meeting product or service delivery or response times, availability levels, and complaint levels.

4.   Comparative data might include industry best, best competitor, industry average, and appropriate benchmarks. Such data might be derived from independent surveys, studies, laboratory testing, or other sources.

Competitive Dominance emphasizes measurements most important to predicting *customer satisfaction,* assuring *market acceptance,* and *linking to key business drivers.* The company should select measures shown in Item 6.1

based on served, natural, and investment market priorities (see Item 7.1). Measuring predictors of customer satisfaction will enable the company to retain customers. Studies have shown that customer satisfaction leads to revenue growth over time achieved from customer loyalty. The question is whether these indicators will enable the company to grow at its projected rates. A company may have high satisfaction with its current customers but may not be gaining new customers, especially if new markets demand different product and service quality requirements. The following example illustrates this.

A company has clear customer satisfaction leadership trends in its served market segments. The requirements for these segments are for high performance, high reliability, and service responsiveness. The company aligns its resources, processes, services, and product plans to be responsive to that segment. Because of this, the company enjoys continued revenue growth and profitability, as well as a commanding share of that segment. This situation would receive high marks in a traditional TQM level Item 6.1 assessment. Consider, however, the situation where the growth rate of these segments will slow from ten percent to two percent over the next five years. If the company wants to continue to grow at ten percent per year, it must either: inject new value that dramatically stimulates demand; gain significant wins from the majority of the competition; choose a niche strategy and downsize accordingly; or enter new markets to sustain a ten percent growth. If it does nothing, it will fail over time. To sustain growth, the company must decide to enter new markets where delivery, cost and service responsiveness drive growth and satisfaction. This example illustrates dramatically the insufficiency of rear-view mirror indicators. It must consider future shifts and changes.

A Competitive Dominance assessment would expect to see all six measures, the first three in the traditional served natural markets driving historical satisfaction and revenue, and the three in new investment markets driving market growth and satisfaction. The prevailing wisdom in traditional quality practice is that customer satisfaction yields business improvement. While Competitive Dominance theory considers customer satisfaction extremely important to business success, it requires demonstration of a clear cause and effect connection between product and service measurements, customer satisfaction, and market growth. A Competitive Dominance evaluation would attempt to link the measures shown in Item 6.1 with Item 7.1 and Item 7.5b (gains and losses of customers, and market share).

6.2 Company Operational and Financial Results *(130 points)*

Summarize results of improvement efforts using key measures and/or indicators of company operational and financial performance *linked to the key business drivers.*

Areas to Address
a.   Current levels and trends in key measures and/or indicators of company operational and financial performance. Graphs and tables should include appropriate comparative data.

Notes
1.   Key measures and/or indicators of company operational and financial performance should **have a direct link to key business drivers in Item 3.2 and** *address the following areas:*

> • *productivity and other indicators of effective use of manpower, materials, energy, capital, and assets;*

- *cycle time, **time to market,** and responsiveness;*
- *financial indicators such as cost reductions, asset utilization, and benefit/cost results from improvement efforts;*
- *human resource indicators such as safety, absenteeism, turnover, and satisfaction **based on key skill categories;** public responsibilities such as environmental improvements; and*
- *company-specific indicators such as innovation rates and progress in **opportunity** or shifting markets or segments.*
- ***indicators of achievement of significant milestones or goals that provide evidence of a successful organizational transformation such as skills competency levels attained, efficiency targets met, win rate in targeted markets achieved.***

2. *The results reported in Item 6.2 derive primarily from activities described in Items **1.3**, 5.1, 5.2, and 5.3, **and in Category 4.***

3. *Comparison data might include industry best, best competitor, industry average, and appropriate benchmarks. For human resource areas such as turnover or absenteeism, local or regional comparative information might also be appropriate.*

In Item 6.2, Competitive Dominance would look for measures tied to revenue growth, productivity, and transformation as key indicators of market acceptance. As per note (1), these indicators should have a clear connection to the key business drivers. Some examples of these indicators are illustrated in Figure 6-8.

A Competitive Dominance assessment would look for a strong correlation between revenue growth indicators, productivity indicators, and the market share indicators in Item 7.5b. In addition, this correlation would demonstrate a strong cause and effect relationship between strategic deployment of the key business factors in Item 3.1, successful transformation, and improved results.

Examples of Indicators

Indicators of Revenue	Indicators of Productivity	Indicators of Transformation
Return on assets	Revenue per employee	Portfolio mix percent change (old-new)
Revenue growth	Expense to revenue	Expense reduction in non-strategic areas
Return on investment	Inventory turns	Diversity tied to key business drivers
Cash flow	Time to Market	Competency growth in strategic skill areas
Days sales outstanding	Sales effectiveness	Win rate in strategic target markets
	Overall morale by key skill category	People's acceptance of change

Figure 6-8 Examples of Revenue and Productivity Indicators.

6.3 Stakeholder Performance Results *(45 points)*

Summarize results of **stakeholder** performance improvement efforts using key measures and/or indicators of such performance.

Areas to Address

a. Current levels and trends in key measures and/or indicators of supplier performance. Graphs and tables should include appropriate comparative data.

Notes

1. *The results reported in Item 6.3 derive from activities described in Item 5.4. Results should be broken out by key **services and key stakeholders**, as appropriate. Data should be presented using the measures and/or indicators described in 5.4a(1).*

2. *If the company's **stakeholder** management efforts include factors such as building **stakeholder** partnerships, or reducing the number of **stakeholders**, data related to these efforts should be included in responses.*

3. *Comparative data might be of several types: industry best, best competitor(s), industry average, and appropriate benchmarks.*

The breadth, depth, and scope of stakeholder measures are what differentiates Competitive Dominance from traditional TQM. Stakeholders is a broader definition than supplier. For each stakeholder group, per note (1), results should reflect the most important measure(s) of key business drivers for the company to achieve its customer satisfaction, market growth goals.

7.0 CUSTOMER FOCUS AND SATISFACTION (*250 points*)

The *Customer Focus and Satisfaction* Category examines the company's systems for customer learning and for building and maintaining customer relationships. Also examined are levels and trends in key measures of business success—customer satisfaction and retention, market share, and satisfaction relative to competitors.

Paradoxically, in Competitive Dominance theory, customer satisfaction becomes both the means and an end. In current quality practice, customer satisfaction is one of the key measures for the effectiveness of quality management. With the focus on Competitive Dominance, customer satisfaction now also becomes the means to obtain market share growth. In addition to customer satisfaction, however, Competitive Dominance articulates a significant difference from traditional quality focus. It differentiates between customer base (the "served market" and the focus of customer satisfaction), natural markets, and investment markets. Natural markets are market segment opportunities where the company is well positioned in customer accounts and product solution fit. Investment markets are potential new growth opportunities requiring investments to address potential new requirements. To achieve Competitive Dominance, companies must focus on all these segments to assure sustainable long term growth and prosperity. Competitive Dominance becomes more than leadership in customer satisfaction. It is customer satisfaction and the application of quality tools and processes to generate demand in future growth markets.

The customer and market expectations may vary significantly between the base of current customers served and new market opportunities. Competition may not be the same. Competitive Dominance recognizes these dynamics and requires processes and models to analyze markets and competition to determine investment priorities. One of the key assessment items is how the company determines where to invest based upon optimum achievement of revenue and market share growth.

In Competitive Dominance the Customer Relationship Management processes expand to encompass all requirements important to the customer. This is to assure that the company has a balanced focus and is able to energize the resources of the company to address the breadth and scope of what is important to customers. Fixing one area important to customers, but still having a problem in another important area, does nothing to improve overall satisfaction. In Competitive Dominance, customer relationship processes demonstrate a synchronized closed-loop link between the customer-contact employees and the rest of the extended enterprise. It also evaluates market leadership in the company's commitment to customers.

Competitive Dominance differentiates itself from current quality practice in *Customer Satisfaction Determination* by extending the concept to *Customer Satisfaction Management* processes. It is not sufficient for leadership to focus on the process of collecting customer satisfaction information from customers and competitor's customers. Nor is it sufficient to focus only on how the company improves the customer satisfaction determination process and how it uses other indicators of improvement. An effective customer satisfaction process includes the use of the results for improvements in products, services, and long term satisfaction and growth. It assesses the actionable nature of the information—the ability to get to accurate root cause determination, the link to operation measurements, and the link to the customer relationship process.

The results from customer satisfaction are important indicators of market share growth. In Competitive Dominance, these results have a direct tie to the natural and investment market segments the company has determined are the growth opportunities.

A highly integrated quality and strategy approach requires a demonstration of a definable, repeatable, predictable relationship between the company initiatives to transform itself to the future and success in targeted market segments. Effective Competitive Dominance deployment is characterized by highly stratified market share trends supported with detailed analysis and the use of effective planning models and tools to perform this analysis.

7.1 Customer and Market Knowledge *(30 points)*

Describe how the company determines near-term and long-term requirements and expectations of customers and markets, and develops listening and learning strategies to understand and anticipate needs

Areas to Address
a.   How the company determines current and near-term requirements and expectations of customers **and natural markets.** Include: (1) how customer groups and/or market segments are determined and/or selected, including how customers of competitors and other potential customers are considered; (2) how information is collected, including what information is sought, frequency and methods of collection, and how objectivity and validity are ensured; (3) how the company determines specific product and service features and the relative importance of these features to customer groups or segments; and (4) how other key information and data such as complaints, gains and losses of customers, and product/service performance are used to support the determination.

b.   How the company addresses future requirements and expectations of customers, **natural, and investment markets, and how competitors and potential competitors are considered**.

c.   How the company evaluates and improves its processes for determining customer **and market** requirements and expectations **including how the company**

determines investment priority for quality, customer satisfaction, natural, and investment market leadership.

Notes

1.   The distinction between near-term and future depends upon many marketplace factors. The applicant's response should reflect these factors for its market(s).

2.   The company's products and services might be sold to end users via other businesses **(stakeholders)** *such as retail stores or dealers. Thus, "customer groups" should take into account the requirements and expectations of both the end users and these other businesses.*

3.   Product and service features refer to all important characteristics and to the performance of products and services that customers experience or perceive throughout their overall purchase and ownership. The focus should be primarily on factors that bear upon customer preference, repurchase loyalty, or **demand generation**—*for example, those features that enhance or differentiate products and services from competing offerings.*

4.   Some companies might use similar methods to determine customer requirements/expectations and customer satisfaction (Item 7.3). In such cases, cross-references should be included. **In Competitive Dominance, the emphasis should be placed on future markets.**

5.   Customer groups and market segments (7.1a) might take into account opportunities to select or **create** *groups and segments based upon customer- and market-related information.*

6.   Item 7.1a(2) should have a direct tie to sources of data referenced in Item 2.1, and to analysis methods in Item 2.3.

7.   Examples of listening and learning strategy elements (7.1b) are

- *relationship strategies, including close integration with customers;*

- *rapid innovation and field trials to better link R&D to the market;*
- *close monitoring of technological, competitive, societal, environmental, economic, and demographic factors that may bear upon customer requirements, expectations, preferences, or alternatives;*
- *focus groups with demanding or leading-edge customers;*
- *training of frontline employees in customer listening;*
- *use of critical incidents to understand key service attributes from the point of view of customers and frontline employees;*
- *interviewing lost customers;*
- *post-transaction follow-up (see 7.2c); and*
- *analysis of major factors affecting key customers.*

8. **Competitor analysis in Item 7.1b includes items such as:**

- **product and service comparisons**
- **Investment and market strategies**
- **Value chain analysis (see Item 5.1), and**
- **Market segment penetration.**

9. *Examples of evaluations factors appropriate for 7.1c are*

- *the adequacy and timeliness of the customer-related information;*
- *improvement of survey design;*
- *the best approaches for getting reliable and timely information—surveys, focus groups, customer-contact personnel, etc.;*
- *Increasing and decreasing importance of product/service features among customer groups or segments;*
- *the most effective listening/learning strategies; and*
- **enhanced modeling tools for market, competitor, and/or investment analysis.**

The evaluation might also be supported by company-level analysis addressed in 2.3a.

10. A continual challenge to the requirements process is how to identify and establish resource and funding priorities between current requirements (Item 7.1a), future requirements (Item 7.1b), and internal imperatives such as investment in technology. These priorities should link solidly to the key strategic business drivers identified in Item 3.1.

This is one of the key items for Competitive Dominance success. This item should have a strong link to these other items:

- Overview—in the description of markets, customers, and competition, and key business drivers;
- Item 1.1—leaders active role and participation in establishing the future vision;
- Item 1.3—company leadership in social, environmental, economic, and political forces;
- Item 2.1—data sources for customer, market, industry, and competitive information;
- Item 2.3—analysis of market and customer data;
- Item 3.1—basic input to establish the strategy;
- Item 3.2—critical link to the key business drivers deployed to achieve the strategy;
- Item 5.1—identification of value chain, stakeholders, and competitors; and
- Item 7.5—gains, losses, and market share.

If Competitive Dominance was the major driver of the guidelines, this item would be added to Category 3 as the basis for a company plan. This would reduce the number of points on Category 7, but it would keep customer satisfaction weight high. More importantly, it would increase the points on Category 3 to reinforce the importance of taking strategic view of quality management, and it would enhance the integration of quality in market planning as a discipline fundamental to Competitive Dominance. In the interest of maintaining continuity with the Baldrige guidelines, the placement of Item 7.1 should not have impact on an effective Competitive Dominance assessment. The links are more important.

In Item 7.1, Competitive Dominance differentiates itself from traditional quality in two areas:

1. focus on natural market and investment market opportunity in addition to current customers (served market); and

2. the process to identify and prioritize requirements and investments to achieve leadership business objectives.

Before going any further, a better understanding of customers and market definitions is in order, as illustrated in Figure 6-9. These concepts are discussed in detail in Chapter 8.

The **Served Market** is the company's current customer base. The requirements for these segments are primarily customer satisfaction improvements and competitive actions and responses. In assessing customer groups and/ or market segments, Competitive Dominance theory evaluates the structure of the current customer base to determine company performance in serving its core customers. Competitive Dominance would also consider competitors placements within these segments, and their growth rates. The company should analyze its own and competitor's strengths and weaknesses in addressing these segments. It would also assess the use of various processes to gather requirements from external and cus-

Markets	Groups of customers who will respond similarly to a given offering.
Served market	A term that identifies customers where a product has been placed. Fundamentally, it identifies an existing customer who has made expenditures for your offering.
Natural markets	A market where there is a fit between the company's capabilities and the critical success factors for that market. Represents a market where the company can sell, but does not have a served market. The served market is a subset of the natural market.
Investment markets	A market opportunity where there is a void between a company's capabilities and critical success factors. To succeed in investment markets, a company must invest to develop a capability where void(s) exist, thereby turning it into a natural market.

Figure 6-9 Market Definitions.

tomer feedback sources to improve its own capabilities to serve these customers.

Natural markets are segments where there is a strong fit between the company's capabilities; for example: product, service, distribution, and sales solutions. In other words, all conditions exist for the company to succeed in this market—if it so chooses. A company should be able to analyze its growth as well as competitors' growth in these natural market segments to compare growth rates, customer "wins," competitor placements, and reasons for wins and losses.

Investment markets are new market segments that represent a potential growth opportunity. These markets may be variations of natural market segments where demand for new value generates growth beyond that already identified. Investment markets can also be entirely new segments where a company identifies new products and services (related or unrelated to existing ones) to capture new customers and create new business. A simple example would be a company that provides industrial cleaning products for restaurants and then moves into the hotel market for carpet cleaning. The products and services are variations of existing ones, the market and competition are different.

New market demand or innovative technologies that provide significant new value in improved quality, features, or function typically drive new investments to address new market requirements. Market segmentation and selection are critical analyses to ensure accurate requirements and investment decisions. The company may not confront traditional competition and most likely will face new competitors in investment markets. Wins in natural market segments will build the customer base. Wins in investment markets will not only increase the customer base, but will also begin to change the structure of the customer base.

One technique to identify investment market trends is **Lead User Analysis**. In lead user analysis, the company identifies leading edge customers (those that set the pace in their industry) and partners with them to understand their specific requirements. These requirements can be anywhere in the value chain; in design, product, technology, manufacturing, sales, distribution, service, and so on. These requirements represent where the rest of the industry will be going in the next few years. By satisfying lead user needs, the company can offer more competitive products and services to provide greater value to all customers in that segment and therefore begin to serve a new market and create new demand for its products and services. The strategic significance of natural and investment markets is discussed in detail in Chapter 8.

Understanding the requirements of these markets requires detailed analysis. It is challenging and hard work. Even more fundamental to company success is the prioritization of investment to implement requirements. Unless the company has unlimited resources, it must determine what requirements will provide the highest short and long term pay back, and allocate resources based on this analysis. The Competitive Dominance Item 7.1c assesses the processes, tools, and models the company uses to systematically prioritize resources to the highest leverage requirements. Figure 6-10 illustrates the prioritization as basic input to the planning process in Category 3.

Three basic Competitive Dominance business indicators of requirements alignment with business goals are: (1) revenue as indicated in Item 6.2; (2) productivity as indicated in Item 6.2; and (3) market share in Item 7.5.

7.2 Customer Relationship Management
(30 points)

Describe how the company provides effective management of its responses and follow ups with customers to preserve and build relationships and to increase knowledge about specific customers and about general customer expectations.

Areas to Address
a. How the company provides information and easy access to enable customers to seek information and assistance, to comment, and to complain. Describe contact management performance measures and service standards and how these requirements are set, deployed, and tracked.

Requirements

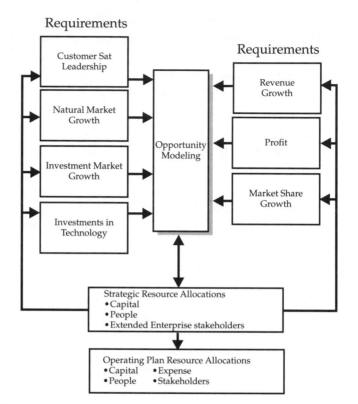

• Along with customer and market external requirements, companies have internal requirements such as research and technology the do not have short term benefits to company bottom line.
• The company process needs to consider the priority of requirements to yield short and long term revenue, profit, and/or market share.
• The process analyses should consider both short and long term objectives. The leadership must agree on basic company goals such as revenue, profit, market share. A profit strategy may conflict with a market share strategy.
• Business models and segmentation tools provide systematic approaches to the prioritization process.
• A Competitive Dominance Item 7.1c evaluation would determine how resources allocations to implement requirements aligned with business objectives.
• Output of this process should directly link to Category 3.

Figure 6-10 Factors to Consider in Modeling to Determine Priorities.

b. How the company ensures that formal and informal complaints and feedback received by all company units are resolved effectively and promptly. Briefly describe the complaint management process and how it ensures effective recovery of customer confidence, meeting customer requirements for resolution effectiveness, and elimination of the causes of complaints.

c. How the company follows up with customers on products, services, and recent transactions to determine satisfaction, to resolve problems, to seek feedback for improvement, and to build relationships.

d. How the company evaluates and improves its customer relationship management. Include: (1) how service standards, including those related to access and complaint management, are improved based upon customer information; (2) aggregation and use of customer comments and complaints throughout the company; and (3) how knowledge about customers is accumulated.

Notes

1. Customer relationship management refers to a process, not to a company unit. However, some companies may have units which address all or most of the requirements included in this Item. Also, some of these requirements may be included among the responsibilities of frontline employees in processes described in Items 5.2 and 5.3. **Managing the relationship with customers may include other stakeholders as critical non-company units between the company and the customer such as retailers or distributors. How the process and information flow addresses these units of the extended enterprise should be described.**

2. Performance measures and service standards (7.2a) apply not only to employees providing the responses to customers but also to other units within the company which make effective re-

sponses possible. Deployment needs to take into account all key points in a response chain. Examples of measures and standards are: telephonic, percentage of resolutions achieved by frontline employees, number of transfers, and resolution response time.

3.   *Responses to 7.2b and 7.2c might include company processes for addressing customer complaints or comments based upon expressed or implied guarantees and warranties.*

4.   *Elimination of the causes of complaints (7.2b) involves aggregation of complaint information from all sources for evaluation and use throughout the company. The complaint management process might include analysis and priority setting for improvement projects based upon potential cost impact of complaints, taking into account customer retention related to resolution effectiveness. Some of the analysis requirements of Item 7.2 relate to Item 2.3.* **Aggregated complaint trends should also be a factor in requirements and investment priorities as described in Item 7.1.**

5.   *Improvement of customer relationship management (7.2d) might require training. Training for customer-contact (frontline) employees should address: (a) key knowledge and skills, including knowledge of products and services; (b) listening to customers; (c) soliciting comments from customers; (d) how to anticipate and handle problems or failures ("recovery"); (e) skills in customer retention; and (f) how to manage expectations. Such training should be described in Item 4.3.*

6.   *Information on trends and levels in measures and/or indicators of complaint response time, effective resolution, and percent of complaints resolved on first contact should be reported in Item 6.1.*

In Item 7.2, there are two key Competitive Dominance focus areas:

1. The broad view of requirements that all requirements for customer and market success be addressed in the requirements process in category 7.1; and

2. Considering customer-contact employees in the journey toward the new vision or future preferred state.

The term "Product and Service" requirements in Item 7.1 implies all requirements that have a meaningful impact on customer satisfaction, expectations, purchase intent, loyalty, and competitiveness. A comprehensive requirements process will determine those elements important to customers and prioritize investments based on the most important customer satisfiers, demand generators, or competitive differentiators. A company cannot adequately determine investment priorities by separating product and service requirements from customer-contact requirements. For example:

IBM Rochester, based on market research, developed a "customer view" model that categorized requirements into six groups most important to customers (Hoisington, Huang, Cousins, Suther 1993). Figure 6-11 shows this "customer view." Each group shows examples of the more specific customer wants and needs. There are about 20 in each group, prioritized in importance. Each of these groups is explained in further detail below.

- **Administration:** Most of these requirements relate to the company's terms and conditions and administrative systems that interact with customers.
- **Sales:** The frontline sales people, account representatives, and systems engineers addressed in Item 7.2.
- **Technical Solutions:** The performance of the products developed and manufactured by the company.
- **Delivery:** The processes for ordering, delivering, and installing products at a customer location.

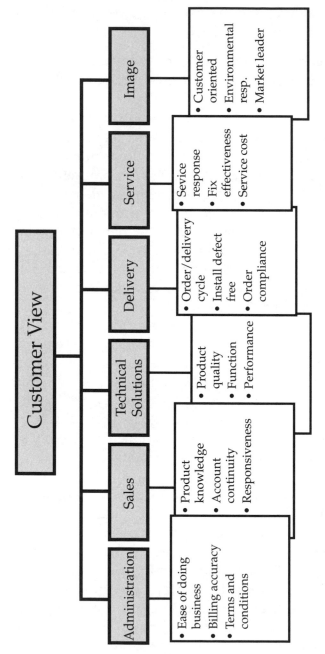

Figure 6-11 Customer View of Important Requirements.

- **Services:** The after-sale service and support addressed in Item 7.2.
- **Image:** The company reputation in the industry as a supplier of choice.

It is not sufficient to prioritize only those requirements strictly defined as "products and services" separate from others. Technical solutions, delivery, and service define "products and services." The prioritization would not cover the scope of what is important to customers. If "account continuity" (sales), were considered a higher priority by customers than "product performance" (technical solutions), the company prioritization process would not recognize this in resource allocations to support "products and services." The concepts and processes for Customer Relationship Management are described in Chapter 8.

Customer-contact employees are a key part of the transformation road map and journey toward the future. The road map must include initiatives directed to, and in support of frontline employees as critical skill categories in Category 4. For example, Competitive Dominance evaluates key links between Item 7.2, Item 1.1, Item 3.2, Item 4.1, and Item 5.1. If a key business driver is to become "market-driven" or externally focused, then customer-contact becomes a major initiative. In Item 3.2, one key business driver is "to become externally focused." The plans to address this action may be to get all people as close to customers as possible through customer involvement initiatives driven by the senior executive team (Item 1.1). The human resource plans would define and address customer contact people as a critical skill group, with the appropriate actions described in Items 4.2, 4.3, and 4.4. Category 5 should address how customers are involved in processes and the interaction with key work units and stakeholder teams, and Item 7.2 should address the continuous improvement of this key business driver.

It is also especially important that customer contact employees be involved in extended enterprise teams (See Item 5.1). Many companies use distributors, retailers, or value-added remarketers to sell and support the product or service to the end customer. The Customer Relationship Management process must address the integration of these stakeholders as critical units to establish, maintain, and build customer relationships, or manage dissatisfaction incidence and recover lost customer confidence. The information flow throughout this process must also address all stakeholders in the process. In Figure 6-11 above, 60% of the Sales and Service components went through non-company channels, yet the customers considered IBM as the supplier in the event of a problem. Having strong process and information links with these non-company partners is a critical component of successful customer relationship management.

Competitive Dominance differentiates itself from traditional practice in note (3) through the requirement to demonstrate market leadership in commitments to customers. It expands the concept of customer trust, confidence, and competitiveness to include terms, conditions, and commitments that, by their leadership nature, generate demand for the company products and services. There is a relationship to the customer view Figure 6-11, "Image" as it affects performance against implied commitments.

7.3 Customer Satisfaction *Management* *(30 points)*

Describe how the company determines **and improves** customer satisfaction, customer repurchase intentions, and customer satisfaction relative to competitors; describe how these determination processes are evaluated and improved.

Areas to Address

a. How the company determines **and uses** customer satisfaction **feedback**. Include: (1) a brief description of processes and measurement scales used; frequency of determination; and how objectivity and validity are ensured. Indicate significant differences, if any, in processes, and measurement scales for different customer groups or segments; and (2) how customer satisfaction measurements capture key information that reflects customers' likely future market behavior, such as repurchase intentions or positive referrals.

b. How customer satisfaction relative to that for competitors is determined. Describe: (1) company-based comparative studies; and (2) comparative studies or evaluations made by independent organizations and/or customers. For (1) and (2), describe how objectivity and validity of studies or evaluations are assured.

c. How the company evaluates and improves its overall processes and measurement scales for determining customer satisfaction and customer satisfaction relative to that for competitors. Include how other indicators (such as gains and losses of customers) and customer dissatisfaction indicators (such as complaints) are used in this improvement process. Describe also how the evaluation takes into account the effectiveness of the use of customer satisfaction information and data throughout the company **for improvement to the customer base, natural and investment markets.**

Note:

1. Customer satisfaction measurement might include both a numerical rating scale and descriptors assigned to each unit in the scale. An effective (actionable) customer satisfaction measurement system is one that provides the company with reliable information about customer ratings of specific product and service features and the relation-ship between these ratings and the customer's likely future market behavior.

2. *The company's products and services might be sold to end users via other businesses (stakeholders) such as retail stores or dealers. Thus, "customer groups" or segments should take into account these other businesses as well as the end users.*

3. *Customer satisfaction feedback should correlate to those factors considered most important to customers in the Overview, Item 7.1, and Item 7.2.*

4. *Customer dissatisfaction indicators include complaints, claims, refunds, recalls, returns, repeat services, litigation, replacements, downgrades, repairs, warranty work, warranty costs, misshipments, and incomplete orders.*

5. *Company-based or independent organization comparative studies (7.3b) might take into account one or more indicators of customer dissatisfaction as well as satisfaction. The extent and types of such studies may depend upon factors such as industry and company size.*

6. *Evaluation (7.3c) might take into account how well the measurement scale relates to actual repurchase and/or customer retention. The evaluation might also address the effectiveness of pre-survey research used in design, and how actionable survey results are—how well survey responses link to key business factors, processes, and cost/revenue implications and thus provide a useful basis for improvement.*

7. *Use of data from satisfaction measurement is called for in 5.2b(4) and 5.3c(4). Such data also provide key input to analysis (Item 2.3) and requirements (Item 7.1).*

The important Competitive Dominance elements of customer satisfaction in Item 7.3 are

1. The determination and collection of information should tie directly to those elements deemed most important to customers;

2. Customer satisfaction process is used to improve the overall customer relationship; and

3. Customer satisfaction data is used for investment markets.

The scope of customer satisfaction determination needs to include all important items, from the customer expectation model (see Chapter 8). In the customer expectation model example discussed in Chapter 8 and Item 7.2, the company collects and aggregates customer satisfaction surveys and other feedback by the six major customer satisfaction headings. To enable correlation and reinforcement of priorities, a customer satisfaction feedback structure should fit the customer and market requirements' model(s) from Item 7.1. Where other stakeholders provide customer value (see note (2), the customer satisfaction determination process should provide customer feedback on stakeholder performance.

The customer satisfaction process needs to be more than a process for determining satisfaction. It needs to be a process that builds the customer relationship. The customer satisfaction determination has to be a subset of an overall customer satisfaction management process. Information collected from satisfaction feedback and analyzed in Item 2.3 must have action taken from the results, otherwise the information collected provides little more than another report circulating across the desk. In the

Figure 6-11 example, each of the six customer view groups had an executive owner responsible for the satisfaction in that group. Because the owners had satisfaction goals tied to executive compensation, the results got plenty of attention and proactive action.

Figure 6-12 represents the third major Competitive Dominance element of customer satisfaction—the use of the information to not only improve customer's satisfaction but as input to determine market investment candidates.

If a company has high satisfaction in a market not currently targeted, then it means that the products and ser-

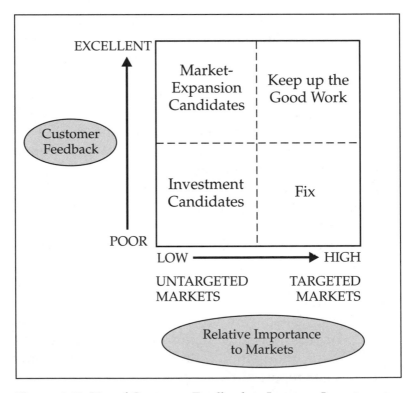

Figure 6-12 Use of Customer Feedback to Improve Investment Market Opportunity.

vices fit well (meet the needs) in that segment. Analysis should be performed to determine the attractiveness of the segment (see Item 2.3) for market share and revenue growth. Longer term actions may lead to the development of new investment markets. If the company has low satisfaction in targeted markets important to growth, then it has significant risk of losing its natural market share. Immediate action is required.

7.4 Customer Satisfaction Results *(100 points)*

Summarize the company's customer satisfaction and customer dissatisfaction results using key measures and/or indicators of these results.

Areas to Address

a. Current levels and trends in key measures and/or indicators of customer satisfaction and customer retention. Results should be segmented by customer group, as appropriate.

b. Current levels and trends in key measures and/or indicators of customer dissatisfaction. Address the most relevant and important indicators for the company's products/services.

Note:

1. Results reported in this Item derive from methods described in Items 7.3 and 7.2.

2. Results data (7.4a) might be supported by customer feedback, customer's overall assessments of products/services, and customer awards.

*3. Indicators of customer dissatisfaction are given in **Item 7.3, Note 4.***

4. Segments should be those addressed in Item 7.1.

Note (4) ensures a link to Item 7.1. The segments describing the customer base and/or natural market(s) should tie to the results shown here. Information on customer satisfaction or customer dissatisfaction in new, emerging market opportunity segments in natural and/or investment markets should be highlighted as key indicators of health in these new company thrusts.

7.5 Customer Satisfaction Comparison *(60 points)*

Compare the company's customer satisfaction results with those of competitors.

Areas to Address
a. Current levels and trends in key measures and/or indicators of customer satisfaction relative to competitors. Such indicators may include gains and losses of customers or customer accounts to competitors. Results may include objective information and/or data from independent organizations, including customers. Results should be segmented by customer group **and/or from targeted markets** as appropriate.

b. Trends in gaining or losing market share **in targeted markets** to competitors.

Note:
1. Results reported in Item 7.5 derive from methods described in Item 7.3.

2. Competitors include domestic and international ones in the company's markets, both domestic and international.

*3.   Objective information and/or data from independent orga-
nizations, including customers (7.5a), might include survey results, competitive awards, recognition, and ratings by
independent organizations and customers should reflect comparative satisfaction (and dissatisfaction), not comparative performance of products and services. Information on comparative
performance of products and services should be included in 6.1b.*

**4.   Item 7.5b assumes that gains in customers come two
ways. One is through competitive win. The other is by
capturing growth in new markets segments with large
opportunity (not highly penetrated). In this case, to demonstrate leadership, the company should demonstrate
that its growth rate is better than the segment growth on
average, and best of the competition.**

**5.   The term "targeted markets" in Item 7.5b should link
back to those identified in Item 7.1.**

The Competitive Dominance enhancement to Item 7.5 is
the demonstration of a definable, repeatable, predictable
relationship between the company initiatives to transform
itself to the future preferred position and success in the targeted markets. A company determines success by growth
in target market segments compared to the leaders in the
competition and the overall segment growth rate. Competitive win rate is another indicator, but it is not sufficient in
itself. The current Baldrige criteria imply that market share
growth comes from wins over competition. This situation
is a result of actions in highly penetrated markets. Competitive Dominance theory supports this approach, but it extends the thinking into market segments with less
penetration and high opportunity. In this situation, the de-
terminant for dominance is growth rates faster than the
segment and faster than any other competition in the segment (refer to Item 3.1). Even segment growth does not

	Revenue $M Year n	Revenue $M Year $n+1$	Growth %
Industry			
A	$ 30	$ 39	30 %
B	$ 70	$ 73.5	5 %
Total	$ 100	$ 112.5	12.5%
Slow			
ALPHA	$ 12	$ 15.84	32 %
BETA	$ 48	$ 51.36	7 %
Total	$ 60	$ 67.20	11 %

Figure 6-13 Market Segment Growth Example.

guarantee market survivability. The following (as illustrated in Figure 6-13) is a simplified case of a real life dominant firm. This example is also described in Chapter 8 in the context of natural and investment markets.

Assume that the industry revenue size is $100 million made up of two segments **A** and **B**. In other words, aggregate customer expenditure in this industry is $100 million. **A** is $30 million, growing at 30% Compound Growth Rate (CGR). **B** is $70 million, growing at 5% CGR. Assume a company called **SLOW** has revenues of $60 million with market share of 60%. Suppose that **SLOW** has two product lines; one in **A**, another in **B**, called **ALPHA** and **BETA**, respectively. Revenue from each is $12 million and $48 million respectively, totaling the $60 million. **SLOW's** revenue growth is 32% for **ALPHA** and 7% for **BETA**, both growing faster than the industry. At the end of one year though, the industry had grown by 12.5%, but **SLOW** had only grown by just over 11%.

SLOW lost market share even though product by product segment growth was faster than the industry. The cumulative impact of erosion of market share in this way is disastrous to the company. Companies that generalize markets and plan from historical projections will find themselves in crisis of this type.

7

Tools for Deployment of Competitive Dominance Theory

While we have described the theory of Competitive Dominance, any managerial principle, unless it is actionable, becomes just another item of pontification for executives and senior management. The ability to act on specific principles is fundamentally important. Our emphasis is consistently on the deployment of Competitive Dominance principles for more effective managerial practice. Chapter 6 describes the deployment of Competitive Dominance through the Malcolm Baldrige template. In this chapter, we describe the use of three tools that we have found particularly useful. They are:

Leadership diagnostic: This tool is an instrument to calibrate a person's leadership capabilities and track progress over time. The instrument is sufficiently granular and discriminatory to identify areas of strengths and weakness. We also describe how to maximize fit between a persons leadership profile to the stage of business life cycle.

Scenario Planning: We have discussed at length the dangers of fixed and rigid assumptions to forecast the future, which is inherently uncertain. Scenario planning is a powerful tool for analyzing environments and situations which have high degree of uncertainties. We discuss an approach to developing a range of plausible and meaningful futures that promotes organizational buy-in and helps improve an organization's deployment capacity to deal with uncertain futures.

Analytic Hierarchical Process (AHP): Business decisions are inherently multi-criteria and multidimensional. In addition the relative importance of each dimension and criteria are different. The increasing complexity and magnitude of the business variables increase the risk of executives making uninformed or anecdotal decisions. AHP provides a systematic and fact-based tool to organize and structure decisions. We describe the AHP process and how it can be used to solve complex business problems in a manner that promotes buy-in and implementation of the decision.

Figure 7-1 demonstrates the intensity of the relationship between these three tools and the ten principles of Competitive Dominance.

The tools we describe are useful in the application of the Competitive Dominance principles and the Baldrige principles as well. The intensity of their applicability is shown in Figure 7-2.

Competitive Dominance Principles			
10 Principles of Competitive Dominance	Leadership Diagnostic	Scenario Planning	Analytic Hierarchical Process
Strategic Leadership	■	■	■
Continuous Environmental Scanning	▲	■	▲
Modeling Trends and Dynamics		▲	■
Listening Posts	■	■	
Change/ Transformation	■	▲	●
Customer-Centric Culture	■	●	
Unified-Systemic Links	■	▲	■
Stakeholder Integration	●	▲	▲
Organizational Energetics	■	▲	
Opportunity Growth	▲	■	■

■=Applies strongly   ▲=Applies Moderately   ●=Applies

Figure 7-1 Relationship of Tools to Competitive Dominance Principles.

Competitive Dominance Principles			
Malcolm Baldrige Categories	Leadership Diagnostic	Scenario Planning	Analytic Hierarchical Process
Leadership	■	■	■
Information	●	■	■
Strategy	■	■	■
Human Resources	■		●
Process		▲	■
Results	▲	●	
Customer Satisfaction	▲		▲

■=Applies strongly   ▲=Applies Moderately   ●=Applies

Figure 7-2 Relationship of Tools to Malcolm Baldrige Categories.

STRATEGIC LEADERSHIP DIAGNOSTICS

One of the most important tools of Competitive Dominance is the strategic leadership diagnostics. The importance of strategic leadership has long been recognized, and it is only recently that the critical role of strategic leadership in quality management has been widely recognized. The Baldrige criteria starts with leadership. The Baldrige guidelines are perhaps one of the first tools that have established specific criteria to asses leadership characteristics. The application guidelines state that "a company's senior leaders must create clear and visible quality values and high expectations" (Malcolm 1994). Winners of the 1994 Baldrige Award have reinforced this requirement in press interviews (Baldrige 1994). The importance of leadership is also emphatically identified as important in Deming's 14 points, and ISO 9000 (Lamprecht 1992, Walton 1986). While all stress the importance of leadership in quality management very few analytical processes exist to evaluate and improve and individual's general leadership and specific strategic leadership capabilities. Most of what's written about leadership improvement has been developed from testimonials by successful leaders as role models, through pontification by quality experts, or because of academic research that is frequently too generic and unactionable for line executives or business leaders. The Baldrige guidelines are perhaps one of the first tools that have established specific criteria to asses leadership characteristics.

We postulate that there are six variables which taken together determine a person's specific leadership profile. The five variables are "character," "brains," "guts," "heart," "muscle," and "knowledge." This is summarized in Figure 7-3, Leadership Variables.

Each of these variables is described in further detail below.

> **Character:** It is that quality which makes leaders absolutely trustworthy even under the most trying circumstances. They can be counted on to put the needs of the others, of the organization, of their people, of the community above their own. Personal considerations will not affect the quality of their decisions (Donnithorne 1994). Character assumes that the leader has internalized and integrated the high moral standards in him- or herself in such a way that these characteristics have become part of them in an instinctive and natural manner.

> It is hard to imagine that people will want to follow someone whose character is questionable, it is also

Leadership Variables	
Character	Integrity, consistent high moral principles, internalized ethical behavior
Brains	Intelligence, capacity to think profoundly and deeply
Guts	Capacity to act decisively, sense of urgency, high energy level
Heart	Ability to get others to act, interpersonal skills
Muscle	Political skills, ability to mobilize bureaucracies and constituencies
Knowledge	Domain specific expertise. In business, e.g. technology, markets, industry. In politics, e.g. demographics, economics, etc.

Figure 7-3 Leadership Variables.

hard to imagine an organization entrusting responsibility on someone who will put his or her own personal needs above others. Ethically, bankrupt organizations frequently demand less, but any advantage they accrue cannot be sustained. Many leaders who fall short of the mark can also gather a following and achieve seemingly impressive results. In those situations, the results are also temporary. Moreover, those who have higher standards vote with their feet. They go elsewhere. Character goes beyond ethics and integrity. Character is an ingrained quality of outstanding leaders where ethics and high moral standards are instinctive.

Brains: This variable is used to determine an individual's mental capacity to conceptualize and deal with ambiguity. It is also used to asses a person's ability to think in a systemic way that links facts into a pattern of thought. It is a capability that permits one to think in a way that is insightful. For this intelligence to be useful, it needs to be complemented with finely honed political skills, with a high energy level and with an ability to motivate and inspire people to act. In other words, intelligence must be action oriented. A tolerance for ambiguity is also necessary to be able to deal with the uncertainties of the future, volatility of markets, realignments in industry structures and the risks of new strategic opportunities. Brains goes beyond the ability to remember facts or the ability to quickly learn something new. Brains is the ability to see the underlying structure and logic of seemingly disparate facts. Brains is also the ability to conceptualize innovatively. Finally, a key attribute of a person with a highly developed insightful intelligence is he or she knows what he or she doesn't know. Taken together, all these characteristics can give the leadership of an organization unique insights into the situation it has to deal with so that they can formulate strategies which are actionable and which will give them unique competitive advantages.

Guts: This variable is used to determine a person's capacity to act decisively and a person's ability to sustain a high energy level to get results. Does the individual have the courage, sense of urgency, goal orientation, and the capacity to act in the face of ambiguity and uncertainty? Leaders who exhibit risk aversion, who desire infinite information, who engage in enormous staff work before reaching a decision, and who cannot make decisions in a timely way are those who are unable to make gutsy decisions. Their capacity to act is inhibited. Competitive dominance requires that leaders have the physical and mental endurance, intellectual and moral courage to stay the course and to create and sustain momentum. Guts is also the capacity to know when one is wrong and to have the courage decisively rectify errors, anything less is cowardice. Cowardice in a leader is a most discernible attribute, specially to subordinates and peers. Competitive Dominance is impossible without guts.

Heart: Leaders care about their people. They have the ability to inspire and motivate to get people to act. Excellent interpersonal skills and sensitivity to the needs of individuals enable a leader to inspire and energize an organization in the arduous and demanding road toward Competitive Dominance. Leaders with unquestionable character and who are able to combine their decisiveness with meaningful emotional appeal and intellectual rigor are more effective in being able to revitalize moribund and lethargic organizations. Leaders also care about the organization of which they are a part. They are ambitious without being self-serving. Good leaders are also good followers. They recognize situations that require a leadership role, and they are able to differentiate them from those situations that require a team player role. They can do both. Every leader must be simultaneously a leader and a follower. A good leader can do both.

Muscle: This variable characterizes the political skills of a leader. No leader can be without some political skills. Political skills are at a premium in Competitive Dominance where transformation is required, where the vast resources of the organization need to be mobilized to bring new levels of performance, where novel and innovative strategies are being implemented and where new approaches to deployment are being implemented. The ability to manipulate bureaucracies, to make business operations function effectively, and to win over new supporting allies are all necessary elements in process management and reengineering.

This political capability must extend beyond the boundaries of the company. It must also include all stakeholders that contribute to the value of the final product or service that the customer sees. At the highest and most refined level, leaders exhibit the ability to influence the industry and the social environment to the greater benefit of all. In this capacity, they create the rising tide that raises all boats.

Knowledge: This variable is used to determine the level of expertise the person has in the specific business the company is in. For example, in a pharmaceutical firm, does the leader have sufficient knowledge about pharmacology and medicine to make strategic decisions? Or is the person a generalist who believes that managing high technology, hotels and baked bread are so similar that domain specific expertise is not required? In our opinion, it is hard to imagine that a leader without such expertise can be effective in achieving industry dominance. This industry-specific knowledge about its technology, about its markets, about the structure of participants, and about its economics, we call "domain specific" knowledge. This knowledge is most frequently acquired in the job. Domain expertise that is narrow is harmful because important knowledge escapes the attention of the leader. Worse yet, this type of leader thinks he or she knows something that, in fact, he or she does not. Leaders of this type don't know what they don't know. Knowing what one doesn't know is one of the reasons outsiders are frequently more effective than insiders. Outsiders are unencumbered with false assumptions; outsiders are able to think laterally and thereby develop new insights.

The above sketches in very broad strokes the variables that can be used to asses the leadership qualities of a person. We segment the levels of attainment broadly in each variable into four broad categories. From the most elementary level to the highest level they are, administrator, manager, leader, and transformational visionary. This is summarized in Figure 7-4, Leadership Variable Attainment Levels. Note that these are only labels for purposes of describing a state of action, not meant as disparaging. Each of these labels is examined in further detail below.

Administrator: An administrator has sufficient skills to implement strategies, initiatives, procedures, processes, and methods with competence. These people are also capable of implementing new directions and innovations, although departures from the well known require a learning phase and many do so with difficulty.

Manager: This individual has the capacity to manage, interpret, and implement a wide range of strategies, initiatives, processes, and procedures. Managers can balance a diversity of business, people issues, and company policies and practices with competence and reliability. They are frequently called upon to create new processes and procedures for implementation to meet specific goals.

Attainment Levels of Leadership Variables	
Administrator	Skilled in following rules
Manager	Competent to manage, interpret rules.
Leader	Capable of making new effective rules.
Transformational Leaders	Reconceptualizes the environment in which the rules apply. Creates new rules that redefines domains for rules.

Figure 7-4 Leadership Variable Attainment Levels.

Leader: This individual can create goals, directions, and initiatives for an organization to achieve. He or she is able to empower people and organizations with resources to attain organizational and business goals. Many others, with varying degree of capability, are also able to mobilize other constituencies to achieve their goals. Leaders are capable of creating and organizing followers for the achievement of goals.

Transformational Visionary: Sowell writes: "vision is a preanalytic cognitive act" (Sowell 1980). Transformational visionaries see what is needed instinctively, intuitively, not necessarily as a result of analysis or study. They set new courses of action to move an organization to a more desirable state. They are able to articulate the journey that is needed to achieve extraordinary results in a way that everyone understands their role and are motivated to participate. The boundaries of the community of shared vision do not end within the company itself, it is within and outside the company. The coverage of their political influence is broad indeed.

These concepts can now be brought together into a leadership calibration matrix. This is illustrated below in Figure 7-5, Leadership Calibration Diagnostic Matrix. Note that the calibration matrix has now decomposed each of the leadership variables into more detailed parameters that specifically characterize that variable. For example, Brains is composed of four parameters: conceptual ability, tolerance for ambiguity, ability to translate thoughts into action, and judgment. We recognize that something as complex as intelligence cannot be determined by only four parameters; but the objective is to find the most salient parameters that are useful. Readers can add those they consider useful.

Character Calibration Matrix

CHARACTER	Administrator		Manager	Leader	Transformational Visionary	
	1	2	4	6	8	10
Integrity	may compromise situationally		adheres to rules, needs support	high standards and sets example	role model, total integration with self	
Moral Standards	situational, may waver		adheres to rules, can sustain with help	high standards	role model, total integration with self	
Courage	deflected on resistance		sustained with help	Sustains others	undaunted, sustained by vision	

Figure 7-5 Calibration Matrix for Character.

The numbers in the row are used later in the description on how this matrix is used. In the same manner, calibration matrices can be developed for the other leadership variables. These are shown in Figures 7-6 through 7-9.

These calibration matrices help us to qualitatively identify milestones of attainment within each of the leadership variables. With these instruments, it is no longer sufficient to say, "This person is very competent in the area of technology, but somewhat weak with people." This is what we characterize as the "buy low, sell high" type comments. They sound good, but are not sound. We are not even sure they sound good. However, with these matrices, we are now able to express ourselves with a higher degree of precision and accuracy. We can say, "This manager knows enough technology to lead a project that crosses functional areas, but needs help in acquiring expertise in the industry and market dynamics of our business. This manager is capable of creating a healthy environment, and therefore can be trusted to lead a major function. We will continue to monitor the people aspect because this manager has a tendency to still make people mistakes, but learns."

This example illustrates how these calibration instruments are used. The usage of these matrices is very straightforward. For each variable, find the descriptor that is the closest fit with respect to the individual, then assign a numeric value that is consistent with that specific individual. The qualitative description is a guide to the numeric value. For example, we use the description in the previous paragraph. For the technology variable, say for Jane Doe, we had calibrated her as follows: Industry and Markets score of 1.8, Technology score of 3, Range of Knowledge score of 3. In the Knowledge area, Jane's average score is $(1.8+3+3)/3=2.6$. In the Heart variable, say that we had calibrated her at a 4 for Sensitivity, a 4 for her

Brains Calibration Matrix

BRAINS	Administrator 1 2	Manager 4	Leader 6	Transformational Visionary 8 10
Conceptual skills	concrete thinker, focus on facts	organizes facts into patterns	organizes patterns into opportunities	creates new patterns into visions
Tolerance for ambiguity	frustrated by it, seeks constant assurance	manages it, flexible and adaptive. Supportive to others.	takes advantage of it uses sanity checks high tolerance, sees clarify where others don't	high tolerance, sees clarity where others do not
Turn thoughts into action	must be given specific roadmap	can develop roadmap and drive action	creates innovative approaches and effective deployment	thinks abstractly and formulates actionable strategies
Judgment	personal experience and directions	considers immediate group and beyond	factors in strategies, and supporting knowledge	instinctive, intuitive and uncannily accurate

Figure 7-6 Calibration Matrix for Brains.

Heart Calibration Matrix

HEART	Administrator		Manager	Leader	Transformational Visionary	
	1	2	4	6	8	10
Sensitivity		does not perceive needs of others or unperceptive	aware but works at it, learns from mistakes	aware of individual/ group needs, knows how to optimize		very perceptive, creates enduring loyalty
Business/people balance		unable to balance, overlooks needs of people	balances both with effort, sometimes needs guidance	makes everyone count, knows when to optimize what		knows when balance is possible and impossible, can make tough calls
Motivate and inspire		conventional carrot and stick	creates healthy environment	creates trust and a sense of mission		creates a cause and a crusade

Figure 7-7 Calibration Matrix for Heart.

Guts Calibration Matrix

GUTS	Administrator		Manager		Leader		Transformational Visionary	
	1	2	4		6		8	10
Goal orientation and Command	imposed from above, and administers rules		high goals, needs support, effective within bounds		takes charge, sets challenging but meaningful goals		reconceptualizes goals, commands natural authority	
Ability to turn Plans into action	can implement, but must be given plans		can formulate and implement plans		can act decisively even under vague direction with meaningful plans		decisive when not apparent why to many. consistent with values and vision.	
Support creation	provided by others		provides and creates within bounds		forms coalitions of diverse nature		redefines common interest & forms new alliances	
Risk aversion	risk averse, needs protection and be prodding		prudent risk taker, acts with known clear alternatives		risk taker, knows when to shift, forms creative alternatives		perceives no risk, due to clear vision and ability to know when to act	

Figure 7-8 Calibration Matrix for Guts.

Knowledge Calibration Matrix

KNOWLEDGE	Administrator		Manager	Leader	Transformational Visionary	
	1	2	4	6	8	10
Industry & Markets		enough to do the job, needs support and tutoring	knowledgeable within the bounds of function, will take initiative to learn	knowledgeable of both including related functional areas, advice sought by many others		intuitive and accurate understanding of structure and forces, formulates effective/dominant strategies
Technology		understands to implement, needs guidance and leadership	knowledge to deploy & improve, skilled to improve other functions	master and competent in related synergistic technologies. Can drive new initiatives		systemic insight to leapfrog and create new businesses and markets, knows competitive impact
Range of Knowledge		within bounds of Functional area	cross functional	spans the whole value chain and the participants.		strategic, technical and business. Macro and detailed. Knows what he doesn't know.

Figure 7-9 Calibration Matrix for Knowledge.

ability to balance the needs of the business and the need of people, and that her ability to create a healthy environment is above average with a score of 5. Her average Heart score is (4+4+5)/3 = 4.33. In this manner, we can determine an average score for each variable, and we can calculate an average overall score. An individual has strengths in those areas that are above the overall average score, and has weakness in those areas that are below the overall average score. The instrument is also useful for executives to provide guidance to subordinates. The individual profile can be illustrated in graphical form using a "spider" diagram as shown in Figure 7-10.

In this example, the average score is 5.8, the individual has strengths in Brains, and Muscle, but has weakness in Heart during the initial base-line calibration. Note that however in this example, the individual has improved in the weak area and elevated the scoring to 6.1.

Note that one of the most important characteristics of leadership is a balanced set of skills. A magnificent vi-

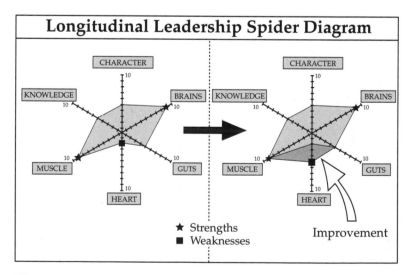

Figure 7-10 Example of a Personal Calibration.

sionary who does not have heart, will never win the loyalty of followers; lack of political skills will also most certainly make cause the most brilliant initiatives to be stillborn. In the same way, rock-solid ability to execute, but no ability to set a new strategic direction, will in all probability doom new, nascent, and fragile opportunities to redefine the playing field to achieve Competitive Dominance. This instrument is therefore, useful to not only calibrate achievement but to guide leaders in their development of new skills to achieve a balance.

By the way, not everybody needs a transformational leader because not all businesses nor all organizations need to be transformed to be effective. But to achieve Competitive Dominance, highly developed skills in all variables will most certainly give a firm a substantial advantage.

SCENARIO ANALYSIS

Generals would not go to war with only plans formulated from mathematical models and numerically intensive analyses. It is also inconceivable that generals would create battle plans predicated on a single set of assumptions, and not know under what circumstances they would launch a different initiative. Yet this is exactly what businessmen have been doing for a long time. No wonder that executives have become disillusioned with conventional forecasting and strategy formulation methodologies (Mintzberg 1994). Complex mathematical models and numerically intensive analysis have not spared business leaders from unpleasant surprises. Nor has it provided them with improved strategic acuity.

Scenario planning seeks to overcome these weakness by a stronger emphasis on the qualitative nature of the environmental forces acting on the firm and by considering a diverse set of potential futures based on different assumptions. In this way, scenario planning provides a number of substantially richer contexts where the impact of strategic decisions can be analyzed. Scenario planning is specially powerful when combined with other analytical techniques, such as those described in this chapter.

A **scenario** is a plausible future, it is not a forecast (Wack 1985 a, b). A scenario is a synthetic future that is developed based on the major uncertainties that face the firm. It is based on a set of logically consistent assumptions which when taken as a whole describe a plausible future. This is illustrated in Figure 7-11, Forces and Alternative Future Scenarios.

The analysis begins by identifying environmental forces relevant to the strategic issues at stake, their qualitative nature, their intensity, the conditions that can cause shifts to occur. Then, by analyzing potential ways in which the forces configure themselves and the trigger points which cause major environmental shifts, a set of plausible fu-

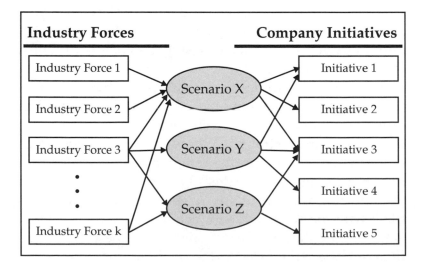

Figure 7-11 Forces and Alternative Future Scenarios.

tures can be postulated. Most useful scenarios deal with alternative futures, not necessarily variations of a single future. These different futures are qualitatively different, they are not just unidimensional variations of a single future. Most useful scenarios are surprising and insightful. They break well-established and implicit assumptions about the environment, the competition, the market and about the capabilities of the firm itself.

Armed with a number of rich and diverse scenarios, decision makers can study and discuss the consequences of strategic initiatives within a wide range of strategic contexts and alternative futures. In this way the robustness of strategic initiatives can be debated, tested, and analyzed. In this same way, decision makers can discuss and gain insight into the strategic options that competitors can exercise under different conditions. Out of all this, improved initiatives can emerge. The diversity and variety of scenarios where the strategic initiatives are analyzed and discussed also provides a learning tool for decision makers.

All executives have key concerns that keep them awake at night. These key concerns are most frequently symptoms of larger strategic issues facing the firm or the business unit. In general, these concerns can be obtained through interviews and discussions with the senior management who are experiencing anxieties about the competitiveness and the strategic performance of the firm. Transformational visionary leaders that we have met can articulate them with great eloquence and clarity. Disguised examples of strategic concerns from high technology firms are shown in Figure 7-12. Note that the examples show the concerns first, followed by the strategic issue. In our experience, we find that the concerns are in reality symptoms of the firm's strategic malaise. Most line executives are more familiar with the symptoms of strategic malaise rather than the strategic issues themselves. In

Concerns	• Dramatic deceleration of revenue growth • Uncompetitive product line in spite of heavy R&D • Loss of key personnel • Steady decline in customer satisfaction
Strategic Issue	• **Market shift: Change in Structure of Demand**

Concerns	• Key new technology deployed by competition first • Product costs and warranty costs above industry average • Recent new products missing the mark • Outflanked by competition in forming key alliances
Strategic Issue	• **Technology Shift: Emergence of Newer and More Effective Technology and New Industry Participants**

Figure 7-12 Examples of Strategic Concerns and Strategic Issues.

practice, the strategic issue is distilled much later from the analysis of the symptoms and during the scenario planning process. In rare instances where the executive in charge has a clear view of the strategic issues, we find that we have been talking with that rare breed—a leader who is also a superb strategist and a business statesman.

These concerns and strategic issues are the result of forces impinging on the firm. We define a force as a factor external to the firm which unless acted upon will cause the firm to lose effectiveness. Any changes in these forces will alter the *status quo* of the environment in which the firm operates. These changes are the root causes of executive's discomfort and concerns. These uncertainties are the result of dislocations and the effect of disequilibrium which astute executives either observe directly, sense instinctively, or discern intuitively.

Forces can be systematically analyzed to determine their nature, direction, and magnitude. Knowledge and insight into the key forces acting on the firm form the foundations for scenario analysis. Being able to describe the key concerns and being able to articulate the strategic issues is the first step in scenario analysis. With this as a starting point, by means of root-cause analysis, a set of forces that are driving the concerns can be identified. That is the starting point. But how can one determine that the set of forces that are going to be analyzed are complete, non-redundant, and useful? How can one know that the set of forces is non-trivial? Three tests apply. One, taken as a whole, do these forces reasonably explain the strategic dilemma that is facing the firm? Two, against the vision that the transformational leader has for the firm, will a rebalance of these forces improve the strategic posture of the firm? Three, as the scenario analysis proceeds, does the logic of the analysis remain internally consistent, and does it pass the reality check against the external environment? If the answers to these questions are affirmative, proceed to the next steps.

Having now a set of forces, it is important to have a clear and unambiguous description of each force, its qualitative nature, its magnitude, and its direction. It is not meaningful to describe a force in a single way. Intuitively, we know this is true. For example, there is no single way to describe the forces of a volatile and changing market. The impact of a market loss in a small metropolitan area is vastly different than the loss of a large geographic area. The competitive pressure of the emergence of a generic drug is substantially different than the sudden appearance of a new and effective drug which has been genetically engineered. Consequently, the description of the force must in some way uniquely capture its magnitude and its direction. To do this we have developed a process that we call **"stratification."** A force can be stratified into different states that describe different levels of intensity and direction. Stratification begins by isolating the critical determinants that establish the magnitude and direction of the force, then proceeds to develop different mixes of the determinants and their values. It is this mix and configuration of these determinants that help characterize the progression and direction of the force in question. To help clarify this, Figure 7-13 provides two examples of forces, their descriptions and distinct stratifications.

Knowledge of the key forces acting on the firm, analysis of their changes, and a descriptions of their stratifica-

---

Force: Increasing Complexity of Product Lines

Description	Products are getting more and more difficult to use. They have more functions and they are more complicated
Stratification	1. Product offers a discrete set of functions 2. The fixed set of functions can interact 3. The product is a system 4. The product is interoperable with other products

Force: Level and Mix of Market Demand Is Changing

Description	The level of demand is more uncertain and volatile. The distribution and mix of demand components is also changing
Stratification	1. Total demand is down and U.S./Europe is down. 2. Total demand is stable and U.S./Europe is down. 3. Total demand is up and U.S./Europe is down. 4. Total demand is up and U.S./Europe is up.

Figure 7-13 Examples of Forces, Description and Stratification.

tion form the foundations for the description of scenario futures. Recall that a scenario is a plausible future; it is not a forecast. A scenario is a synthetic future that is developed based on a specific configuration of forces, each of which is described by a specific stratification. Different scenario futures are created by distinct configurations of different forces at different levels of stratification. The scenario must be logically consistent so that when the scenario is taken as a whole, it does describe a plausible future. A scenario is like a story, it is thematically driven by a consistent logic.

It is useful to give each alternative scenario a descriptive name. It captures a mental image and it facilitates communications. For example, the Royal Dutch Shell scenario: "$15 a barrel" is fairly dramatic and descriptive (Wack 1985 a, b). The most useful and interesting scenarios are the following: (1) Those that deal with qualitatively different alternative futures rather than variations of a single future. For example, it avoids the high, medium, low, status quo, optimistic, pessimistic, etc. These are fundamentally "variations on a single theme." (2) Those that break stereotypes and are surprising. These are the scenario futures that "speak the unspeakable." They shatter implicit assumptions which are accepted as universal truths. They demolish myths, thereby causing the management team to think very deeply and profoundly about the strategic issues facing them. (3) Those that are developed in a participatory way with complete and committed engagement from the top management team that is responsible for guiding the firm and setting the strategy. A fatal flaw of scenario analysis is for the top management team to delegate the work to their staff. Unfortunately, this is the most frequent mistake that senior executives make. This is similar to doing your child's homework—a brilliant paper is turned in, but there is a complete lack of learning. As a savvy executive from a respected high technology firm said, "thinking cannot be outsourced." Figure 7-14 provides an example of scenario futures.

In this example, we have shown an example of different scenarios of a potential market for a specific industry. These scenarios are disguised from a high technology industry where new technology is emerging that has the potential to dramatically alter the economics of their products and services. In addition, legislators and agencies are drafting new laws that are changing the legal and regulatory frameworks. Scenario A describes a market where a new structure emerges and displaces the old as new classes of competitors appear on the scene. Scenario B describes the situation where the entry barriers and the exit barriers are still so high that new entrants do not appear, and the competitive intensity of existing

Scenarios on Models of Competition		
Scenario A	**Title**	**New Class of Competitors Emerge**
	Description	A new market structure emerges with completely new rules driven by new entrants deploying different technologies and radical channels of distribution.
Scenario B	**Title**	**Competitive Intensity**
	Description	Driven by high entry barriers and high exit barriers, competition among traditional competitors intensifies as they struggle for limited profits.

Figure 7-14 Example of Scenario Futures.

competitors intensifies. These are two different futures, not variations of a single future.

In the next example (illustrated by Figure 7-15), we have an industry that is also undergoing change also a result of new technology emerging on the scene. The indus-

Scenarios on Industry Futures		
Scenario A	**Title**	**Brave New World**
	Description	Shifts accumulate and accelerate sooner and more forcefully than anticipated. Customer values change, supplier products and services change. Instability in both the supply-side and demand-side leave the industry and the market in a turmoil.
Scenario B	**Title**	**World of Customer Leadership**
	Description	Leading customers—under the pressure of cost, competition, and time to market—form consortia to set standards for products, services and new business practices. Suppliers are driven by customers' leadership.
Scenario C	**Title**	**World of Supplier Leadership**
	Description	Visionary and aggressive vendors drive change by cooperating with leading customers. They introduce new technology, products, and services with convincing value propositions. Leadership is driven by visionary suppliers and customers.

Figure 7-15 Examples of Scenario Futures.

try is in a dramatic state of flux, and there is a high degree of uncertainty as to which technology and which standards are likely to prevail. How customers deploy the technology and what products they will buy are profoundly influenced by this state of flux. Scenario A says that turmoil will continue unabated as both suppliers and customers remain paralyzed by the uncertainty and stunned by the speed of change. We call this scenario the "Brave New World." Scenario B says that certain aggressive customers decide to take destiny into their hands and assert leadership. This has a catalytic effect and they are able to develop a following. Suppliers decide tacitly to follow their lead. We call this scenario the "World of Customer Leadership." Scenario C is the situation where the reverse is true. Suppliers decide to take destiny into their own hands and they are smart enough to do so with leading customers who have influence. This allows them to develop new, convincing, and compelling value propositions which facilitates their ability to lead. Appropriately, we call scenario C the "World of Supplier Leadership." Again these are different futures, not variations of the same future.

All these concepts can now be brought together to show how to construct a **scenario table**, This is illustrated in Figure 7-16, Alternative Scenario Futures. In this illustration we show only five forces. There is no limit to the forces that can be considered. We find that more than a dozen forces makes the analysis and discussions reach a very high level of complexity very rapidly. It is also our experience that when there are less than six forces, the scenarios lack sufficient texture and richness. We suggest that planers construct their own scenario tables with a number of forces that are consistent with the strategic issues at stake for them, and the tolerance for complexity of their own executive team. With a scenario table, we now have a meaningful structure with which to begin the

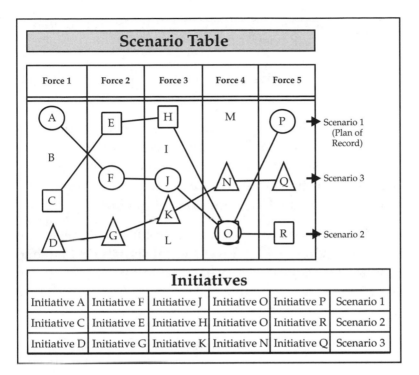

Figure 7-16 Alternative Scenario Futures.

strategy analysis. Figure 7-16 illustrates how a scenario future is constructed by selecting specific stratifications of forces into a logically consistent group that collectively describes a plausible future. It is useful if one of the alternative futures be the "Plan of Record Future." This future represents the official and documented plans of the firm. This is the future for which the firm has a committed investment stream.

On the bottom half of Figure 7-16 we see that for every scenario, there are potential company initiatives and the plan of record that have been identified against that scenario. This row of initiatives should accurately reflect the strategy of the firm. The objectives of the analysis of the company's strategy are to test its current and committed initiatives against the alternative futures. Top management should ask itself questions like:

1. Are my initiatives sufficient to cover the environmental forces at play?

If the answer to this question is negative, then there is a serious strategic gap. There are forces at play and there are no company initiatives to act either on the threat or the opportunity. In this case there are some fundamental flaws in the strategic assumptions of the firm.

2. Are my initiatives sufficiently robust in the event of shifts in environmental forces? What signals do I have to monitor to know that a shift is taking place, has taken place?

One must not only know that a shift is afoot, one must know when it has reached a level which warrants decisive action or a change in strategy. There is a shift in a force when there is a change in stratification. There are indicators that can be monitored that signal a transition in stratification. In Figure 7-13, in the Market Demand example, there is a transition from stratification 2 to 3 when the total demand increases. This indicator we call a "trigger point."

The inability of top management to focus attention on triggers is the fundamental cause of the "boiling frog syndrome" (Tichy, Devanna 1986. 44). The ability to monitor triggers is one of the most important and most neglected aspects of scenario analysis. Finding the right triggers is very hard work, requires deep analysis and substantial domain expertise. Triggers can be leading, coincident or lagging. Namely they signal that the transition will occur, is occurring, or has occurred. Leading triggers are the most useful because they allow executives to take proactive action. Triggers can be readily, although not easily, isolated by analyzing the determinants of a force and identifying the measurable condition which will cause a force to move from one level of stratification to another.

3. What are my leading competitors doing against these forces? What do their behavior indicate about their assumptions of current stratifications? What forces are they are leveraging to their competitive advantage?

Analyzing the answers to these questions can shed significant insight into competitors' strategic assumptions. With this kind of insight it possible to predict their behavior and to significantly improve a firm's ability to design strategic countermeasures. The executive management should ask itself the question: Given this array of forces, what unforeseen and new competitors can now emerge? Most firms suffer the most serious competitive setbacks from firms that have escaped their radar screen. The incumbent gave them the time and the freedom to establish themselves.

4. Considering the alternative scenario futures and the triggers that have been identified, are the assumptions in the "plan of record" appropriate?

The test here is whether the initial strategic assumptions embodied in the "plan of record" remain valid when one considers the potential scenario futures, the volatility and stability of the trigger points.

5. Does my plan of record reflect a good strategy?

A good strategy is one that is competitive, addresses the major forces, is sufficiently robust to deal with environmental change. A good strategy is also one which is not so rigid and inflexible that it cannot accommodate changes in the environment. They are effective within an envelope or band of environmental change. The width of the band or envelope of uncertainty which the executive team can tolerate is a good indicator of their attitudes toward risk. A strategy has to be to some degree consistent with the executive teams ability to undertake risk. Finally, and most importantly, a good strategy is one that is doable, affordable, and will make the firm better off.

6. What contingency plans can I formulate? What forces and specifically what trigger points will put them into effect?

One of the key features of scenario analysis is that it provides an effective analytic construct to explicitly identify contingency initiatives would certain conditions occur. The conditions that can be monitored are trigger points, competitive actions within the context of forces and trigger conditions, etc.

Scenario Analysis is a powerful instrument to analyze strategy that are anchored in current decisions but must produce results in the future. It is an effective mechanism to analyze strategic approaches, to asses whether the conditions for successful deployment exists, and to intelligently test whether the expected results will be there in the future.

THE ANALYTIC HIERARCHY PROCESS (AHP)

Most important decisions in the business world are complex because they are multi-criterion, multi-organizational, multi-disciplinary, multi-period, and they require the judgment and expertise from many experts. AHP is an approach that facilitates the process of making such decisions with improved quality and buy-in. It does so through a rigorous and disciplined process that decomposes complex decisions in a structured and hierarchical manner (Saaty 1990; Saaty, Kearns 1985). The decision in question is parsed and deconstructed into its elemental units, so that the elemental units reflect the many criteria and factors that must be considered. AHP permits the scaling of each elemental unit at each level of the hierarchy against another elemental unit at the next highest level in the hierarchy. From this, a matrix of pairwise comparisons of the elemental units can be constructed where the entries indicate the strength with which one element dominates another with respect to a given criterion. This scaling information is translated into a largest eigenvalue problem which results in a normalized and unique vector of weights for each level of the hierarchy (always with respect to the criterion in the next level). This, in turn, via a series of multiplications, results in a single composite vector of weights for the entire hierarchy. This vector measures the relative priority of all elemental entities at the lowest level that enables the accomplishment of the highest objective of the hierarchy. These relative-priority weights can provide insight into the relative importance and the leverage of each elemental unit in the final decision. In this manner AHP provides to the decision maker and the participants the insight and guidelines for the analysis of the factors and criteria that go into the final decision.

The hierarchy is constructed by the group which needs to make the decision and which needs to implement and execute the decision. The group also determines the relative weights of all the elemental units in the hierarchy relative to each other at the same level and relative to the higher elemental units. This is done by a combination of group discussions and balloting. Therefore, this collaborative group process gives AHP some salient advantages:

1. It is a participatory process that increases management buy-in.

2. The process produces a model whose results are repeatable and self-documenting, so that explanation to executive management is easier than conventional approaches.

3. The model can be continuously refined, improved, and expanded so that more meaningful results can be derived constantly.

4. The model combines the cumulative expertise, experience, and judgment of the whole group while simultaneously allowing for hard facts to be used in the model when necessary.

5. There is a comprehensive and deep body of research and practice that shows the efficacy of the methodology.

Figure 7-17, by way of an example, illustrates how a top level goal can be decomposed into a hierarchical

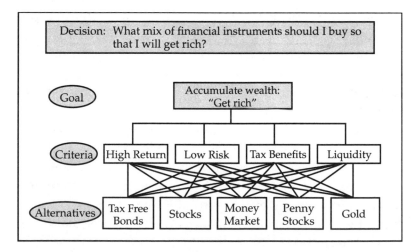

Figure 7-17 Decision Hierarchy for Accumulating Wealth.

structure that identifies all the major factors that go into the final decision. The goal is to accumulate wealth, this is shown at the top of the hierarchy. At the bottom of the hierarchy are shown the alternatives by which this objective can be achieved. One can buy tax-free bonds, stocks of companies, money market instruments, speculative penny stocks, and gold. But one does not want to get rich arbitrarily, one needs to consider the level of return, low risk, tax benefits, and liquidity. These elements then become the criteria at the second tier of the hierarchy.

Having a hierarchy of the decision, pairwise comparisons using the 9-point scale[1] used in the AHP methodology can be executed. The pairwise comparison of the criteria are shown in Figure 7-18. First, the table shows

Pairwise Comparison of Decision Criteria
Portfolio Investment Example

	Return	Low Risk	Tax Benefits	Liquidity	Weights
Return	1	1/5	3	3	0.21
Low Risk	5	1	5	4	0.59
Tax Benefits	1/3	1/5	1	1	0.09
Liquidity	1/3	1/4	1	1	0.1

Figure 7-18 Portfolio Investment Example.

[1] 1=equal importance
3=moderately more important
5=strongly more important or essential
7=very strong importance
9=extremely important
2,4,6,8 are intermediate values
See Saaty 1990.

that the diagonals are 1, in other words they weigh equally, which is obvious. For example, consider the third row, Tax benefits. The importance of Tax Benefits relative to tax benefits is identical, or equal. Consider the second row, Low Risk. The person who is doing the pair-wise comparison, is risk averse and would rather mini-mize risk than gamble on a higher return. For that individual, Risk's weight is stronger than return, and therefore a 5. If we turn the relative weighing around, in other words, return's weight relative to Risk, we get 1/5. Clearly if A=5B, then B=1/5A. By solving the eigenvalue problem, we get the weights that are shown on the right hand column. The column adds to 1.0. What this sug-gests is that 21% of the portfolio ought to have instru-ments that provide return, 59% low risk instruments and roughly 1% each in instruments, that provide tax bene-fits and liquidity.

Figure 7-19 illustrates a substantially more complicated example from a high technology company. It shows how to choose from a series of alternatives to achieve an objec-tive that contain factors that have a high degree of subjec-tivity. This example shows what criteria are used to judge the achievement of the goal. Because this example is more complex than the first one, it shows what factors deter-mine the degree to which the criteria are met or not. But note that the process is similar in each case, the goal is successively decomposed hierarchically into the elemen-tal units which in total address all key issues of the com-plex decision.

In this example, the company has a very large number of potential strategic initiatives, which are illustrated at the bottom of the hierarchy. The fundamental question that this company was trying to understand was how to rank the initiatives from most important to least impor-tant. First, the goal was defined as "Company Leader-ship." This was a goal that was uniformly agreed to by the

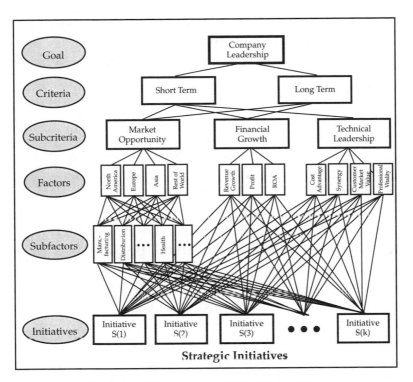

Figure 7-19 Decision Hierarchy for Prioritizing Company Initiatives.

vast majority of management and by the rank and file. After many work sessions and surveys within the company
itself, it was determined that the second level of the hierarchy was the time frame in which this leadership goal
was to be attained. The decision was made that the time
frame would be decomposed into "near term" comprising the next three years, and "long term" comprising the
following three years, for a total time horizon of six years.
The next level of the hierarchy was determined by the senior executives of the company who agreed that three major criteria would be used to judge the achievement of
leadership within each of the two prescribed time frames.
The three major criteria were: market opportunity, finan-

cial results, and technical leadership. Market opportunity was further decomposed into the major geographic segments as shown, and then further decomposed into major industry sectors which were judged to be important to gain market share. Financial results were decomposed into revenue, growth, profitability, and return on assets. Technical leadership was decomposed into cost advantage, degree of synergy with other important technologies, customer and market perception, value to the customers, and professional vitality.

Basically these elements permit the decision to be parsed in the following way. For example, does a technical initiative enable the reduction of product cost? Does the new technology synergize in a positive mutually enforcing manner with the other existing technologies? Will customers value this new technology, will it be visible to him or her, and will the benefits be apparent to him or her? The element of professional vitality was considered important because engineers and scientists do not want to work in a technology which is not at the cutting edge, and also because it is difficult to attract the best talent with projects that are focused on tired and antiquated technology. At the bottom of the hierarchy are the strategic initiatives, which are identified as $S(1),...,S(k)$. In actuality, each of the strategic initiatives was decomposed further into subinitiatives. Each strategic initiative $S(k)$, was decomposed into $S(k)1$, $S(k)2$, $S(k)3$, etc. This was very important for the buy-in into the process by the rank and file of the company. By very finely grained aggregation of initiatives, the overwhelming majority of the people could identify their specific work in the decision making process.

Figure 7-20 illustrates the overall work flow that was used for this process. The following narrative is keyed to the numbers in Figure 7-20. We have chosen a narrative style as if we are giving instructions.

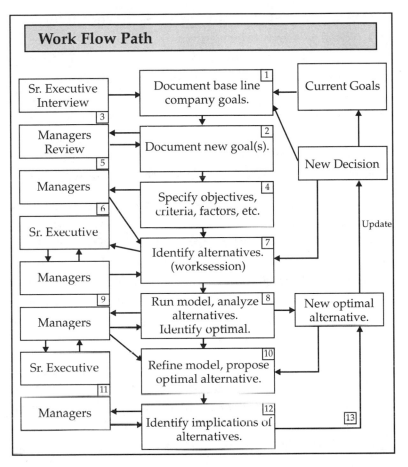

Figure 7-20 Analytic Hierarchy Process Work Flow.

1. Document the current company goals. Four primary sources of input should be used: (a) documentation that exists, (b) interviews with the senior executive management, (c) interviews with the middle managers and first line management team, and (d) the rank and file. For smaller companies this can be done readily. For larger companies, the senior executive management interviews are mandatory, interviews with lower levels of management and with the rank and file can be selective.

2.   As a result of the interview, document the desired and new goals that are required. Additional discussions with selected executives and managers and additional group discussions may be required to distill a new and modified perspective. The results from steps (1) and (2) are documented. This is an important step because it specifies the superordinate goal, forms the boundary conditions for the hierarchy and serves to establish the broadest base of consensus among the decision makers.

3.   Review and discuss with the executive team, key members of the management team, and representative selected rank and file the results of step (2). This should de done in small groups so that the ideas are clearly communicated and all participants know and feel that their input has been fully considered. One-way lecture-type meetings do not work well, these meetings should be interactive with ample opportunity for all to raise questions.

4.   Develop a first pass at the potential general structure of decision hierarchy and potential objectives, factors, and criteria to achieve new strategic goals. Frequently, this step can be combined with step (3). When the complexity of the hierarchy is high and the scope of the goal is broad, a separate step may be required to make the whole process more digestible for the organization. The objective of this step is not to arrive at a final hierarchy but to introduce the thought process of stepwise decomposition of goals and objectives. It will also allow the group to express their specific personal priorities and map them into the appropriate level of the hierarchy. The objective is still to maximize buy-in.

5.   The senior executive who owns the goal forms a team from the executive team and selected managers. The senior executive should brief the team, telling them that they are there not to represent their organizations, but to represent the whole company and bring their specific functional knowledge and general management experience. At this point an intensive work session is required with this new team. The senior executive should lead the debate on the initial proposal and output of step (4). The outcome of this meeting is a consensus on the structure of the decision hierarchy and specify the objectives, criteria, factors, and subfactors. We have found that throughout this work session, it is useful to form workgroups to identify the elements at a specific level of the hierarchy and to form different groups to identify elements at a different level of the hierarchy. This allows the broadest possible participation, and widest possible range of input from the group.

6.　　The senior executive directs general managers to identify the alternative choices which will be at the bottom of the decision hierarchy. The alternatives should be narrowed down and held to a manageable number. If the alternatives are a very large number, they should be grouped into classes of alternatives, as we discussed earlier.

7.　　During the wrap-up of this intensive work session, the leader and the team agree on a decision hierarchy and the final pass at the objectives, criteria, factors, and subfactors and the alternatives, which are at the bottom of the hierarchy. With these fundamental underpinnings in place, the group is ready for the weighing process of the elements in the hierarchy. There are fundamentally two ways to do the weighing process. One is by balloting, the other is by group discussion. Both processes involve basically the same people, but the balloting process is faster than having group discussions. The key advantage of discussions comes from the inherent nature of discussions, namely everybody gets to hear the opinions of others. There is a degree of bonding that takes place during discussions that has distinct advantages. In the discussion that follows, we will describe a balloting process. The senior executive in charge of the meeting should at this point describe the balloting process.

8.   Ballots are sent out and the participants vote for the overall criteria importance, and then for all elemental units. Figure 7-21 shows a sample ballot and instructions for voting. A model is built using the decision hierarchy and the balloting from the participants of the team. The model is run and analyzed. Preliminary findings and observations are summarized for discussion.

9.   A summary report is developed and submitted to the senior executive for discussion. The initial findings and preliminary conclusions are discussed. This discussion is focused on answering questions, clarifying points, and discussing recommendations for further analysis. Discussions with the general management team are held off-line as appropriate.

10.   Based on the discussions of step (9), additional analysis is performed on the model. In addition to findings and conclusions, alternative "what-if" cases are run on as many cases as necessary to determine the sensitivity of the analysis and conclusions. These alternative cases are run by altering the relative weights of the elements of the hierarchy to determine at what point does the model show sharp and different conclusions. In our experience it is very useful to perform these alternatives to anticipate dissension from potential antagonists in the team. Showing the effect of major variations elemental weighing and discussing the implications will frequently convince a potential dissident.

To achieve the goal of **FINANCIAL RESULTS,** compare the relative importance of **Revenue Growth, Profit, and Return on Assets (ROA)**

Circle one number per comparison below using the scale:
1=equal   3=moderate   5=strong   7=very strong   9=extreme

	9	8	7	6	5	4	3	2	1	2	3	4	5	6	7	8	9	
Revenue	9	8	7	6	5	4	3	2	1	2	3	4	5	6	7	8	9	**Profit**
Revenue	9	8	7	6	5	4	3	2	1	2	3	4	5	6	7	8	9	**ROA**
Profit	9	8	7	6	5	4	3	2	1	2	3	4	5	6	7	8	9	**ROA**

Balloting Instructions

1. Select a rating for each pair-wise comparison.
2. Circle the scale number 1-9 depending on which element weighs the most. For example, if **revenue growth** is extremely more important than **profit** to financial results, then circle 9 on the left. For example, if **ROA** is moderately more important than **revenue growth** for financial results, then circle 3 on the right.

Note 1. If you cannot make a decision, leave it blank. A blank is better than to answer without accuracy or knowledge.
Note 2. Choose the right or left, in the way which is most natural for you in the decision. For example, if it is more natural for you to compare revenue against profit, rather than profit against revenue, do so.

Figure 7-21 Sample Ballot for Weighing Elements in a Decision Hierarchy.

11. Plan and prepare for another intensive work session with members of the team. Develop an agenda for the meeting. Focus the agenda of the meeting on the following (i) the findings and conclusions of the analysis of the model (ii) discuss the implications of the decisions, and (iii) identify the actions required as a result of the identified implications.

12. Hold the intensive work session with the senior executive and the team to execute the agenda described in (11). As in step (5), it useful to break the team into work groups to analyze the implications and to formulate the action plans.

13. At this point the first pass at the decision has been made. Document the decision hierarchy and the major conclusions with especial emphasis on the implications and action plan identified in step (12). Reiterate and update periodically the model with new information and reexamine whether the original decision is still valid.

The fundamental value of the AHP process is that it allows a disciplined and systematic parsing of business objectives into its elemental components. Furthermore, it permits this decomposition to be carried out in a hierarchical manner. The relative importance of each of the elemental units can be calculated so that the contribution of each element to the overall objective is appropriately weighed. The other key benefit of the process is that this process must be carried out with a team whose composition is made up of those who have a stake in the decision and who must ultimately implement the decision. As such, it promotes teamwork and buy-in, all of which facilitate the ultimate implementation of the decision. A good decision that can be implemented with speed by people who believe in it are the hallmarks of competitive and successful firms. It is necessary for Competitive Dominance. AHP is an effective tool to achieve those characteristics.

8

Methodologies for Deployment of Competitive Dominance Theory

It is our conviction that managerial principles must be actionable for them to rise beyond executive exhortation or theory. We believe that good tools and effective processes combined can render managerial principles actionable. In the preceding chapter, we discuss three tools which can be used in the application of Competitive Dominance theory. In this chapter we will discuss three processes that can make a difference in business effectiveness and managerial practice. Reengineering and business transformation is a hot subject in business. Here we demonstrate how to engineer three pivotal business processes that can make a difference. They are:

Customer Satisfaction Management: The fundamental weaknesses of the vast majority of customer satisfaction management processes are that they are "after-the-fact" processes, and they are targeted at only the symptoms of dissatisfaction. We show that it is necessary to drive this process across the life-cycle of the product or service. We discuss in this chapter how to do that.

Natural and Investment Markets: Most businesses suffer from the tyranny of "served markets." Their attention is overwhelmingly dominated in the protection of the existing base. This precludes them from addressing new opportunities which can launch their business into a new growth trajectory. The process of Natural and Investment Markets describes how to identify lucrative unaddressed opportunities in a systematic way.

Organizational Energetics: After years of line management and consulting, we have observed that high performance groups have high energy and enthusiasm that is sustained through the trials and tribulations of difficult and challenging projects. The pivotal issue is the degree of external focus that is maintained throughout. We discuss how this can be achieved and, more significantly, we discuss the pitfalls and blunders to avoid.

There is no magic in these processes themselves; the magic is in the managerial will and tenacity to make them work. Figure 8-1 describes the intensity of the relationship between these methodologies and the ten principles of Competitive Dominance.

The Competitive Dominance methodologies described have a strong relationship to the Malcolm Baldrige principles as illustrated in Figure 8-2.

CUSTOMER SATISFACTION

Customer satisfaction is at the center of strategy and quality. In the final analysis it is customers who judge quality,

Competitive Dominance Principles

10 Principles of Competitive Dominance	Customer Satisfaction	Natural and Investment Markets	Organizational Energetics
Strategic Leadership	▲	■	▲
Continuous Environmental Scanning	▲	■	●
Modeling Trends and Dynamics	▲	●	
Listening Posts	■	■	■
Change/Transformation	■	●	■
Customer Centric Culture	■	■	■
Unified Systemic Links		●	■
Stakeholder Integration	●	■	▲
Organizational Energetics	■		■
Opportunity Growth	■	■	

■=Applies strongly   ▲=Applies Moderately   ●=Applies

Figure 8-1 Relationship of Methodologies to Competitive Dominance Principles.

it is customers—current and new ones—that ultimately determine the effectiveness of a company's strategy, and new customers drive a company's growth. Customer sat-

Competitive Dominance Principles

Malcolm Baldrige Categories	Customer Satisfaction	Natural and Investment Markets	Organizational Energetics
Leadership	■	■	■
Information	■	■	●
Strategy	▲	■	▲
Human Resources	●		■
Process	■	▲	●
Results	■	■	■
Customer Satisfaction	■	■	▲

■=Applies strongly   ▲=Applies Moderately   ●=Applies

Figure 8-2 Relationship of Methodologies to Malcolm Baldrige Categories.

isfaction is a powerful instrument by which a company can differentiate itself from the competition. It is therefore a strategic concept. Customer satisfaction is not a one-time thing, it demands constant management attention, and it requires disciplined and rigorous planning.

Customer satisfaction goes well beyond error detection, error reduction, better warranties, reducing complaints, or improving after-sales service. Customer satisfaction demands a much broader perspective. It demands a perspective that considers the entire product life-cycle. Therefore, customer satisfaction begins at the market planning stages of the product life-cycle, it is followed by the product development stage, continues to product-launching into the market, and then proceeds to the service and support stage.

Conventional thinking considers customer satisfaction the final stage of the product life cycle. However, a strategic and a quality intensive approach requires that the process must continue through a closed-loop mechanism that seeks to continuously improve the product/service and to continuously enhance organizational processes to intensify customer satisfaction. Consequently, we reject the notion that customer satisfaction is a process that a firm undertakes at only one phase in the product life-cycle. Customer satisfaction must be part of a closed-loop strategic process whose goal is to ensure market success, continuous learning and improvement. This is illustrated in Figure 8-3, Customer Satisfaction Process.

The customer satisfaction process shown in Figure 8-3 is divided into three distinct stages that mirror the life-cy-

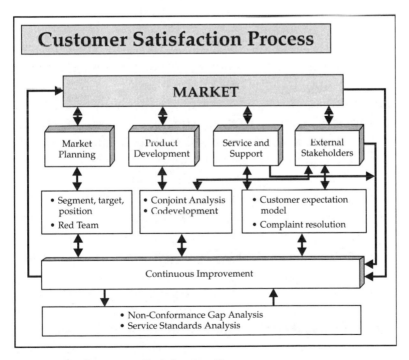

Figure 8-3 Customer Satisfaction Process.

cle of a product or service. The first stage we call the Market Planning Stage, the second we call the Product Development Stage, and the third we call Customer Service and Support Stage. There is a need for a key additional process, including external stakeholders called the Continuous Improvement Process. For each stage that we have identified, there are tools that are effective in elevating customer satisfaction and improving competitive advantage. To simplify the discussion that follows, we will use the term "offering" to denote a product or service or a combination of both. For example, a car is a product offering, a packaged five-year warranty is a service offering and a combination is simply called an offering.

Customer satisfaction must begin at the market planning stages with the analysis of the market segments that the company is electing to serve. With a clear view of that segment's needs and wants, a company is able to develop an offering to squarely address the specific needs of customers in those segments. Clearly, the more insightful the understanding of customer behavior in those segments, the better the chances are for the company to achieve customer satisfaction. The wrong product will not achieve customer satisfaction no matter how good you try to make after sales service. Having selected a segment to serve, the company must now develop an offering. This is the fundamental function of the Product Development stage. The key functions of the Customer Service and Support stage are to provide key after-sales functions: provide customer assistance in the use of a product or service, rectify defects caused by defective products or services, and undertake actions to ensure satisfactory performance of the product or service. For example, in the purchase of a home computer, customer service and support via an 800 telephone number provides assistance to those customers who may have difficulty installing an intricate and complex software application. An automobile dealer will perform product maintenance to ensure a car will run smoothly and will perform warranty work when there are defective parts.

The most important process is the Continuous Improvement Process. The existence of this process differentiates a good company from an exceptional company. This process is put in place to make sure that no error occurs more than once, that customer satisfaction can be improved continuously, and that the company is able to anticipate future drivers of customer satisfaction.

The following table, Figure 8-4, identifies the key tools that we have found useful across the life-cycle of the product or service and that are useful for the Continuous Improvement Process. Many of these tools are well known; however, it is their systematic use in an organized way to satisfy customers and to create a competitive advantage that is important.

Segmenting, Targeting and Positioning: The principal tools during the market planning stage are segmenting, targeting and positioning (Kotler 1191). This is the so-called the STP process, named after the first letters of the three functions in market planning. This is classical market analysis so we will be brief. After a firm has identified a market opportunity that it wants to go after, it must decompose that market into **segments**. This is necessary because no market opportunity of any significance is homogeneous. There are subsets of customers that react in a similar manner to a given offering. An element within these groupings of customers is called a segment. Once a useful segmentation has been developed, a company must decide which segments it wants to serve. This process is called **targeting**. A good strategy is to target those segments where the company has advantages that the competition either does not have or has trouble matching. This

Life-Cycle Stage	Tool/Process	Use and Function
Market Planning	• Segment, Target, Position	• Identify customer set to serve, their needs and the basis for competition
	• Red Team	• Identify weakness and develop competitive countermeasures
Product Development	• Conjoint Analysis	• Determine product requirements
	• Codevelopment	• Joint development with stakeholders
Service and Support	• Customer Expectation Model	• Align internal resources to exceed customer expectations
	• Complaint Resolution	• Ensure errors occur only once
Continuous Improvement	• Quality Service Gap Analysis Model	• Diagnostics for process engineering errors
	• Service Standards Analysis	• Improve standards

Figure 8-4 Key Tools for Customer Satisfaction.

is called a differential advantage. It is useful to think of advantages in customer terms, namely: "What are the distinctive benefits that my firm is uniquely able to provide in a way that no one else can?" In the next discussion on Natural and Investment markets we describe a technique to find segments where a firm has known and proven advantages. How a company wants to differentiate its offering and make it distinctive from the competitors' offerings is called **positioning**. Positioning articulates the place an offering occupies in a market segment. The most effective positioning strategies are those that draw a very sharp and convincing contrast of an offering from the competition. These unique benefits of the offering provide the compelling reasons for a consumer to select an offering. For example, "Bufferin, the pain-killer that does not upset your stomach" is a simple compelling and memorable positioning statement. Positioning is therefore, fundamentally, an issue of capturing shelf-space in the mind of decision makers (Mutert 1993). A few simple illustrations will make all these ideas clear. The consumers who want to drink beverages is a very large market. This market can be segmented, for example into those who want to drink only diet drinks, those who drink to show their socio-economic status, those who will only drink alcoholic beverages, etc. Perrier has elected to serve the upscale natural water drinker and has positioned its offering as the beverage that shows the consumer is affluent and sophisticated.

Red Team: During the market planning and product planning stages a real danger is for a company to believe its own propaganda and develop blind-spots which can cause irreversible damage later. To avoid this, the Red Team approach is useful. The Red Team concept comes from the military. In the U.S. military, there are squadrons of American pilots that fly planes with enemy markings and use enemy tactics to train pilots in aerial combat. In the business world, a Red Team is composed of experts from within the firm who assume the role of the competition. They address all functional areas, research and development, marketing, service and support, etc. Their mission is to critique the offering and to find all the detractors to competitive effectiveness and customer satisfaction. In this way the company is able to identify shortfalls in their offering, weakness in their support and services processes, flaws in their business processes, etc. Armed with this knowledge the company is now able to predict competitive moves and their likely reaction on the part of customers, and develop countermeasures to blunt the impact of competitive moves (Bauer, Collar, Tang 1992).

Conjoint Analysis: The most effective way to achieve customer satisfaction and to win over new customers from competitors is to have an accurate and precise view of customers' needs and wants, currently and in the future. The firm can then embody in their offering the attributes that customers will find irresistible. Conjoint analysis is a proven and effective technique for gaining insight into customers' desired product features in an offering. Conjoint is a statistical technique that improves decision making about creating an offering (Greene, Nkonge 1989; Greene, Rao 1971). It does so by determining prospective customers' perceptions on the importance of the offering's attributes during their purchase decisions. This is accomplished through customer surveys that measure consumers' trade-offs among the offerings attributes. Although to the casual observer it may seem like that a few dominant attributes determine a purchase decision, in fact, consumers make, consciously or subconsciously, many trade-offs about attributes. We are all familiar with the trade-off decisions in the purchase of a house where the attributes of school district, architectural style and distance from in-laws come into play. A family with school age children may decide that the most important attribute is the fact that the school consistently sends its top students to the Ivy League colleges and judge distance from in-laws as relatively unimportant. This example illustrates that consumers in their trade-off decision also consider the **level** of the attributes. We are all familiar with the price versus quality trade-off decision. But how much quality at what price? This is the attribute level decision that consumers make constantly. For example, consider a product whose quality is measured in mean-time-to-failure (MTF), the average elapsed time between product failure. Consumers may judge that for a ten times improvement in MTF, an increase of two times in price is justified. But for an increase of four times the base price, the product is expected to have 100 times improvement in MTF. Conjoint analysis seeks not only to determine the trade-offs that consumers make, but also seeks to determine the value they assign to various levels of the attributes. In economics, this is called the consumers' utility function. Armed with a set of attributes that describe the offering and also with a description of the levels for each of the attributes, the analyst can create various combinations of various attributes at different levels to create different potential offerings to determine which combination produces the most irresistible offering. The analyst can do this by applying the power of conjoint statistics to find the optimal offering that will attract the maximum number of future potential customers.

Codevelopment: There are situations where an offering is so complex and innovative that even market research cannot fully predict *a priori* potential customers' reactions. This is specially true for high technology products which are "new to the world." In these situations, it is very effective to invite key "stakeholders" to participate in the development process. Stakeholders are participants who are at risk if the offering fails. In other words, they have a stake in the success of the offering. Stakeholders include the major functions from the firm that is part of this offering.

More importantly, they also include external participants, such as business allies, marketing channels, service groups, etc. Broad participation from stakeholders
in the value-chain ensures that there are no missing
links in the participation and therefore no blind-spots.
This process we call **codevelopment.** This process was
very successfully deployed in the development of the
IBM AS/400 minicomputer family. During the development of this product, dozens of stakeholders from
around the world participated in the planning, refined
the priorities of functions, and even helped develop a
pricing strategy. Literally hundreds of business partners tested their own applications and the new minicomputer systems before they were shipped or even
announced (Bauer, Collar, Tang 1992).

**Customer Expectation Model and Customer Com-
plaint Resolution Model:** For the Service and Support
Stages there are two key tools, Customer Expectation
Model and Complaint Resolution Model. These two
models interact synergistically. The objectives are to
fully understand the expectations of the market segment that is being served and to be prepared to effectively mobilize the resources of the company to ensure
that customers' expectations are met, specially when
complaints occur. Too often, companies analyze customer expectations in a piecemeal fashion. They focus
only on a few elements, such as after sales service, on-
time delivery, accurate billing, etc. All of these are individually important, but insufficient. Many companies are unable to visualize the total picture and as a
result they are unable to mobilize the right organizations to make their offerings a success or to improve
customer satisfaction. Figure 8-5 illustrates the customer expectation model that is used with the IBM
AS/400 (Bauer 1991, Boyette 1993). There are six areas

of expectations that customers judged to be most important. The specifics identified in Figure 8-5 also reflect customers' prioritization. The expectation categories should be determined during the stages of Market Planning and Product Development. As we discussed before, this is most effective when done jointly with customers and stakeholders. The company must group these expectation areas into logical categories that tie back to internal company structures and business processes. It must then design a management system to drive customer satisfaction from this model. This management system forms the foundation the Complaint Resolution Model.

A key and vital element of this management system is the assignment of an executive "owner" who is responsible and accountable for each expectation area, and who is expected to drive internal improvement and customer satisfaction actions in a way that addresses customers' needs. The owner is responsible for orchestrating any and all cross-functional processes within the company in a way that it is completely transparent to the customers. Periodic reviews must be held so that all the cross-functional elements can come together in one meeting so the executive team of the company is capable of addressing the problems and opportunities from an external customer perspective, not an internal functional piecemeal fashion. At these meetings, the priorities of the customers must be used to determine the decision making priorities. All internal operations must be aligned to external customer expectations and their priorities. These models are very useful for detecting inefficiencies and gaps in business processes. Customer expectation models are, therefore, very useful for determining what business processes need to be reconceptualized and reengineered, or what new processes are required that will improve customer

Customer Expectation Model—Customer View

Expectation Area	Focus	Specifics by Priority
Administration	• Administrative systems that customers interact with • Terms and conditions	• Ease of doing business • Billing accuracy • Terms and Conditions • ......
Sales	• Front line sales people and systems engineers	• Product Knowledge • Account continuity Responsiveness • ......
Technical Solutions	• Product Performance	• Product Quality • Function • Performance • ......
Delivery	• Order, delivery and installation of products in customer's location	• Order/delivery cycle time • Defect free installation • Order compliance • ......
Service	• After sale service and support	• Service response • Fix effectiveness • Service cost • ......
Image	• Company reputation as a supplier of choice	• Customer oriented • Environmental responsibility • Market leader • ......

Figure 8-5 Example of Customer Expectation Model.

satisfaction. Customer satisfaction surveys can be designed based on the structure of this model. These expectation models are also very effective as a communications vehicle for all employees to improve their understanding of customer needs and to be able to relate the impact of their job to customer expectation areas.

It is reasonable for a company to have multiple customer expectation models. IBM has multiple models for the AS/400 computer system. There is another model for business partners which differs substantially from the expectation model illustrated here. Within each geographic location and country there were models that were tailored and specific to meet local conditions and competitive requirements.

It is hard a imagine that there exists a company that executes so flawlessly that customer complaints never occur. Every company must have a meaningful customer complaint process to ensure that customer satisfaction is maintained and constantly improved. The importance of handling customer complaints cannot be overemphasized. A study of over 2400 customers of AS/400 computers evaluated those customers' experiences that had no problem and those that had problems with a company's products. Those that had no problems said that 84% of the time they would purchase from that company in the future, and 91% of the time they would recommend the system. Those that had problems but were satisfied said that 92% of the time they would purchase and 94% would recommend system to someone else. The difference between customers with no problems and customers that had problems is that customers felt the company was responsive to their needs. Of those who had a problem and were still dissatisfied, 50% said that they would purchase in the future and less than 50% said they would recommend the system. Those that were satisfied would tell 3 other people about the product, and those that were dissatisfied would tell seven other people. This is illustrated below in Figure 8-6. IBM Rochester estimated that a 1% increase in customer satisfaction would generate additional revenues of over $250 million.

> **Service Standards Analysis:** For continuous improvement two major tools ensure that the standards for service quality are continuously improving. Figure 8-7 illustrates a process of service standards improvement. Through early involvement, service planning personnel work with product development people and customers and stakeholders to integrate new serviceability objectives into the products. These are based on the field experience of the service personnel and are documented in the service support plans of new products. From these objectives service standards

Importance Of Customer Satisfaction

Experience from IBM AS/400, n=2400 +

Customer Experience	% Who Will Make a Future Purchase	% Who Will Make a Recommendation	Number of People They Tell
Satisfied Never had a problem	84%	91%	3
Satisfied Had problem, but resolved	92%	**94%**	3
Dissatisfied Still have unresolved problems	46%	48%	7

Figure 8-6 Importance of Customer Satisfaction.

are established. These should be tracked periodically. Defects should be captured immediately close to their source, reported and root-cause analysis immediately performed, and once problem identification is completed, owners would be immediately identified as discussed earlier. The standards should be compared against the competition, customer feedback, survey results, and by service cost analysis. This information should be used to improve service offerings.

Quality Service Gap Analysis Model. The next important tool for analysis is an overall model to determine where the gaps in customer service quality are actually occurring at a systemic level. The model that is useful is

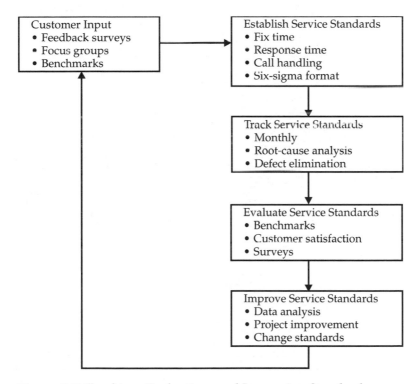

Figure 8-7 Tracking, Evaluating, and Improving Standards.

the gap Analysis model developed by Zeithamel, et al (Zeithamel 1990). This model is illustrated in Figure 8-8. The model identifies systematically the causes which lead to customer disappointments. The fundamental thesis of this model is that a company must deliver what it promises. The model is useful as a diagnostic instrument in identifying systemic and structural gaps in a firms business processes that give rise to customer dissatisfaction. Figure 8-8 identifies five fundamental gap areas. These are summarized in Figure 8-9.

Possibly the most important factor in customer satisfaction is that the work begins when a company is trying

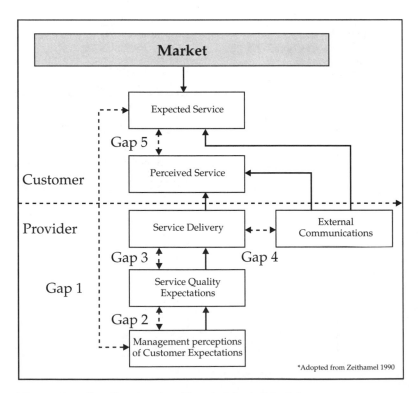

Figure 8-8 Quality Service Gap Analysis Model.

Gap #	Gap	What & Why
1	Not knowing customers' expectations	• Management fails to deliver what customers expect. • Caused by weak market research, management is out of touch, ...
2	Wrong Quality Standards	• Unable to meet or exceed customers' expectations • Caused by lack of commitment, short term view, lack of resources, false belief in false standards, ...
3	Implementation and execution short of the mark	• Unable or unwilling to rise to the occasion • Caused by systemic problems in the management system, organization, culture and processes, training, ...
4	Promises do not match delivery	• Propensity to over-promise, and inconsistent messages to customers • Caused by ad hoc communications channels to customers from too many uncoordinated sources.
5	Customers' shortfall perception	• Customers perceive discrepancy between expected service and what they perceive they are getting • Mainly driven by prior experiences, work-of-mouth, personal needs, ...

Figure 8-9 Customer Satisfaction Gap Analysis Model.

to decide what markets to enter and what customers to serve. The work then continues when you are planning and designing the offering, proceeds to when it has the product in the market, and the hardest work is to continuously improve **all** business process so that customers experience a continuously rising level of satisfaction. This aspect of continuous improvement is fundamental and critical to competitive effectiveness because if a company does not continually improve, the competition most certainly will.

NATURAL AND INVESTMENT MARKETS

The purpose of business is to keep existing customers and to constantly create new customers faster than the competition. These are the fundamental points of departure for this methodology: keep pre-existing customers, win over the new ones, and do so from positions of strengths. We describe a disciplined and systematic approach to continuously grow market share. The methodology presents an approach to accurately and precisely target marketing investments to remove growth inhibitors to grow market share for the firm.

The first step is to unambiguously identify those market segments where the firm is strongly positioned to compete and therefore able to dominate without heroic efforts or investments. These markets are called **"natural markets"** because in a very real sense the firm is a natural in these markets. During the second step of this analysis, identify those market segments where the firm, relative to natural markets, is weaker in competitive ability. Then the firm can, with a great deal of precision, target marketing investments aimed at the specific weakness in those segments in order to overcome them. The effect of these investments is to create natural markets from those where previous weakness existed. These markets are called **"investment"** markets because the firm must invest in order to expand its presence and occupancy. This process provides a simple but effective blueprint for a market expansion strategy. Defend and expand occupancy in natural markets, but invest at a faster rate in investment markets to gain new market share. In this manner, a firm's natural markets are protected against competitive incursions, while at the same time investments are continuously directed at establishing beachheads in new markets.

A natural market is found by evaluating company's competitive strength in the critical success factors of that market. Clearly a knowledge of the critical success factors of that market is a prerequisite. Figure 8-10 illustrates the concepts described above using the IBM AS/400 as an example. When this product was being planned in 1987, four critical success factors were identified in the targeted markets. They were:

1.   a technically outstanding product;

2.   a rich repertoire of mission-critical applications that spanned the key industrial sectors of the market;

Critical Success Factors	Capabilities
Product Excellence	Hardware and software technology unmatched by the competition.
Industry Applications	Repertoire of 5000 mission critical applications across key industry segments.
Distribution Channels	High coverage on all key channel, geographic territories, major metropolitan areas and industry segments worldwide.
Support Services	7500 loyal and highly competent business partners worldwide. Consistent presence with application and channel requirements.

Figure 8-10 Illustration of Fit Analysis of Critical Success Factors.

3.   pervasive channels of distribution; and

4.   responsive and competent support services for the system and its applications (Bauer, Collar, Tang 1992).

A summary of the capabilities are shown in Figure 8-10.

Finding the critical success factors of markets is an undertaking that must be researched thoughtfully. It requires an analysis of the market dynamics, namely an understanding of the forces that are driving demand, the behavior of buyers, their value propositions, how value is delivered, the economics of the offerings, etc. Scenario Analysis is a very effective tool to use to find the critical success factors. Whereas in our previous discussions of scenario analysis we focused on the industry at large, for critical success factor analysis of markets tightly focus the application of Scenario Analysis on the market to gain insight on the success factors. That is to say, perform Market Scenario Analysis, concentrate only on the forces which are driving and influencing the behavior of the market. A serious and common mistake is to describe the firm's capabilities in only generic and vague terms, and then to stop there. It is also necessary to substantiate the qualitative descriptions with meaningful quantitative analysis. For example, in the Industry Applications factor shown in Figure 8-10, the company was able to determine that although there was demand for its product line in all industry sectors, only slightly over a dozen drove 85% of the demand. Further analysis of the applications that were critical in those industries, revealed that less than a hundred addressed the overwhelming percentage in the short term. Digging deeper, the company discovered that it had strong business relationships with the most important business partners that were supplying these applications, and that in fact they were present in all the territories that were important for our future product. This is an example of the laborious analysis that is necessary to be able to support the statements of capabilities for a critical success factor.

Note that, in general, natural markets are firm specific. Universal natural markets exist only for commodities where the goods and services are fungible and where the competitive firms have strikingly similar capabilities. Coca Cola and Pepsi Cola comes to mind. Obviously, a firm's current customer base is a subset of the firm's natural market, but it is not THE natural market, unless the firm has 100% occupancy. These concepts are illustrated in Figure 8-11, Natural and Investment markets. The area where the market opportunity and the capabilities of the firm overlap identifies the natural market. But note that there is another area which is a subset of the natural mar-

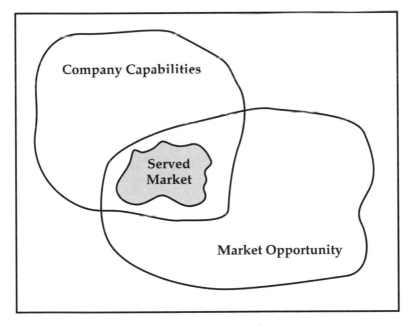

Figure 8-11 Natural and Investment Markets.

ket, that is the **served market** of the company. The served market is the subset of the natural market which a company has the ability to occupy but does not. This is opportunity that has been forfeited to competition or which remains as latent demand. Clearly, the first marketing imperative of a firm is to occupy as much as possible of their natural markets. The second imperative is to analyze investment markets. The first thing to understand about investment markets is that aggregate capabilities do not translate into universal capability from the atomic territorial level of markets. With the AS/400, IBM Rochester found that although in the aggregate it had an overall advantage in the target markets, there were many situations where it could not press its apparent advantage. For example, although IBM Rochester had over 7500 business partners, many of them could not cover specific territories. Some had only country coverage, such as Japan or Mexico. Others could only cover major metropolitan areas, such as New York and Boston. Unfortunately, many of its competitors served with distinction many of those territories that the business partners could not reach. IBM Rochester learned that to be able to formulate actionable plans, the analysis must continue to drill down to the territory level where execution takes place. Insightful and analytic understanding of the critical success factors of a market, down to the territory level helps determine how a firm can fine tune and optimize its capabilities in an actionable way. Leadership and dominance are established territory by territory.

We generalize these principles about natural markets and illustrate them below in Figure 8-12. Company A has an overall superiority, and specifically it is stronger than Company B. However this advantage does not translate automatically to all territories where Company A competes. In Territory Alpha, Company A has a weakness in Factor 5. Note that although Company B is overall weak-

Critical Success Factors	Company A Capability	Company A Capability	Company B Capability	Company B Capability
	Overall	Territory Alpha	Overall	Territory Alpha
Factor 1	++	++	++	++
Factor 2	+	+	−	+
Factor 3	++	++	++	+
Factor 4	+++	+++	+	+
Factor 5	+++	−	+	+++

+++	capabilities leads all key competitors
++	among the key competitors
+	average among the key competitors
−	competitively weak relative to key competitors

Figure 8-12 Aggregate Natural Markets and Territory Natural Market Analysis.

er than Company A, in this territory Company B has a substantial advantage in Factor 5. Company B can compete vigorously in Territory Alpha and it can legitimately expect to win over Company A. In effect, Company B has a natural market in Territory B. Many companies forfeit attractive territories under the false belief that an apparently stronger competitor can win because they are more capable in the aggregate. However aggregate strength does not necessarily translate automatically into local capabilities.

Every firm should perform a Natural Market analysis to identify the weakness of its competitors in specific territories by critical success factors. This also explains the situations where "market leaders" are often confounded by the inexplicable success of a "weaker" competitor. Ev-

ery competitor should confound its adversaries in this
way. This example highlights the importance of Natural
Market analysis down to the territory level where the
skirmishes for customers take place. It is this kind of
thoughtful analysis that enables apparently weak companies to win consistently in specific territories.

As we have seen, a market is classified as an investment
market where the firm falls short in one or more critical
success factors. In other words, the firm does not meet the
conditions to establish a sustainable competitive foothold,
and if present, its ability to defend that market is weak.
The firm must invest to acquire or develop the capabilities
that are missing in their competitive repertoire. It must invest in acquiring competency in critical success factors.
Company A in Figure 8-12 must make investments in Factor 5 in Territory Alpha to mitigate its competitive weakness relative to competitor Company B. Although
Company B is not as strong as Company A, in this specific
territory it has an advantage if it leverages Factor 5 intelligently. Clearly then, the degree to which the fit between
the firm's abilities and the critical success factors is not optimal determines the intensity of investments required to
transform an investment market into a natural market.

Expanding from the concepts illustrated in Figure 8-11,
this analysis technique provides the foundations for a
very actionable and meaningful market strategy. This is
illustrated in Figure 8-13.

A firm must begin with a clear understanding of the
aggregate market opportunity it wants to compete in,
and it must know that market's critical success factors.
With this knowledge, it knows what it takes to win. Next,
it must determine its capabilities territory by territory.
With this knowledge, it knows whether it has the ability
to win in a specific territory, it knows where there is a fit
between its capabilities, and it knows the success factors
for a specific territory. This is the process of "fit analysis"

that is illustrated in Figure 8-13. In those territories where the firm has competence in all the critical success factors, the company has a fit. Those territories where the company has customers, its served market, it must retain the loyalty of those customers and not take them for granted. The strategy there should be to defend against competitive excursions. In these territories that are a natural market but not a served market, the company must adopt a

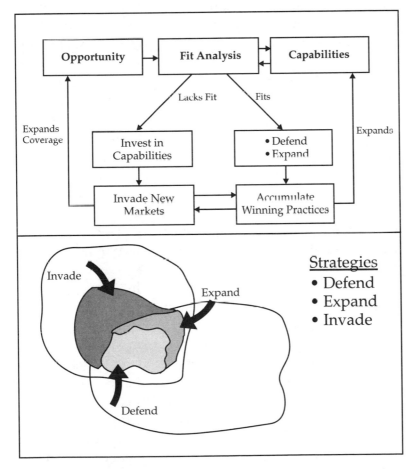

Figure 8-13 Natural and Investment Market Strategy Dynamics.

strategy of expanding its occupancy of natural markets, which it can do because it has all the requisite capabilities. Regardless, in both of these markets, the company must sell vigorously, it must be a very tough competitor and adopt a strategy of Competitive Dominance.

Smart companies accumulate practices that are effective defenses, that win against the competition, and that create customer loyalty and high satisfaction. These winning practices can be deployed in other territories and in investment markets. This is the means by which new natural markets are continuously expanded from a base of served markets. This process of accumulation and propagation of effective winning practices significantly accelerates a firm's ability to achieve the goal of dominance of natural markets. It reduces the opportunities for "reinventing the wheel" and other false starts. In a similar way, another territory which has to develop a capability in a critical success factor for an investment market, can learn from another unit that has been successful. Because the firm is continuously accumulating practices which are known to work, scare resources are invested with great efficiency to develop competencies in critical success factors. In this way investment markets are continuously turned into natural markets from a basis of strengths and proven knowledge.

This is an effective first step to achieve Competitive Dominance. Continuously create natural markets. Apply what works to investment markets. The second step is to invest in the capabilities required to turn investment markets into natural served markets. Invest to develop capabilities in critical success factors specific to that territory or which will enhance overall capabilities to improve the companies abilities to create new natural markets from investment markets. This is what we call an "invasion strategy." As before, the competitively effective winning practices are accumulated.

As Figure 8-13 shows, the combined effect of these actions produce four synergistic results. One, because the capabilities of the firm are continuously expanded, its "fit" continuously improves with an ever increasing number of territories. Two, this fit increases the company's ability to expand its occupancy in natural markets. Three, invading new investment markets expands the company's market share in the overall market opportunity. Four, the accumulation of winning and best practices in both natural and investment markets continuously turbochargers the capabilities of the firm in the marketplace. Competitive Dominance is the result of a clear sense of direction and relentless and purposeful action. Sustained dominance is attained by purposeful and determined accumulation and sharing of winning practices. This way the firm can learn more quickly and with greater efficiency than its competitors, it is now able to sustain its Competitive Dominance. This is organizational learning in its finest form.

A word of caution is necessary at this point. Mindless market expansion can be fatal to a company. Many companies that do not recognize this adopt a strategy of growing at the rate of each market segment that is faster than the segment growth rate. This can also be fatal when one does not consider both the rate of growth of the segments as well as the mix of the segments that comprise the overall opportunity.

The following is a simplified case of a real life dominant firm. This is illustrated below in Figure 8-14, Market-Segment Growth Example. Assume that the market opportunity is calibrated at $100 Million in year 199x, and that it is made up of two segments **A** and **B**. **A** is $30 million with a growth of 30% annual growth rate and **B** is $70 million with an annual growth rate of 5%. Consider a company called **SLOW,** whose revenues in 199x are $60 million. SLOW has two product lines targeted at seg-

		Year X Revenue $M	Year X+1 Revenue $M	Growth %
Market	A	$30	$39	30%
	B	$70	$73.5	5%
	Total	$100	$112.5	12.5%
Slow	**Alpha**	$12	$15.84	32%
	Beta	$48	$51.35	7%
	Total	$60	$67.20	11%

Figure 8-14 Example of Market Segment Growth.

ments A and B respectively, Alpha and Beta. Alpha produces revenues of $12 million and Beta produces revenues of $48 million. Alpha's annual growth rate is 32% and Beta's annual growth rate is 7%. Clearly, Alpha is growing faster than the market segment A, 32% versus 30%. Beta is also growing faster than the market segment B, 7% versus 5%.

But wait, let's see what happens at the end of one year. The market has grown to $112.5 million at a rate of 12.5%. SLOW has grown to $67.2 million at an annual rate of 11%. SLOW has lost market share even though it exceeded the growth of each market segment! What happened? SLOW's proportion of its product line was out of alignment with the market. The A market is the fastest growing segment in the market growing at 30% per year, but SLOW has only 20% of its revenues in the growth segment. It has 80% of its revenues from product Beta, which participates in the B market segment which is growing at glacial speed. SLOW has adopted the mindless growth strategy by electing to grow faster than the market rather than growing faster than the market in aggregate. Needless to say, the cumulative impact of years of market share erosion in this way is disastrous to a company. Companies that generalize markets and plan from historical projections will find themselves in a crisis. SLOWs strategy should have been to grow Alpha at a rate of say, 50% and Beta at its 7%. At the end of the year, Alpha would reach $18 million and Beta $51 million, for a total of $69 million. This growth would be 15%. Market growth strategies must consider the percentage of the mix of the market segments and their growth, and it must consider the mix of revenues of the company itself as well. It cannot ignore these factors. We call this **"the revenue mix conundrum."**

Natural and Investment Market Analysis is a powerful means to expand market occupancy and improve market share position by determining the fit between a companies capabilities and the success factors in the market. Through disciplined and systematic targeting of unoccupied natural markets and development of capabilities in investments markets, a company can significantly improve its competitive position. With proper attention to the growth dynamics of the market segments and the mix of the segments, a company can gain market share in a meaningful and significant way.

ORGANIZATIONAL ENERGETICS

High performance organizations, extraordinary teams and high achievers all have one characteristic in common. They are committed to a goal, which they pursue relentlessly with a high level of energy and enthusiasm. Less frequently observed, but perhaps more important, they are also able to overcome emotional deprivation. They can draw emotional support from many sources to sustain that energy and commitment they set for themselves. Embryonic or emerging companies tend to have these characteristics. One can feel it when walking in the door.

On the other hand, mature companies exhibit the opposite. The prevailing wisdom is that all companies go through an inevitable corporate life cycle as illustrated by Figure 8-15 (Miller 1989). When companies reach the Bureaucrat or Aristocrat stage, they become less competitive, typically go through a crisis, downsize, and begin renewal, eliminating the old ways and perhaps beginning a new life cycle.

The theory of Competitive Dominance refutes the down side of the corporate life cycle theory. To the extent that you accept this life cycle theory, it becomes a self-fulfilling.

Can a company create an environment that nourishes and sustains these characteristics over an extended period of time, thus avoiding the down side of the corporate life cycle? The answer is yes, and one of the keys to successful Competitive Dominance is organizational energetics, so let's examine how organizational energetics can help overcome the corporate life cycle downturn.

Successful companies tend to become internally focused, building infrastructure and making decisions to

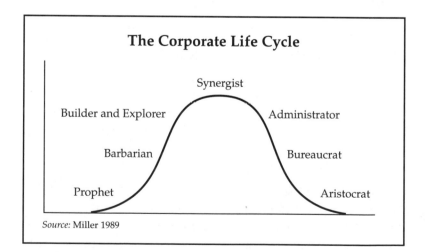

Figure 8-15 The Corporate Life Cycle.

support the needs of the company first, not the needs of the market. Brand image of successful companies can carry sales and lull the company into a false sense of security and complacency about the correctness of the internalized decision they are making. The workload of companies in this situation becomes biased in support of the bureaucracy and administrative minutia created by growth in size of the organization and business controls procedures. In many cases, companies that have emerged to become major industry participants don't recognize that the marketplace which they created has continued to mature or change, and that new industry participants have changed the playing field. They continue to do what made them successful, without recognizing that the external environment continues to change. In effect, they have become excessively internally focused as illustrated in Figure 8-16.

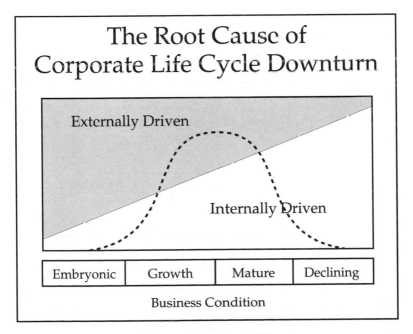

Figure 8-16 Impact of Excessive Internal Focus.

When companies emerge into major industry participants, they do so because they recognize a market shift or
new opportunity, and they are able to seize a commanding position. They are driven by external markets and
forces that create the prophet, barbarian, builder, and ex-
plorer mentality in an organization. The business world
defines these companies as entrepreneurial. More simply
stated, all areas of embryonic and growth organizations
are involved and driven by external factors as shown in
Figure 8-17. They are able to anticipate the downward
trends by continuously monitoring external signals and
by taking decisive proactive actions that create a new
growth curve for them.

In many ways, the characteristics of markets is similar
to the left side of the corporate life cycle curve. They are
in continuous change, adjusting and adapting to a multitude of external forces. The nature of growth organiza-

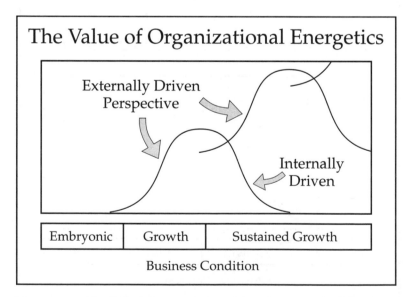

Figure 8-17 Applying Organizational Energetics to the Corporate
Life Cycle.

tions must be the same. Their management systems and method of operation must map closely to the dynamics of the industry and markets they serve in order to anticipate and fluidly respond to changes. Large segments of the organization must have continuous external contact to avoid internal bias and to keep a pulse on the environment. The company must foster an internal environment of innovative thinking, energy and enthusiasm.

Organizational energetics is a tool of Competitive Dominance to create and sustain an embryonic and growth environment in an organization, to continuously replicate the left side of the corporate life cycle curve and avoid the downturn. The following set of processes help to create this adaptive organization.

1.   Ensure a cross/extended enterprise management system at the business unit level. Every business unit has measurements and regularly scheduled meetings to understand the status of the business against plans, and to address operational gaps. Too often though, these set of measures and reviews are limited to those operational units within direct control of the organization. All non-direct reporting units are managed via plan dependencies once or twice a year. When unit executives relinquish their responsibility to run a business in order to protect their controllable turf, they bestow the responsibility to run the business on the bureaucracy. Administrative and bureaucratic structure grows to support and coordinate groups of independent units. Bureaucracy becomes the business entity and the company operation adjusts to support it, internalizing their management systems. When the product group is in one operating unit, sales is in another, and distributors in another company altogether, it is imperative that they must work together as teams at the operational level, not just at senior executive levels.

In a dynamic marketplace, all organizational elements important to success must meet regularly to review plans and operational status, discuss performance, focus on dependencies and address gaps. The management system must include all elements important to success and operate as a business, not as an piece of a larger unit. Customers and stockholders do not see independent units; they see a business. It is from that view that they decide how to spend their money.

2.   Craft objectives that are grounded in a vision that can inspire people to achieve. The objectives must be clearly stated and understood in a broader context than simply a metric that can be measured. It must explain how it contributes to the overall goals of the organization. This way, objectives acquire meaning and significance. The objectives must pass the test of successive and step-wise decomposition as it moves down the organization, where ownership and accountability can be brought to bear. People at the lowest levels in the organization must be able to directly relate their job to some aspect of overall company goals achievement. Most importantly, owners of the objectives must be empowered and enabled to meet and exceed them through skills development, tools, effective business processes, etc. Conventional wisdom says that people perform only that which is inspected, not what is expected. That is false, and it reflects a cynical view of people's motives. People perform that which is respected, by them, by their peers, and by their management.

3.   Create an organization-wide customer-centered culture. One of the most important actions a company can take to implement organizational energetics is to initiate methods and systems that create broad-based customer involvement—regular customer contact with all aspect of the company. In the past, customer contact was the domain of sales and service, requiring administrative systems and processes to ensure that customer needs and wants were interpreted accurately. Embryonic and growth companies recognize that keeping close contact with customers enables them to keep a pulse on consumer expectations and market dynamics, anticipating changes and responding more accurately. Direct customer feedback to those performing the work ensures that nothing is lost in the translation of customer needs and wants. Those employees also can now directly tie the output of their actions to customer response. There is no more effective way to create organizational enthusiasm and morale than to have regular positive customer feedback to employees. There is no more effective way to get employees to accept change than to have negative feedback from customers. Figure 8-18 illustrates some customer-contact processes that can be effective through every part of the organization.

4.   Beware of emotional deprivation and create processes to overcome it. One of the fundamental reasons organizations cannot sustain a high level of energy and enthusiasm is because, over time, discouragement sets in, people get burned out. They lose heart. People need to be emotionally nourished. They not only need to know that what they do has meaning, but they need confirmation that what they do is valued. The flaw of current practice is that management does not have good internal "listening posts" or overlooks other key sources of emotional energy, support and affirmation. Employees working shoulder to shoulder with customers and stakeholders and experiencing first hand how they react to their work is one of the most effective means of overcoming emotional deprivation. Suddenly you do not

Organizational Unit

Planning	Product Development	Product Introduction	Manufacturing	Sales and Installation	Service and Support
• Customer Councils • Market studies • Focus groups • Conferences	• Customer laboratory • Codevelopment • Conferences	• Early ship programs • Customer briefings • Conferences	• Branch Office visits • Customer tours • Customer visits • Conferences	• Plant employees assist in customer installations	• User Groups • Owners groups • Customer satisfaction monitoring

Figure 8-18 Methods to Achieve Broad-based Customer Contact

need so many "attaboys" from management. Another way is having employees of the firm participate directly and actively in external activities that reaffirm the value and significance of their work.

5.   Create and closely monitor internal listening posts. The objective of listening posts is to monitor the morale, attitude, and commitment of people and management. The traditional method of performing this task is the widely practiced yearly morale or attitude surveys. These are effective for gathering and analyzing large amounts of information to assess trends, but they are usually not done frequently enough to keep a pulse on attitudes or emerging issues. There are other effective means to continuously assess the level of buy-in and enthusiasm and to actually build a high level of commitment. Periodic roundtable discussions, luncheons, step-level interviews, and having an open door where people can just walk in are effective ways to do this. Giving people the opportunity to listen to other people's questions and to participate in open and frank discussions with management, is a sure way to build understanding, morale and commitment.

6.   Avoid Overreacting to Morale Indices. Many organizations use opinion surveys and other mechanisms to determine the morale level of the employees. The conventional wisdom is that the indices ought to be consistently increasing. This intuitive evaluation schema is correct only for organizations where changes are stable and predictable. On the other hand, decline of morale indices is to be expected for organizations that are facing major shifts, such as large scale reorganizations, new and unfavorable regulatory legislation, or accelerating erosion of market share. For organizations that are being led into new directions and that are being transformed into a different kind of company, it is important to understand the dynamics of morale in those environments so that management does not overreact to declining indices. Our experience has been that morale goes through four phases when a company is trying to take an organization into new directions which people are unfamiliar with or which require a cultural and mid set shift. Figure 8-19 illustrates the four phases. During the initial phase, when the leadership is indicating that a new direction is being set, frustration sets in, and morale indices trend downward. In the second phase, people begin to defy this new direction, whether consciously or subconsciously as they try to revert to the familiar comfort zone. At the third stage, people begin to change as they begin to understand the new directions and explore the ways that they can contribute in a positive and constructive manner. At that point morale indices begin to improve. Finally at the fourth stage, the understanding and buy-in is pervasive and commitment becomes widespread. Morale turns up strongly at this time. We have observed in our experience that there is a time lag between the morale indices of the employees and that of management.

When the overall indices are trending down, people morale will move down first. It is therefore a leading indicator. When morale is about to turnaround, management indices will turn up first. In that situation, management morale is a leading indicator.

Figure 8-19 highlights the management implications of the dynamics of morale in an environment of transformational change. There are specific actions that management can take during different phases of morale to manage it a meaningful way. There is one key lesson: *Management must manage differently at different stages.* The return arrow reminds everyone that the transformation

Managing Morale in an Environment of Transformation

Frustration	Defiance	Change	Commitment
Environment:			
• Know change is taking place	• Testing management resolve	• Realize management is committed	• Results reinforce management direction
• Feel threatened, fear sets in	• Hoping it will go away	• Good old days are over	• Hope and enthusiasm
• Initial enthusiasm declines	• Resisting change or passive resistance	• Taking ownership	• Setting aggressive goals
• Wishing for the good old days	• Morale plunges	• Become change agents—explore	• High learning and high sharing
	• Cynicism and blame	• New behavior taking root	• Excitement and high morale

Repeat the cycle

Figure 8-19 The Four Phases of Morale.

Managing Morale in an Environment of Transformation

Frustration	Defiance	Change	Commitment
		Repeat the cycle	

Actions:

Frustration	Defiance	Change	Commitment
• Communicate Need	• Communicate constancy of purpose	• Communicate progress	• Communicate success and follow on actions
• Establish goals and checkpoints	• Reinforce	• Focus on Management morale	• Avoid complacency
• Prepare for the worst	• Recognize new actions	• Recognize Achievement	• Recognize breakthrough approaches
• Set up listening posts	• Do not let up	• Celebrate progress	• Celebrate Success
• Do not overreact	• Avoid "you" and "them"	• Disciplinary action on non-supporters	• Adjust, establish new goals

Figure 8-19 The Four Phases of Morale. (*continued*)

Managing Morale in an Environment of Transformation

Frustration	Defiance	Change	Commitment

— Repeat the cycle —

Management Implications:

- Manage differently at different stages.
- Establish listening posts and a system to continuously monitor the environment and attitudes.
- Communicate strategy and maintain constancy of purpose.
- Do not lose faith or display lack of confidence in the direction.
- Celebrate and recognize achievement no matter how modest.
- Recognize that some will not make it.
- 5% and the top layer needs to be with management at the start.
- Recognize that management morale is the leading indicator of turnaround.
- Recognize that people morale is the leading indicator that change is in progress.

Figure 8-19 The Four Phases of Morale. *(continued)*

process is a continuous cycle of change but the more the process is repeated, the more the organization becomes accustom to change as a standard improvement process.

7.   Make it easy to succeed by providing variety of learning and teaching opportunities. It is demoralizing to be asked to do extraordinary things but not be given the means to succeed. Builders and explorers need tools, education, and training. Investing in skills of the people and the management team is a very effective morale builder, because it not only tells the people that they are important, but it also equips them to achieve higher levels of performance. It renews them, gets their innovative juices flowing, and creates enthusiasm for the task at hand. Companies can provide incentives for learning and vitality such as awards for patents, technical publications, and promotions for outstanding technical and academic achievements.

The other side of personal learning is organizational learning. Effective organizational learning systems require internal and external listening posts that provide continuous information for improvement. Once again, these are not events, but systematic processes that provide the organization with information to anticipate shifts that create gaps in expected behavior. Internal listening posts have been described in Chapter 5 and Chapter 6, Item 4.4). External listening posts can be through continuous customer contact, effective market intelligence systems, participation in industry groups, or benchmarking. Collecting, analyzing, propagating, and learning from best practices is the essence of a learning organization. Externally focused organizations usually have effective organizational learning systems grounded in closed-loop listening posts. The administrative and bureaucratic elements of internally focused organizations will squash or distort feedback that signal shifts or change.

8. Celebrate achievements at every opportunity. Achievements, no matter how modest, must be recognized and celebrated. People understand role models far better than abstract ideas. Emulation and imitating a winner is easier than imagining and risking how to reach a new standard of behavior or performance. But these winners must also be protected from the negative criticism of those who oppose change and renewal. Bureaucratic systems do not like winners or those that stand out. Giving credence to critics with outdated attitudes is the fastest way to inhibit change and progress. Bureaucracy will systematically seek to destroy winners credibility because they are a threat to the status quo. Winners establish an existence theorem. They define what is possible, and what can be done. When a business unit or pilot project succeeds in accomplishing stretch goals, recognition will reinforce the learning and establish the expected level of performance—the benchmark the company is striving for.

A company must celebrate the key checkpoints and milestones that are indicators of progress toward their future goals. These become the opportunities to drive home to everyone that the company is progressing, change is taking place, and the direction is correct. It becomes increasingly more difficult for those that are not buying in to change to justify their position with others when clear progress is being made. The facts demonstrate that the objectives are correct and the train is moving from the station, so all those who want to participate in the new direction better be on it. These checkpoints and milestones also present an opportunity to address changes in direction or modifications to plans. The market and the industry is not static, therefore the best laid plans require modification over time. By using checkpoints and milestones, these modifications appear to be planned and anticipated rather than reactions. One caution for the company is to not create paper tigers. Do not celebrate shallow victories or create mythical success stories. A company may be able to get away with it one or two times, but over time people will realize that progress is not being made at the expected rate, and they will lose confidence in the direction. This situation is characteristic of the "Magic Wand" malpractice described in Chapter 9.

Figure 8-20 illustrates a closed-loop process that embodies the eight principles described.

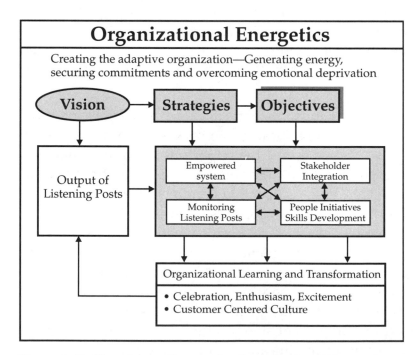

Figure 8-20 Closed-loop Process for Organizational Energetics.

High performance and extraordinary results requires energy and enthusiasm. The result is an organization that achieves and has high morale. Sustained energy, enthusiasm, and morale are possible with common sense management that focuses on the emotional needs of people. The process for organizational energetics is a tool that managers can use. We have found it particularly effective during organizational transformation and periods of high uncertainty and stress.

9

The Dirty Dozen: Management Malpractices to Avoid

We have experience with many manufacturing and services organizations that have attempted to develop and implement strategy and quality improvement initiatives—both successfully and unsuccessfully. From the unsuccessful efforts, we have distilled specific patterns of ineffective management practices; or what we call "malpractices." These can be grouped into a dozen common characteristics. Here are the dirty dozen, the twelve most commonly made mistakes of managerial malpractice that we have found to be singularly ineffective and that are in fact, damaging to the business. In exceptional cases, although results can be achieved, they are not sustainable. These practices cannot withstand the test of time, unforeseen environmental change, or changes in leadership.

LEAPFROGGING

This the practice where management attempts to skip an intermediate stage of maturity and tries to apply the practices of several subsequent stages. This is the moral equivalent of trying to learn advanced calculus without having mastered algebra: You can imagine how it could be done, but anyone who has tried it will tell you how fruitless and frustrating it is. Just as mathematics has prerequisites, strategy and quality practices build on, and complement, each other. It is necessary to acquire fluency and mastery of certain techniques before more advanced ones can be tried in a way that will yield sustainable results. For example, it is hard to imagine that a company can engineer and implement a closed-loop corrective action system to continuously improve quality if it does not have experience with in-process and end-process measurements. It is also hard to imagine that the management team of a company can deploy scenario analysis when they do not have any experience with planning. Leapfrogging is doubly hard when a company must synchronize strategy and quality initiatives and align them. A company cannot successfully apply strategic management without developing a base for environmental analysis and monitoring. It is possible that a company can develop an excellent maturity at the level three or four of strategy capability that enables it to anticipate the development of nascent opportunities in emerging investment-markets. But if its quality systems are only at a maturity level one, it cannot leap to quality maturity level three or four without some preventive capability and process efficiency. For this company, strategy implementation will be difficult. This is because at such a low level of quality maturity, the company does not have the ability to reengineer its processes to implement and make actionable a strategic direction, it will lack many of the basic process management and analysis capability. This does not imply that it takes long, evolutionary time to implement an effective Stage 4 strategy quality system. It means that a refined strategy requires fundamentals to be well deployed in order to sustain improvements and achieve results. Refinement in one area such as strategy, can also act as a stimulus to accelerate quality learning and maturity. And the converse is also true.

The flaw of leapfrogging is in adopting an ambitious and aggressive approach but failing to recognize that the approach must be coupled in a balanced and consistent way with deployment. Consequently, the following results are obtained:

Leapfrogging	Maturity
Approach	++
Deployment	--
Results	--

Typically, "young men in a hurry" fall prey to this practice. Worse still, we have seen "old men in hurry" who succumb to this practice and fail when they can least afford it.

MAGIC WAND

This is one of the most common malpractices of strategy. In this situation, companies develop a "grand strategy" and "vision" that demonstrates the potential to capture a large segment of some opportunity and gain significant advantage over the competition. As a result of having spent much time spent discussing the opportunities and directions, this strategic vision is embraced by the executives who originally conceived of it. The strategy and vision are documented and communicated to operational and business unit executives and managers to ensure their understanding and commitment, but communication is as far as it goes. Many of these business unit managers believe the strategy is correct because it sounds so good. Many will support the concept, but because the connection to the operational side is tenuous; they will focus on other priorities that require immediate attention. While they may be responsible for some of the strategic initiatives, there is no regular management review system to monitor progress on strategic initiatives, nor are any physical resources deployed to implement them. The topic of progress on strategic initiatives comes up periodically as part of operational performance reviews where the business unit managers tap dance their way through a ritual of response that satisfies the executives as long the their current business results are good. This not unlike central planning in Communist economies where "the leaders pretend to know what it takes to make progress, and the managers pretend to make progress." Even when executives apply pressure to carry out strategic initiatives, they take a shotgun approach, not a disciplined and comprehensive set of organization-wide transformational actions. They wave the magic wand but nothing happens, and as long as the business is meeting its current objectives, everything is OK. Approach sounds great, but with marginal deployment, no strategic initiative will be implemented that provides substantive results.

In this situation, one of two things, or both, is going to happen. Opportunities will be lost, or the executives will realize, too late, that they should have spent more time on the deployment of strategy as crisis begins to loom on the horizon.

A good test to determine if a company uses the magic wand approach is to identify the top 4–6 key strategic initiatives from the strategy development work. Then identify the number of people directly applied to each and who the owners of theses initiatives are. This is illustrated in Figure 9-1.

In the case of magic wand malpractice, two or three initiatives will have minimal direct resources actively working on strategy deployment, nor anyone who can be identified as directly responsible. Strategy requires a disciplined approach to change and transformation. All stakeholders within the company, and those that provide value outside company walls must be included in the transformation to the future preferred state. The transformation process must be integrated into the day to day management system.

The reason that the Magic Wand does not work is that it is fundamentally a wish-driven approach to strategy and quality. Just because a company wishes something to be true, it will not necessarily make it so. It takes work. In strategy and quality work means being able to translate goals and objectives into actions, being able to monitor progress, being able to learn and adjust continuously. In this case, approach is weak, it may sound good, but it is

Strategic Initiatives	Number of People	Owner of the Initiative
Initiative number 1	55	John Jones
Initiative number 2	130	Jane Smith
Initiative number 3	44	Kathy Yeu
•	•	•
Initiative number (n)	20	James Washington

Figure 9-1 Deploying Strategic Initiatives.

not sound. Deployment is weak, and results are weaker still. Consequently, we see the following:

Magic Wand	Maturity
Approach	– –
Deployment	– –
Results	– –

SILVER BULLET

This is the situation where management tries to find the "one thing" to achieve quick results as if business problems were werewolves. This approach is most frequently tried by managers looking for "the quick fix" with the expectations of "instant gratification." A systematic process gives way to "task forces" and "special studies." This approach overlooks one of the most important characteristics of quality and strategy integration, namely, that it requires a prioritized, systemic integration of processes to improve operational and business performance. Experienced managers know that mindless concentration on "one thing" creates unforeseen dislocations elsewhere in the enterprise and generates a great deal of unproductive effort. A holistic approach that thoughtfully integrates a meaningful combination of initiatives is necessary to produce sustainable results. For example, speed is an important element of quality and successful strategy execution. But a single-minded focus, to the exclusion of other considerations, such as on "cycle-time reduction" as a silver bullet will cause unnecessary and unproductive effort in many areas of the business.

A silver bullet approach to cycle time reduction is one where an executive sets an across-the-board goal of 30%

cycle time reduction in every key process, without regard for the benefit derived from one process over another. The result is that everyone is scrambling to improve cycle time, but in only a few areas would the effort yield any results. The fact may be that 50% cycle time reduction is required in one area to meet market demand, while reductions in other areas have no significant business benefit. A more thoughtful approach would be to understand thoroughly the competitive requirements and value that speeding up specific process would bring, and then to develop a set of integrated initiatives that concentrates on speeding up the processes that have the maximum leverage. This requires a root-cause type analysis to determine the processes most effecting time to market and with the optimum competitive impact. From this, the company can prioritize the improvements needed. This approach of addressing business problems is not conducive to silver bullets.

Now that the company has a prioritized approach, it is able to target where to drive improvements. For example, it may find that the problem with time to market lies in sub-optimized distribution systems between company operations and non-company distributors. These stakeholders must then team together to optimize the process throughout the system. This is an integrated and synchronized approach to strategic planning and quality management.

The silver bullet malpractice is weak on approach as it is not prioritized to key business imperatives. It is strong on deployment in that it is broad-based involvement from all parts of the organization. In fact, deployment is too strong, for it causes wasted effort in areas where there is small impact. But the lack of results will speak for themselves. Typically, executives who are strong on operational experience but limited in strategy and visionary

skills fall victim to this malpractice. This malpractice can
be characterized by the following:

Silver Bullet	Maturity
Approach	− −
Deployment	+
Results	− −

LOPSIDED APPROACH

A lopsided approach is the sophisticated version of the
Silver Bullet approach. Instead of selecting a silver bullet, a specific functional area is selected in the false hope
that this concentration will produce long lasting quick
results. This approach is insufficient because it fails to
consider all the functions of the enterprise, as a whole.
The deployment is insufficient because it is too narrowly
focused. The results will be predictable—no improvement. For example, one of the most common lopsided
approaches is to focus on manufacturing product defects, their detection, and the indicators of cost of quality.
This is a quality maturity level one focus. There are situations where this approach is necessary, for example, for
a manufacturer with major defects problems, a lopsided
approach may be required for a period of time. Lopsided
approaches are also adopted to position a company or a
product in a unique way to establish themselves as a
"role model." Too often, though, companies continue to
overemphasize these areas, far beyond continuous improvement actions, when they no longer become differentiators in the market.

Another example is the single-minded obsession on sales to existing and well known customers. The company forgets that in addition to the served market, there are other potential customers it is not winning. Another example is the quest to "set the right expectations" with customers to narrow the gap between what the company can deliver and what customers will experience. This also fails because it overlooks the fact that customers are able to compare products/services from the competition. This arrogant approach assumes that customers have neither the means nor the ability to form their own judgments.

Lopsided approach is an example of "a little bit of knowledge is a dangerous thing." It is fallacious to think that attacking one aspect of an enterprise can provide permanent advantages or improvements. The reasons this malpractice does not work are similar to that of the Silver Bullet approach. A company is comprised of functions and organizations that interact systemically. Very few groups work in complete isolation. Consequently, no matter how impressive the improvements in one area may be, they cannot make a lasting, positive, fundamental contribution to a business. This malpractice is usually found in companies whose executive resource systems have been built on functional heritage or where strong functional staff organizations exist. The "leaders" of these organizations lack the general management experience or perspective to consider the business processes as an interrelated and dynamic system. In a very real sense, these organizations have moved people beyond their level of competence. In their to zeal to contribute, they resort to the areas they knew something about neglecting others. In this case, the approach is weak, but not as weak as in the Silver Bullet case. The deployment is strong, stronger than the Silver Bullet, and the results are also mixed as in the Silver Bullet case, as shown in the following.

Lopsided	Maturity
Approach	−
Deployment	+
Results	−

To avoid the lopsided approach, leaders need to "know what they know, and they need to know what they don't know." They need to put a team of complementary skills and experiences to meet the specific strategy and quality needs of the organizations. Who would field a football team made up entirely of quarterbacks? Likewise, it does not make sense to organize a symphony orchestra made up entirely of cellos.

IMPATIENCE

Impatience is a corollary of the Silver Bullet, and it is a sure sign of a lack of strategic maturity and of quality management sophistication. Impatient management overlooks the inherently time-consuming nature of strategy and quality. This is true because both strategy and quality require process reengineering and renewal where internal functions and external constituents have to work together to rethink the business. This is in general a counter-cultural process that takes time and requires persistence. Impatient management also overlooks the nature of cultural transformation where years of ingrained habits and rote business processes have to be changed. Leaders that lack a tolerance for uncertainty and ambiguity and the capability for conceptual insight required for long term strategic thinking tend to become impatient with the unobvious. Fresh thinking and new thoughts diffuse slowly.

A characteristic of this malpractice is to first establish a set of measurements without thinking through what needs to change and why. It is almost as if people were like Pavlov's dogs. Ring the right bells, and the right behavior will follow. This is old thinking, a leftover from the Taylor school of scientific management. In this day and age this approach still works, but the behavioral change is not sustainable. People will do what is inspected and not what is expected for sustainable results. At this point, managers learn to play the game; instead of managing and leading, they learn to manage the indicators.

For example, in most business, market share is an important metric of business success. One way to measure market share is to calculate the ratio of the company's revenues (numerator) divided by the revenues of the industry (denominator). We have seen cases where senior executives redefine the denominator when they are unable to show share growth any other way. By making the denominator smaller a miracle occurs, they have sustained market share growth. When this occurs, there is lack of alignment and integration between improvement in internal measures and business results. A strong focus on results without an equally strong focus on approach may lead to "measurement blindness," where every organization has a set of operational measures that show improvement, but the overall business results do not get any better. The simple fact is that results will always lag effort. On strategy and quality initiatives, positive and impressive results take a long time to materialize. Impatience often leads directly to Leapfrogging and Silver Bullets. It is also frequently the result of Magic Wands when the leader wonders why results are not materializing in spite of waving the magic wand. In this case, the following results:

Impatience	Maturity
Approach	– –
Deployment	=
Results	=

It is not reasonable, nor is it possible, to expect instantaneous results. Although it is always important that management have a sense of urgency, it does not mean that they should be mindlessly impatient. Take the first steps that are appropriate and consistent with the quality and strategy maturity levels of a company, monitor progress, and recognize and reward those who take those steps because they are marking the road to progress and pointing in the direction of a larger opportunity for change. The momentum of small successes accelerates the pace of change, but remember that change is always difficult, and with it come phases of frustration, resistance, and defiance.

COWARDICE

Business results, morale, cost of quality, and other organizational indicators will always lag behind effort. In other words, efforts must come first, frequently significant effort, and at times heroic effort must be exerted before results emerge. People's and organizations' ability to understand and deploy strategy and quality initiatives will vary. Initially, only a very small percentage will enthusiastically start implementation, the majority will view it with some degree of skepticism, and others will openly resist. Because new initiatives take effort, change the status quo, and make people uncomfortable, resistance increases and overall employee morale plunges. This is also precisely the time when the organization has arrived at the turning point.

Unfortunately and frequently, this is also the point when managerial cowardice sets in. This is the time to be decisive and show convincingly, and perhaps dramatically, that there is no turning back. This is illustrated above in Figure 9-2. The Spanish conquistador Cortes did that when he was faced with a severe morale problem among his soldiers in Mexico. He burned his ships. He clearly showed them there was no way to return to Spain. They were in Mexico for the duration. Many managers loose heart as resistance sets in, and they compromise or give up to return to the old ways. Employees begin to describe strategic and quality initiatives as "Another program of the year!" Often when cowardice and impatience are combined, the leadership will blame "them." If only "they" had the same sense of urgency, there would be no problem. If only "the frozen zone"

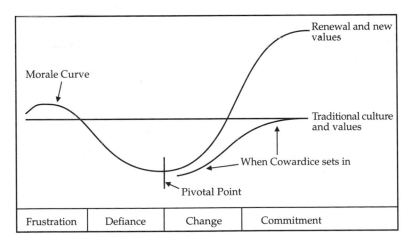

Figure 9-2 Stages of People Attitude.

would move off dead-center, there would be real progress. If "they" made a real effort to shed the past, progress would really accelerate. When the "we" and "they" dichotomy sets in, cowardice is evident, and this will doom the best approaches to failure.

Leaders have the responsibility to stay the course without being deflected and the slightest signs of resistance or temporary setbacks. They should draw courage from the cold facts and rigorous analysis that has been developed from strategic analysis and they should draw strength and stamina from the fact that thoughtful deployment plans are actionable. Leaders need that inner confidence and courage because risk can never be entirely eliminated, and because gaps in the analysis and deployment methodologies can never the completely closed. In dynamic and unpredictable environments, that is inevitable. This is why Hamel and Prahald (1992) talk about strategy as an "expedition:" as a decision-maker, you know the direction, you know it is going to be hard, but you move on because you must. The methodology of Organizational Energetics is particularly helpful to avoid falling in the trap of cowardice. Listening posts provide scanning information to continuously assess direction and attitudes. Adjustments can be made to respond to unanticipated changes without backing down from the goal. With cowardice, the results are weakest, and approach and deployment are never given an opportunity.

Cowardice	Maturity
Approach	+
Deployment	− −
Results	− −

BOIL THE OCEAN

This approach is the antithesis of all the above. It seeks to do too much, instead of not enough. Management tries to launch an excessive number of ad-hoc initiatives without an apparent focus; without an overarching integration of all the efforts. Management finds itself without sufficient time to do justice to all the initiatives underway. Many initiatives are deployed, and measurements are identified without a disciplined and focused approach. And, although a lot is being done, the tragedy is that nothing is being done really well. At the end of the day, it is impossible to declare victory on any meaningful initiative. The organization has redoubled its efforts having lost sight of its goals! RCA and ITT are good examples of companies that tried to boil the ocean. RCA, the company that made televisions, owned NBC, and made computers, went on a buying spree that included a carpet business. ITT made digital switches for telephone networks, owned and ran a worldwide chain of hotels, and baked and distributed bread as well. Although ITT was able to show impressive financial results, the performance was not sustainable beyond the tenure of their CEO.

When GM decided it was going to deploy technology in a massive scale in its factories and cars, it was undertaking a task that was monumental in its scale. Although impressive in its scope, it has yet to produce the financial results anticipated.

Boil the Ocean is the result of lack of strategy analysis and thoughtful consideration of the implications of all the initiatives being launched. Lack of strategic analysis creates a lack of clarity on what is important, what is most important and what can be postponed. Without this kind of unclouded perspective, it is not surprising that energy and efforts can be dissipated in many directions, potentially many of which are unproductive. Even without a good sense of direction, disciplined and systematic analysis of deployment plans and their implications on resources investments will lead one to conclude that not everything is affordable or necessary. In this case, the following results can be seen:

Boil the Ocean	Maturity
Approach	–
Deployment	+
Results	–

This practice is particularly undesirable because it causes people to become cynical. People work hard, but have nothing to show for it. This negative pall makes any subsequent but meaningful initiatives more difficult to launch. Inexperienced managers are most susceptible to Boiling the Ocean. Experienced managers who are new to a specific industry or product line are also susceptible. Weak managers under the gun from dictatorial or unreasonable supervisors also engage in this malpractice. At the tactical level, detailed analysis and presentation of the resource implications caused by fractured and divergent directions is an effective countermeasure. At the macro level, our experience is that strategy analysis and Baldrige are useful instruments to determine where the major weakness are, to create a smaller number of initiatives.

BUY-LOW, SELL-HIGH

Buy-Low Sell-High comes from the retail brokerage business. To get rich, a client is advised to buy stocks at a low price, then sell them at a higher price. The formula is clearly unassailable and foolproof. The fatal flaw is, of course, that it is unactionable. In business, this malpractice is very frequently encountered with the magic wand. Where the magic wand approach identifies initiatives but fails to deploy them, the buy-low, sell-high approach does not get that far. This malpractice can also be called **"PONTIFICATION"** as the leader "Pontificates" theory but cannot articulate concrete and specific actions that people can relate or rally around. The initiatives remain at the abstract and conceptual level with impressive sounding names that only an MBA from a consulting firm can understand. This occurs most often when the leaders have visionary capabilities but lack operational experience. Buy-Low, Sell-High is characterized by pontification of theory and hype; therefore:

Buy-Low, Sell-High	Maturity
Approach	– –
Deployment	– –
Results	–

With this approach there is an observable lack of follow-up, and when it exists, the emphasis is on style, not substance. This managerial malpractice also creates cynicism. People begin to believe that slogans, vision statements, exhortations, and shallow reporting is all there is to quality and strategic management. In this malpractice, the approach is extremely high-level, with no deployment or results. When there is action, people are fundamentally going through the motions. The number of presentations and programs are overwhelming, but are mostly empty of content and substance. To avoid this malpractice, concentrate on deployment plans, and continuous monitoring of progress. Emphasis is on learning, progress, and most importantly on actions.

THE 500-POUND GORILLA

This is the management style that ignores the transformational and cultural dimensions of organizations, the issues of employee morale and well-being, and the participatory and process nature of strategy and quality improvement. Simply stated, this is the management style that believes that if one dictates to people what to do, they will do what they are told; if one manages by the numbers, and if one disciplines those that fail, one will get what one wants; if one reorganizes and puts strong task masters in place, both efficiency and effectiveness will follow. A manger does not need to explain to people where you are taking the organization or why, just tell people what to do. There are no listening posts to monitor attitudes and acceptance. When in doubt, use the stick and throw away the carrots. Speak loudly, carry a big stick, and use it. The weakness of this approach is that the leadership will get what it wants, but not always what it needs. 500-Pound Gorillas completely overlook the fact that everybody can contribute, and that people and organizational transformation are required to achieve sustained business leadership. They tend to operate in the old style of management where a contention system existed between management and labor. Results are the overriding objective; systematic approach and deployment are secondary.

There are situations where 500-Pound Gorillas are needed and effective. They are useful when the leader has a very specific task that needs to be accomplished. The gorillas are given a brief to execute, the parameters and boundaries of jurisdiction are clearly delineated, and the desired results are unambiguously understood. In other words, they are on a short leash. In a way, they are like the Navy Seals, they are there to do a task, and they do it well—like no one else. But think twice about asking them to plan or implement the invasion of Normandy. Here we have:

500-Pound Gorilla	Maturity
Approach	– –
Deployment	=
Results	=

ROTATING BALD TIRES

In this practice, management establishes new objectives and goals, and inspires the organization to achieve new levels of excellence. Then it uses the same initiatives, methods, management systems, and processes of the past, and expect different results. To paraphrase Einstein, "You cannot solve a problem (or create an opportunity) by applying the same level of thinking that created the problem in the first place." Initially, the potential for accomplishment excites the people, but over time they realize that the outcome is inevitably the same. Nothing really ever changes in their tasks, nor in the way management carries on day-to-day business. One of the characteristics of this practice is reorganization at the beginning of the action to better deploy resources, then when progress is lacking, explain it away and reorganize again. Management reviews still run on the same schedules with the same participants reviewing the same measures. People begin to believe that the original objectives and goals, while inspiring, were just another "program of the year"—and "this too shall pass." The organization drives for the new goals, but if they meet them, they cannot trace the achievement back to any substantive changes put in place. In this case, the following results are seen:

Rotating Bald Tires	Maturity
Approach	++
Deployment	− −
Results	− −

Here, an excellent approach fails because of lack of deployment and a focus on those elements important to transformation. Why do organizations rotate bald tires? One reason is that they have not mastered the intellectual substance of strategy and quality and the fundamentals of deployment in a new environment. The strongest indicator of substance is deployment and action that is consistent with the new direction. This takes rethinking the business processes and thinking through to what extent they add to customer value, to what degree they are enhancing competitiveness and how they contribute to quality. Drilling down on these questions will quickly convince the executive or line manager that rotating bald tires may not be the choice approach. How does a company know it may need to rotate bald tires? Its results may not be consistent with its intentions and aspirations. The results are too modest or non-existent. Is management listening to the people who have to make it work? They are on the firing line, listen to them and consider their suggestions. They may surprise you.

The above is the internal manifestation of Rotating Bald Tires. The external manifestation is when a company presents the "same old stuff" to its customers and parades it as new. This can be a product, a service, or a combination of both. This never works, because it assumes that customers are unable to judge what is different and new. Sometimes this is done quite innocently when decision makers are out of touch with customers. Sometimes this is done deliberately, in which case, they are "perfuming the pig" in the hopes that somebody is fooled.

You can fool some of the people some of the time, but not all the people all the time. So the malpractice is not effective, nor is it sustainable, and it borders on the unethical. A word to the wise is: organizations that subscribe to the practice of rotating bald tires should first ensure that the spare tire has air.

REAR-VIEW MIRROR

This practice is less obvious, yet has the potential for turning success into disaster. Why do some successful companies all of a sudden find themselves in crisis? It's because they plan their future goals on historical projections and experience of past success. The malpractice of Rear-View Mirror is actually "rotating intellectual bald tires." This malpractice does not take into account forces affecting the future position of the company, the industry, or the market. These forces and shifts change the predictability of the past. The "Achilles Heel" of successful companies is that they continue to do what made them successful in the past. They become predictable, based on history, to the competition and the industry. Executive development programs teach the emerging leaders to emulate the things that made the company successful.

The momentum and excitement of success lead the organization to spend more time gloating about what it has accomplished than what it will do next. The excellence achieved has lulled the company and management into a false sense of security and impenetrability. While looking in the rear-view mirror, the company does not see the bend in the road—until it's too late to respond. They go into the ditch. They begin layoffs, downsizing, and/or portfolio restructuring. In this malpractice, approach, deployment, and results were strong, but the company forgot that the marketplace and competition are not stagnant.

Rear-View Mirror	Maturity
Approach	– –
Deployment	=
Results	–

How do you prevent from managing through the rear-view mirror? What it takes is an awareness that the old recipes won't work. To make sure that this awareness develops, cast the old recipes in the new evolving environment and demonstrate that they will be ineffective. Another, less ambitious way is to identify a major emerging force in the environment, such a new innovative competitor, a new hot product, etc., and show the damage that this new force will inflict on the company. Scenario Planning is a good instrument to understand the efficacy of Rear-View Mirror Strategies in a new and emerging environment. Continuous scanning, adjustment, and improvement are required. Changing the course of a business will not be easy. CEOs will be taking the executive management out of its "comfort zone," and moving it into what it perceives as being the "danger zone." What does not work is the alarmist and dooms day approach. Where redirection and new alignment are required an analytic approach, compelling logic, and building coalitions of supporters are the means to achieve what effectively is a business transformation.

Full Speed Ahead and Damn the Torpedoes

In this malpractice, management executives do not implement systems and processes to recognize warning signs or triggers that signal a shift in status quo. This malpractice is frequently seen with the malpractice of Impatience, it is a favorite one for 500-pound Gorillas and those who are Rotating Bald Tires. They have set a course, and no matter what occurs, they will stay that course. They will persevere through diligence, dedication, and commitment. They spend all their time developing excuses for problems rather than analyzing the causes and looking for weakness in approach or searching for opportunities to improve deployment. Their persistence gives the organization short term confidence in the direction set, but this confidence erodes when the course of action does not begin to deliver promised results. No one can predict the future.

The Big Three automobile manufacturers were "going full speed ahead" in the 1970s and 1980s. While they were busily adding fins to their cars and building gas guzzlers, the consumers were looking for fuel efficiency, economy, and a vehicle that was manufactured with fewer defects. Simultaneously, the countries in the Gulf were taking control of their oil deposits and raising the price of petroleum crude. The warning signs and triggers that were signaling a shift in the status quo did not register on the radar screens of the Big Three, they were going full speed ahead.

Digital is another example. Personal computers sales were clocking regularly high double digit growth, customers wanted systems that did not have proprietary and closed architectures. Yet Digital persisted in staying with their proprietary architecture and ignoring personal computers. "Full steam ahead" with Digital's minicomputers and "damn the torpedoes" of personal computers and open systems" without convenient personal computer connections was not a sustainable recipe for success.

The best one can do is identify trends and forces affecting the environment and anticipate alternative futures. A vision of the future can be developed from a strategy process, but this is not a one time event. To achieve a vision in a highly refined and mature stage of strategy, executives must have processes and systems that continuously monitor key indicators and anticipate situations that validate their course and direction, or cause them to make adjustments to respond. The ability to effectively and efficiently make these course adjustments on a long term journey to achieve a vision is a hallmark of a mature quality system. Most major battles are won because of a systematic and integrated approach between strategy and quality implementation. The overall strategy is planned based on factual analysis of the environment and the participants, but the difference between winning and losing is the ability to identify situations or changes from what was planned, and respond efficiently and effectively. In this case:

Full Speed Ahead	Maturity
Approach	+
Deployment	− −
Results	−

❖   ❖   ❖

There you have them. The "dirty dozen." The twelve
more frequently made mistakes in strategy and quality.
The reason they are ineffective is that their approach and
deployment are drastically out of alignment and therefore
do not yield the sustainable expected results for Competitive Dominance. Hence, the term "malpractices."

10

Summary and Conclusions

Competitive Dominance is about winning and staying a winner. It is about a style of management that seeks to achieve sustained leadership by outthinking the competition with more effective strategies and by outperforming the competition with superior quality and customer satisfaction. The core concept of Competitive Dominance is that strategy and quality are two sides of the same coin. Competitive Dominance is about doing the right things: strategy, Competitive Dominance is simultaneously about doing things right: quality. Competitive Dominance is also an attitude. It begins with the axiomatic principle that leadership is temporary. This means that the incumbent can be dislodged by the innovative, aggressive and hungry upstart who aspires to be the leader. This also means that to stay the leader, one must relentlessly create more customer value and one must constantly and continuously surprise the competition. Finally, Competitive Dominance is not about unethical or illegal business practices. It is really about making companies the undisputed winners in the global marketplace.

Another central theme of this book is that managerial principles are not useful unless they are also actionable. We place a heavy emphasis on a unifying structure for the integrated practice of strategy and quality. In this chapter we summarize with an overall blueprint of how to put this book to work for you in an actionable manner. This book has tried to address five of the most pressing questions managers and business leaders ask themselves:

1.   What is my current situation?

2.   What approach should I use given my current situation?

3.   How do I act on the approach that I have taken?

4.   What are the pitfalls that I should avoid in the implementation?

5.   How I do know whether I am getting the right results?

We diagram these questions into a flow diagram that is illustrated in Figure 10-1, the Competitive Dominance Learning Process. Let us briefly discuss each of the blocks in this diagram.

> **Situation:** This block seeks to address the question: What is my current situation? This question is motivated by the uncertainties in the managers' minds about whether they are doing the right things and/or whether they are doing things right. Managers must

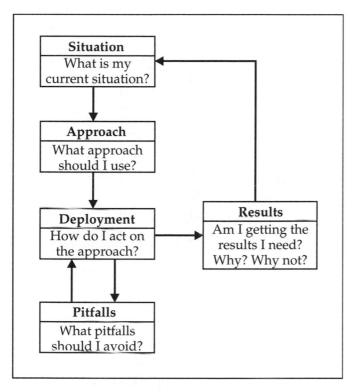

Figure 10-1 The Competitive Dominance Learning Process.

know their company's position in the Competitive Dominance Alignment Map. As we discussed in Chapter 1, there are four regions of the matrix (labeled regions I, II, III, and IV) in which companies can be positioned. We also described in Chapter 1, that a company's position is determined by the combination of its strategy and quality maturity.

Chapter 2 presents empirical evidence of the value of integrating strategy and quality. This is illustrated in Figure 10-2, Competitive Dominance Alignment Map.

Approach: This block addresses question number two which is: What approach should I use given my current

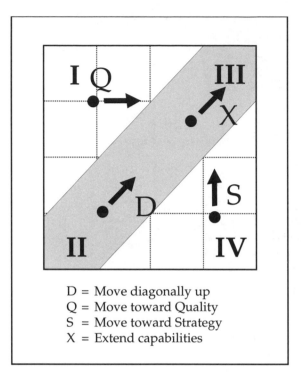

Figure 10-2 Competitive Dominance Alignment Map.

situation? In Chapter 1, we show that there were four stages of strategy maturity and four stages of quality maturity. The discussions and descriptions of each of the four stages will provide managers with the ability to adopt an approach to improve their position depending upon where they are positioned in the Alignment Map.

If their company falls into Region I, then they are weaker in quality and relatively stronger in strategy. For guidance, the managers of those companies can read Chapter 4, Quality and Competitive Dominance, to improve their quality initiatives. Properly designed quality initiatives can reposition the company in a more optimal alignment. This is illustrated by the arrow labeled Q, for Quality.

If on the other hand, companies fall in Region IV, these companies have stronger quality maturity than strategy. They need to improve on their strategy maturity. The managers of those companies can read Chapter 3, Strategy and Competitive Dominance, to improve their strategy initiatives. These new actions can move a company's position up along the diagonal. This is shown by the arrow labeled S, for Strategy.

If the company falls in Region II, then it is aligned, but it is low in the maturity of both strategy and quality. This type of company needs to undertake new and innovative strategy and quality initiatives. Chapters 3 and 4, Strategy and Competitive Dominance and Quality and Competitive Dominance, describe how this can be done. Balanced actions that consider both strategy and quality initiatives can move the company into an improved and aligned position that can position the company further up along the 45 degree diagonal. This is illustrated with the arrow labeled D, for Improvements.

Those exceptional firms that are positioned in Region III of the Alignment Map need to make sure that they can sustain their position. Figure 10-2 illustrates the reasons why leadership of companies in position III are so vulnerable, and why leadership is temporary. Companies in Position III are subject to competitive threats from three directions. These companies in position III need to take action to extend their lead. Chapter 5 provides the fundamental principles for Competitive Dominance. Application of these principles provide Position III companies the approaches needed to extend their lead. This is illustrated through the arrow labeled X, for extension of capabilities.

Deployment: This block of the flow diagram address the third question: How I act on the approach that I have taken? The three chapters in this book that address this question are Chapters 5, 7, and 8. We have taken four chapters in order to reinforce the importance of actionable management principles. Chapter 5 provides the fundamental principles for Competitive Dominance; advanced and leading-edge deployment should adhere to these principles. Chapters 7 and 8 present very concrete and specific tools and methodologies that make the principles outlined in Chapter 5 actionable. We do not claim that these principles are new, but we do claim that their unified practice does elevate the excellence of strategy and quality initiatives. Neither do we claim that these principles displace known and proven quality and strategy principles. Rather, they supplement what is known to be effective and make those known practices and methodologies even more effective.

Pitfalls: The fourth question that lead to the block diagram in Figure 10-1 was: What are the pitfalls that should be avoided in the implementation? The corollary to a bias toward action is a concern for implementation pitfalls. We observe that when it comes to strategy and quality, there are some common errors are made consistently. Chapter 9 identifies more frequently made errors which we call managerial "malpractices." Analysts and staffs have a tendency to down play this kind of discussion, but those who have line responsibility have told us that they find this discussion an accurate depiction of common mistakes.

Results: Any business is concerned with results. This is question five: How I do know whether I am getting the right results? Chapter 6 provides the unifying framework for this analysis. In that Chapter, we have integrated the principles of Competitive Dominance into the Baldrige framework. In Chapters 2, 3, and 4 we have discussed in substantial detail the reasons why we think that integrating our Competitive Dominance principles into the Baldrige framework is the right approach. The simple reason is that the Baldrige framework has the scope to cover an enterprise and its activities, end-to-end in a sufficiently rich and robust manner. To render this explicit, we have shown in very detailed and instructive manner how the integration is actually accomplished. Consistent with the Baldrige principles, and all other worthy strategy and quality principles, this block loops back to the Situation block. This closed-loop process provides the means for a company or organization to achieve the levels of Competitive Dominance.

We introduce Figure 10-3, which is a refinement of Figure 10-1, identifying the chapters in the book that address the key questions that every business must consider. This figure also describes the architecture and the unifying logic of the book.

The major concepts of this book can be summarized with the ten principles of Competitive Dominance. Figure 10-4, Highlights of Competitive Dominance, below provides that summary.

The core concept of Competitive Dominance is simple. Strategy and Quality are two sides of the same coin. The theme of this book is that to become and to stay a winner, a company must drive both. Business leaders and managers cannot neglect either one. The practice of both requires discipline and commitment. We have tried to share with our readers how this can be done. It worked for us, and there is no reason why readers cannot do better. After

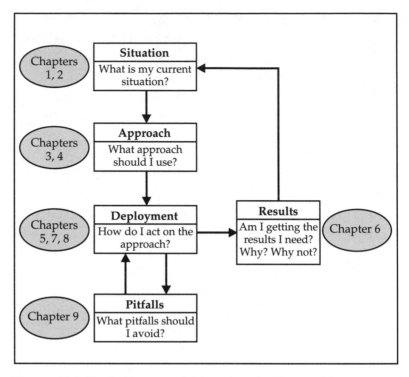

Figure 10-3 Book Chapters Addressing the Competitive Dominance Learning Process.

all, continuous improvement is a fundamental concept in strategy and quality. Our real hope is that your business becomes the sustained and undisputed global winner.

Competitive Dominance Principle	Highlights
Strategic Leadership	• Rejection of the separation between strategy and quality. • Integration of Strategy and Quality as a single concept and managerial practice. • Balanced and simultaneous leadership necessary in both.
Continuous Environmental Scanning	• Market intelligence for strategy and quality. • Extend environmental scanning input to quality processes. • Extend quality scanning input to strategy processes.
Modeling Trends and Dynamics	• Rejection of "rear-view" mirror as sufficient basis for action. • Rejection of fixed-point forecasting. • Adopt stochastic/dynamic models such as scenario analysis.
Listening Posts	• Continuously monitor internal and external stakeholders, customers, competition, and markets. • Have a system to diagnose attitudes and rapidly respond.
Change & Transformation	• Necessary for strategy and quality. • Systematic Strategy and Quality change from today to tomorrow. • Rejection of "rear-view" mirror as sufficient basis for initiatives.

Figure 10-4 Highlights of Competitive Dominance

Competitive Dominance Principle	Highlights
Customer-centric Culture	• Focus on keeping customers and creating new ones faster than • competitors. • Focus on customer value and satisfaction. • Scope is throughout the life-cycle of the offering.
Unified-Systemic Links	• Integration of strategy and quality processes to achieve extended enterprise, cross-functional processes. • Extend process scope to life-cycle boundaries.
Stakeholder Integration	• Integration of stakeholders into strategy and quality processes. • Integration scope covers the life-cycle of the offering. • Stakeholder view is the company, not the function.
Organizational Energetics	• Organization and employee morale, excitement, and commitment as strategy and transformation metrics. • Different morale management approaches at different stages of the change and transformation.
Opportunity Growth	• Quality has equal emphasis on today as tomorrow. • Revenue growth, market-share growth, and capturing new opportunity as fundamental quality metrics.

Figure 10-4 Highlights of Competitive Dominance *(continued)*

Bibliography

K.R. Andrews, Editor, *Strategic Management.* 1983. New York: John Wiley & Sons, Inc.
Classical collection of papers on the subject of strategy formulation and implementation issues.

ASQC/GALLUP. 1992. Survey on Quality Leadership Roles of Corporate Directors and Executives. *ASQC/Gallup Survey.*
Survey of opinions of top corporate executives and outside directors in American Business Organizations. The survey explored their views with regard to quality.

Baldrige Winners: Quality Starts with CEOs. 1994. *USA Today.* February 10.
Two winners of 1994 Baldrige discuss the fundamental importance of leadership in deploying quality improvement initiatives. They are from Ames Rubber and Eastman Chemical.

J.M. Bardwick. 1991. *Danger in the Comfort Zone*. New York: AMACOM.

Insightful model of the behavior of people in situations and organizations where they have learned "helplessness" through a combination of organizational climate and personal choices.

R.A. Bauer, E. Collar, V. Tang. 1992. *The Silverlake Project: Transformation at IBM*. New York: Oxford University Press.

The authors present the ten general management principles that created the AS/400 product success and won the 1990 Baldrige Award. They describe the links between strategy and quality and how they are deployed and practiced. Foreword by Tom Peters, the management guru.

R.A. Bauer. 1991. IBM Rochester Malcolm Baldrige Award Lectures. Unpublished.

Lectures on strategy and quality initiatives and practices in IBM Rochester that helped win the Baldrige Award.

R.A. Bauer. 1992. *A Vision for Quality Management*. Paper read at National Quality Month Presentation, October 1, 1992, at Minneapolis, Minnesota.

The concept of stages of quality and the meaning of competitive dominance are first presented to a group of quality practitioners.

G. Bounds, L. Yorks, M. Adams, G. Ranney. 1994. *Beyond Total Quality Management: Toward The Emerging Paradigm*. New York: McGraw-Hill.

A comprehensive and thoroughly researched textbook on TQM from the academe. Authors propose the concept of Strategic Quality Management to go beyond TQM. The development is in the right direction. This book is skewed to quality; more on strategy would provide parity between the two.

J.H. Boyette, S.B. Schwartz, L.L. Osterwise, R.A. Bauer. 1993. *The Quality Journey: How Winning the Baldrige Sparked the Remaking of IBM*. New York: Dutton.

Another look at how IBM Rochester went about winning the 1990 Baldrige Award. The appendix contains the application that won the award.

Betting to Win on the Baldie Winners. 1993. *Business Week.* October 18.
As a reply to Juran, the editors of Business Week show that a hypothetical investment on Malcolm Baldrige winners would have made the investor a tidy profit.

The New Breed of Strategic Planner. 1984. *Business Week.* September 17. pp. 62–68.
Identifies the dissatisfaction with strategic planning delegated to staffs. Discusses the increasing trend of line managers as strategists to close the gap between formulation and implementation.

Return on Quality. 1994. *Business Week.* August 4. pp. 54–58.
Article discusses the emerging approach that is being adopted by more companies in the US, which consists of measuring the cost of quality initiatives, and then translating the return of those efforts in financial or other terms.

R.D. Buzzell, B.T. Gale. 1987. *The PIMS Principles: Linking Strategy to Performance.* New York: The Free Press.
From market research covering 3000 businesses in Europe and North America, this book establishes the link between quality and positive business results.

R. Charan, N. Tichy. 1991. How Networks Make Organizations Boundaryless—And Deliver Superior Results. *Harvard Business Review.* September–October.
Describes how an organization must transform itself by breaking down artificial boundaries or rigid structures to close the gap between CEO vision and excellence.

C.R. Christensen, K.R. Andrews, J.L. Bower, R.G. Hamermesh, M.C. Porter. 1982. *Business Policy: Text and Cases.* Illinois: Richard D. Irwin.

A text book of cases from the faculty of the Harvard Business School. Introductory chapters useful for understanding key concepts.

R.F. Clark, A.D. Hovanassian. 1993. A Unified Hypothesis for Quality: A Closed Form Equation for Customer Satisfaction, Employee Satisfaction, Productivity and Quality. IBM Technical Report No. TR 03.522. Santa Teresa: IBM Santa Teresa Development Laboratory.

Four year longitudinal data on a large scale quality initiative shows that there is are direct links among quality, customer satisfaction, employee satisfaction and productivity. Very convincing empirical data that most only conjecture about.

P.B. Crosby. 1979. *Quality is Free.* New York: McGraw Hill.

A classic by one of the early advocates of quality. One of the early formulators of the concepts that quality is conformance to requirements, that quality initiatives do not "cost," and that it is the lack of quality that is financially costly.

T.H. Davenport. 1993. *Process Innovation: Reengineering Work Through Information Technology.* Boston: Harvard University School Press.

From the original thinker on the subject of organizational transformation through process innovation.

W.E. Deming. 1986. *Out of the Crisis.* Cambridge, Massachusetts: MIT Center for Advanced Engineering Study.

This large tome is a comprehensive elaboration of the theory, methodologies, and management practices from the leading thinker of quality.

Does the Baldrige Award Really Work? 1992. *Harvard Business Review.* January–February. pp. 126–148.

Lively letters from readers of the Harvard Business Review that debate a wide range of issues about Baldrige. The level of knowledge of comments range from the naive to the sophisticated, and shallow to profound.

Does Quality Really Work? A Review of Relevant Studies. 1993. *Report Number 1043.* New York: The Conference Board.

A survey of quality in American business. It shows that TQM and Baldrige are increasingly practiced in the U.S., and that many firms are benefiting. It appears that a contributing factor to the variance in benefits obtained is the result of differences in the practice.

L.R. Donnithorne. 1994. *The West Point Way of Leadership.* New York: Doubleday.

We like this book because it places such a strong emphasis on character in leadership. The author draws a distinction from ethics which he views as a lesser attribute.

P.F. Drucker. 1994. The Theory of Business. *Harvard Business Review.* September–October. pp. 95–104.

Describes what constitutes a business. Most interesting aspect of this paper is the argument that firms fail not because they do things poorly, but because they do the wrong things so well. They do things by rote, long after those things have ceased to be important.

When Slimming Is Not Enough. 1994. *The Economist.* September 3. pp. 59–60.

The article points out that corporate anorexia is effective in slimming the corporation, but it is fatally flawed because it fails to address growth. The writer, is in fact, too tactful. The described practice is more bulimic than anorexic.

A.V. Feigenbaum. 1983. *Total Quality Control.* Cincinnati, Ohio: Association for Quality and Participation.

The TQM emphasis is on quality as defined by the customer at the most economical cost. Genuine management involvement is another hallmark of his method.

E. Fontela, A. Hingel. 1993. Scenarios on Economic and Social Cohesion in Europe. *Futures.* March.

This paper illustrates very lucidly the construction of scenarios from forces which are stratified at different levels of intensity. Excellent illustration of scenario creation process.

D.A. Garvin. 1991. How the Baldrige Award Really Works. 1991. *Harvard Business Review* November–December. pp. 80–93.

A very readable survey of the Baldrige criteria. Convincingly knocks off the criticisms and uninformed myths that surround Baldrige. Longitudinal data shows that Baldrige is having an effect on American industry.

D.A. Garvin. 1993. Building a Learning Organization. *Harvard Business Review.* July–August.

Article describes the attributes of a learning organization and the maturation process which learning organizations go through.

F. W. Gluck, S. P. Kaufman and A. S. Walleck. 1985. Strategic Management for Competitive Advantage. In *Strategic Management,* ed. K.R. Andrews, New York: John Wiley & Sons, Inc.

Authors postulate and describe stages of strategic maturity.

C. Scott Greene, J. Nkonge. 1989. Gaining a Competitive Edge Through Conjoint Analysis. *Business.* April–June.

Describes how conjoint analysis is useful in the marketing functions of a business. In particular how it is useful in the specification of product features.

P.E. Greene, V. Srinivasan. 1990. Conjoint Analysis in Marketing: New Developments with Implications for Research and Practice. *Journal of Marketing,* October.

More on the use of conjoint analysis for marketing. Not light reading.

P.E. Greene, V.R. Rao. 1971. Conjoint Measurement for Quantifying Judgmental Data. *Journal of Marketing Research.* August.

Dated, but still very useful paper to aid the understanding of the concepts of the conjoint methodology in the analysis of statistical information.

G. Hamel, C.K. Prahalad. 1989. Strategic Intent. *Harvard Business Review.* May–June. pp. 63–76.

Seminal paper that is among the first to sound the clarion call to think about strategy in a different way. Thought provoking and stimulating.

G. Hamel, C.K. Prahalad. 1993. Strategy as Stretch and Leverage. *Harvard Business Review.* March–April. pp. 75–84.

Authors take the next step from their original Strategic Intent manifesto and provide actionable prescriptions for leveraging resources within and outside the firm for strategic advantage.

G. Hamel, C.K. Prahalad. 1994. *Competing for the Future.* Boston: Harvard Business School Press.

Elaboration of the notions of core competence, strategic intent, stretch and leverage. Cogently argues that downsizing is not enough to build a future, but that a vision is necessary.

M. Hammer, J. Champy. 1993. *Reengineering the Corporation: A Manifesto for Business Revolution.* New York: Harper Business.

The popular and readable book on the need for business to rethink and rearchitect their business processes. Shows how to find the opportunities for doing so and provides corporate examples.

R.G. Hamermesh. 1986. *Making Strategy Work: How Senior Managers Produce Results.* New York: John Wiley & Sons, 1986.

A book from the Harvard Business School on how to implement strategy and mobilize organizations to do it. Highlights the disconnect between formulation and implementation, but useful and actionable for those who must deal with this issue.

J. C. Henderson, N. Venkatraman. 1993. Strategic Alignment: Leveraging Information Technology for Transforming Organizations. *IBM Systems Journal*. Vol. 32, No. 1., pp. 4–16.

The paper addresses the issue of information and business processes that use the information within a context of business transformation.

J.L. Heskett, T.O. Jones, G.W. Loveman, W.E. Sasser, Jr., L.A. Schlesinger. 1994. Putting the Service-Profit Chain to Work. *Harvard Business Review*. March–April.

This article shows that by putting customer satisfaction first, profit, quality, and employee satisfaction will follow. Demonstrates this by showing longitudinal empirical data, but does not provide a closed form analytical linkage.

The Horizontal Corporation. 1993. *Business Week*. December 20. pp. 76–81.

Surveys the phenomenon of downsizing, managing across functional boundaries and the importance of teams that drive business processes. Identifies the importance of employee empowerment.

S. Hoisington, T. Huang, T. Cousins, T. Suther. 1993. Customer View of Ideal Business Machine Enterprise. *IBM Technical Report*. January.

A series of technical reports that define a customer satisfaction model and the methodology to develop that model Also, results of a study to mathematically correlate customer satisfaction, people satisfaction, market share, productivity, and quality.

K. Ishikawa. 1985. *What is Total Quality Control?: The Japanese Way*. Englewood Cliffs, NJ: Prentice-Hall.

TMQ from the father of wishbone diagram. Required reading for anyone serious about quality and root cause analysis.

J.M. Juran. 1988. *Juran On Planning for Quality*. New York: Macmillan.

A widely read volume by one of the leading thinkers and advocates of quality.

J.M. Juran. 1991. Strategies for World-Class Quality. *Quality Progress.* pp. 81–85

From the guru himself, how to reach world-class quality.

C. Kaplan, R.F. Clark, V. Tang. 1995. *Secrets of Software Quality: 40 Innovations from IBM.* New York: McGraw-Hill, Inc.

The authors show how a four-year quality and organizational transformation journey not only improved quality and improved financial position, but it also improved employee morale and customer satisfaction. They show empirical evidence that these variables are linked systemically. This book is also a case study in the stages of quality maturity and the links with strategy.

J. Kay. 1993. *Foundations of Corporate Success: How Business Strategies Add Value.* Oxford: Oxford University Press.

Provides a very thought provoking discussion of the meaning, significance, and practices of strategy. Subject matter developed with tightly reasoned and argued framework and models. Makes no claims that are not supported either with empirical data or structured framework.

K. Kelly. 1993. Turning Rivals into Teammates. *Special Bonus Issue Business Week.*

How companies of different sizes and financial resources can team up to address opportunities. Another example of how to rethink who is a competitor or an ally.

R. Koselka. 1993. Evolutionary Economics: Nice Guys Don't Finish Last. *Forbes.* October.

Article argues that teamwork and altruistic motives may be the best strategy after all.

U.S. Knotts Jr., L.G. Parrish Jr., C.R. Evans. 1993. What Does the US Business Community Really Think About the Baldrige Award? *Quality Progress.* May. pp. 49–52.

Article shows the impact of Baldrige in raising the literacy and awareness of quality in the US.

B.R. Kosynski. 1993. Strategic Control in the Extended Enterprise. *IBM Systems Journal.* Vol. 32, No. 1. pp. 111–142.

Paper discusses how strategic linkage among businesses must consider the information technologies that are deployed and the nature of the process linkages. Identifies the critical role of data and business processes—key Baldrige criteria.

P. Kotler. 1991. *Marketing Management.* Englewood Cliffs, New Jersey: Prentice Hall.

This is the definitive textbook on the subject.

T.S. Kuhn. 1962. *The Structure of Scientific Revolutions.* Chicago. University of Chicago Press.

Required reading for strategists and anyone who is a transformational agent. The construct of paradigm analysis is one the most original contributions in critical thinking and analysis. This paradigm is frequently misused. Here is the source.

J.L. Lamprecht. 1992. *ISO 9000.* Wisconsin: ASQC Quality Press.

Survey of the ISO 9000 standards and the processes for certification.

C.N. Madu, C. Kuei. 1993. Introducing Strategic Quality Planning. *Long Range Planning.* Vol. 26. pp. 212–131.

The authors propose extensions to Total Quality Management and formulate ten principles of Strategic Quality Management. The proposals are skewed to quality. The principles are a step in the right direction, although the article does not go far enough in the area of strategy.

J. Main. 1994. *Quality Wars: The Triumphs and Defeats of American Business.* A Juran Institute Report. New York: The Free Press.

Very readable and thoroughly researched on the practices of TQM by American companies. These are not just stories. The author analyzes why TQM is hard, and why it is rewarding. A must for executives seeking to undertake the quality and strategy transformation journey.

Malcolm Baldrige National Quality Award Criteria. 1994. *US Department of Commerce, National Institute of Standards and Technology.* Gaithersburg, Maryland.

Specifies the principles of Baldrige quality and the criteria for applying for submitting an application.

Malcolm Baldrige National Quality Awards Review. 1992–1995. Unpublished Presentation. *US Department of Commerce, National Institute of Standards and Technology.* Gaithersburg, Maryland.

Discusses the practice of Baldrige quality in the US and the increased level of awareness on the subject of quality. Identifies the hopeful signs as well as areas of disappointment. Identifies lack of quality vision and strategy as area of disappointment.

Malcolm Baldrige National Quality Award Office. 1988–1994 Distribution of Written Scores for Malcolm Baldrige Participants. *US Department of Commerce, National Institute of Standards and Technology.* Gaithersburg, Maryland.

Seven years of trend data showing the scores of Malcolm Baldrige participants. Data shows a declining trend in points achieved.

Management Practices: US Companies Improve Performance Through Quality Efforts. 1991. *Report to the Honorable D. Ritter, House of Representatives, GAO/NSIAD-91–190.* Washington DC: United States General Accounting Office.

Discusses the Baldrige framework and shows survey data supporting the benefits that US companies have derived from the application of Baldrige Principles.

M. Maruyama. 1987. New Economic Thinking. *Futures.* August.

This paper is particularly interesting because it illustrates so well the concept of causal loops, in other words, how forces interact with each other either reinforcing or attenuating the strengths of others. This is a critical aspect of robust scenario development.

L.M. Miller. 1989. Barbarians to Bureaucrats: Corporate Life Cycle Strategies. New York: Fawcett Columbine.

The author presents a life cycle theory of corporations. The theory argues that corporations must eventually all lose competitiveness, suffer decline, and atrophy.

H. Mintzberg. 1994. *The Rise and Fall of Strategic Planning.* New York: The Free Press.

Persuasively argues that the pitfalls of classical strategic planning and the conventional processes have created dysfunctional management practices. Proposes new roles for planners.

Cara Chang Mutert. 1993. *Sales and Marketing Strategies and News.* Vol. 3, No. 6. November–December.

A very lucid article of how thoughtful positioning creates differentiation and competitive advantage. Very readable and useful.

C.A. Montgomery, M.E. Porter. 1991. *Strategy: Seeking and Securing Competitive Advantage.* Boston: Harvard Business Review Publishing Division.

A superb collection of articles from the Harvard Business Review on the subject of strategy. Many of the articles are still rooted in the classical orthodoxy of strategic fit.

H. Mintzberg. 1987. Crafting Strategy. *Harvard Business Review.* July–August. pp. 66–75.

Persuasive argument for continuous development and refinement of strategy. Strategy is crafted not formulated or implemented.

J.S. Neves, B. Nakhai. 1994. The Evolution of the Baldrige Award. *Quality Progress.* June. pp. 65–70.

The article identifies the yearly improvements and refinements that have been made to Baldrige. Dispels the myth that the Baldrige criteria are static and unchanging.

R. Normann, R. Ramirez. 1993. From Value Chain to Value Constellation: Designing Interactive Strategy. *Harvard Business Review.* July–August.

Describes how to create and reinvent value for customers and innovative ways to create value by engaging participants outside the walls of the firm.

K. Ohmae, *The Mind of the Strategist*: The Art of Japanese Business. 1982. New York: McGraw-Hill Book Company.

Very readable book on strategic thinking and strategy formulation processes. Presents the 3-C model for strategy analysis and formulation. Three Cs are customers, competition, and company.

T. Peters. 1988. *Thriving on Chaos.* New York: Alfred A. Knopf.

Parts II, IV, and V provide a lively discussion on how to maintain the energy and enthusiasm in an organization with actionable recommendations.

T. Peters. 1993. *Liberation Management.* New York: Alfred A. Knopf.

More from Tom Peters on new ways of thinking about management and business. Lively and thought provoking.

M.C. Porter. 1985. *Competitive Strategy: Techniques for Analyzing Industries and Competitors. New York*: The Free Press.

This is the celebrated book that introduced the 5-forces approach to industry analysis and the concept of strategic groups. Readable and useful. A must for anyone seriously interested in strategy.

M.C. Porter. 1985. *Competitive Advantage.* New York: The Free Press.

Discusses how to create sustainable advantage by concentrating on the structure and economics of the value chain and by creating the right interrelationships among companies from related industries.

J.T. Rabbitt, P.A. Berg. 1993. *The ISO 9000 Book: A Global Competitor's Guide to Compliance and Certification.* White Plains, New York: Quality Resources. New York: AMACOM.

A readable and popular guide on what and how of ISO 9000.

M.E. Raynor. 1992. Quality As A Strategic Weapon. Journal of Business Strategy. September–October

The author argues that the strategies ought to be quality-driven, customer-driven and not product centered and also argues that Baldrige framework is useful for adopting his concept.

E.M. Rogers. 1983. *Diffusion of Innovations.* New York: The Free Press.

Very lucid and insightful discussion on the factors that accelerate and inhibit acceptance and practice of new and innovative ideas that may run counter to accepted conventional wisdom.

R. P. Rumelt, D.E. Schendel, D.J. Teece. 1994. *Fundamental Issues in Strategy: A Research Agenda.* Boston: Harvard Business School Press.

Leading researchers from the academe focus on the questions of strategy for multibusiness firms, multinational competition, and the organizational implications.

T.L. Saaty. 1990. *Decision Making for Leaders: The Analytic Hierarchy Process for Decisions in a Complex World.* Pittsburgh: University of Pittsburgh.

Discusses the multidimensional nature of management decisions and goes on to describe the Analytic Hierarchy Process (AHP) for parsing those decisions into its constituent parts and structuring them hierarchically.

T.L. Saaty, K.P. Kearns. 1985. *Analytical Planning: The Organizations of Systems*. New York: Pergamon Press.

New conceptual framework for planning is presented and tools for integrating the concepts of systems and planning. Great discussion on the shortcomings of traditional planning.

T.L. Saaty. 1987. *Rank Generation, Preservation and Reversal in the Analytic Hierarchy Process*. Decision Sciences, Vol. 18., No. 2, Spring.

AHP description and discussion, which is much more mathematically intense and rigorous. Not light reading.

S.P. Schnaars. 1987. How to Develop and Use Scenarios. *Long Range Planning*. Vol. 20. pp. 105–114.

Paper describes how to develop and create scenarios. Readable and useful introduction to the subject.

P.M. Senge. 1990. *The Fifth Discipline: The Art & Practice of the Learning Organization*. New York: Doubleday.

Long overdue book on the application of systems thinking to business and strategy. A must for those who are into strategy, scenario analysis, and those trying to understand how to knit quality initiatives into an approach that hangs together.

Graham Shorman. 1992. When Quality Control Gets in the Way of Quality. *Wall Street Journal*, February 25.

This article from McKinsey & Co. describes management frustration with getting quality initiatives off the ground and making them effective in delivering business results.

T. Sowell. 1980. *Knowledge and Decisions*. New York: Basic Books.

Very thoughtful book on the role of knowledge, whether accurate, biased, or informed, in decision making in social institutions.

G. Stalk. 1988. Time—The Next Source of Competitive Advantage. *Harvard Business Review*. July–August. pp. 41–53.

Time as a new dimension of strategy advantage is presented very persuasively.

R. Stanat. 1990. *The Intelligent Corporation.* New York: AMACOM.
The book describes the intelligence function of an enterprise. Discusses the sources, analysis, and reporting of information.

T.A. Stewart. 1993. Reengineering, The Hot New Management Tool. *Fortune.* August 23. pp. 41–48.
Article focuses its attention on reconstructing business processes in such a way that it streamlines the operations and drives cross-functional teamwork.

T.A. Stewart. 1994. Reegineering: The Hot New Managing Tool. *Fortune.* August 23.
Shows that it may be for everyone. Provides straight forward and common sense how to manage the process to succeed.

P.R. Stokke, W.K. Ralston, T.A. Boyce, I.H. Wilson. 1990. Scenario Planning for Norwegian Oil and Gas. *Long Range Planning.* Vol. 23. No.2. pp. 17–26.
A good example of scenario creation in the petrochemical industry.

Strategists Confront Planning Challenges. 1990. *Journal of Business.* May–June. pp. 4–8.
Interview with Bell & Howell's I. A. Marquardt who makes the insightful observation of the lack of linkage between strategy and quality and correctly identifies this as a major weakness.

B. Stratton. 1994. Goodbye, ISO 9000; Welcome Back, Baldrige Award. *Quality Progress.* August.
Editorial points out the difference between ISO 9000 as a tool and ISO 9000 certification as a goal attainment. Argues that Baldrige is the best framework for a business to improve quality.

G. Taguchi, D. Clausing. 1990. Robust Quality. *Harvard Business Review.* January–February. pp. 65–75.
Paper discusses how to improve product quality through design methodologies and disciplined management of specifications and parts.

V. Tang, E. Collar. 1992. IBM AS/400 New Product Launch Process Ensures Satisfaction. *Long Range Planning.* Vol. 25, No. 1. pp. 22–27.

Authors show inter-enterprise and intra-enterprise cross-functional teaming improves strategic positioning as well as product quality. The paper documents practices that helped win the 1990 Baldrige Award. The paper is a good example of systems thinking in the area of strategy.

N.M. Tichy, M.A. Devanna. 1986. *The Transformational Leader.* New York: John Wiley.

Book describes the stages of transformation of an organization and the characteristics of leaders that can effect those transformations.

Total Quality Research Report. 1993. *Teknologisk Institutt.* Oslo: Norway.

Broad analysis of quality initiatives worldwide linking TQM, ISO 9000 and other quality methodologies. Reports on the links between quality and business results.

A.H Van de Ven, H.L. Angle, M.S. Scott Poole. 1989. *Research on the Management of Innovation:* The Minnesota Studies. New York: Harper & Row.

Excellent longitudinal study on what management practices work and do not work in the quest of creating new markets with new products. Discussion on the necessity of an industry infrastructure for rapid product acceptance and diffusion of innovation is very insightful.

P. Wack. 1985. Scenarios, Uncharted Waters Ahead. *Harvard Business Review,* September–October. pp. 73–89.

The seminal paper on scenario planning, what scenarios are, how to think about them, and why they are useful. One of the first, most cogent, and very influential arguments against developing better and better forecasts, which is the wrong problem to solve.

P. Wack. 1985. Scenarios, Shooting the Rapids. *Harvard Business Review*, November–December. pp. 139–150.

The seminal paper that shows how to think about scenarios and their construction. Excellent exposition on what is a good and a mediocre scenario on how to get executive buy-in.

M. Walton. 1986. *The Deming Management Method.* New York: Putnam.

Summary of the 14 points of the Deming's management method.

B. Yavitz, W.H. Newman. 1982. *Strategy in Action: The Execution, Politics, and Payoff of Business Planning.* New York: The Free Press.

The center of gravity of this book is on implementation of formulated strategies. Discusses processes and organizational dynamics.

V.A. Zeithamel, A. Parasuraman, L.L. Berry. 1990. *Delivering Quality Service: Balancing Customer Perceptions and Expectations.* New York: The Free Press.

The authors present an elegant model for determining process gaps that result in customer dissatisfaction and provide prescriptions on how to close those gaps.

Index